WILL
GENOCIDE
EVER
END?

OTHER PARAGON HOUSE BOOKS ON
GENOCIDE AND THE HOLOCAUST

Against All Hope: Resistance in the Nazi Concentration Camps, 1938-1945
    Hermann Langbein
Courage to Remember: Interviews on the Holocaust
    Kinue Tokudome, Foreword By Richard L. Rubenstein
Different Voices: Women and the Holocaust
    Carol Rittner and John K. Roth, eds.
Ethics After the Holocaust: Perspectives, Critiques, and Responses
    John K. Roth, ed.
Holocaust: Religious and Philosophical Implications
    John K. Roth and Michael Berenbaum, eds.
Narrow Escapes: A Boy's Holocaust Memories and Their Legacy
    Samuel Oliner
The Road to Hell: Recollections of the Nazi Death March
    Joseph Freeman

WILL GENOCIDE EVER END?

EDITED BY

CAROL RITTNER   JOHN K. ROTH   JAMES M. SMITH

MANAGING EDITOR
WENDY WHITWORTH

aegis

in association with

PARAGON HOUSE
St. Paul, Minnesota

First Edition 2002

Published in the United States by
Paragon House
2700 University Avenue West
St. Paul, MN 55114

Produced by Aegis Trust
Laxton
Newark
Notts
United Kingdom
http://www.aegistrust.org

Aegis is a non-governmental organization whose purpose is to help
reduce the incidence of genocide by promoting cooperation and
scholarship between and among all those who have an interest in
preventing genocide, including governments, national and international organizations, and the media.

Library of Congress Cataloging-in-Publication Data

Will genocide ever end? / edited by Carol Rittner, John K. Roth, and
James M. Smith.
    p. cm.
Includes bibliographical references and index.
  ISBN 1-55778-819-7 (Paperback : alk. paper)
  1. Genocide. I. Rittner, Carol Ann, 1943- II. Roth, John K. III.
Smith, James M., 1969-
  HV6322.7 .W545 2002
  364.15'1--dc21

                               2002007312

Manufactured in the United States of America
10 9 8 7 6 5 4 3 2 1

For current information about all releases from Paragon House,
visit the web site at http://www.paragonhouse.com

To
Philippe Gaillard,
Chief Delegate of the International Committee
of the Red Cross in Rwanda (1993-1994),
and to
all those who tried to save lives
during the 1994 genocide

"AND WHO IS MY NEIGHBOR?"

Luke 10:27

TABLE OF CONTENTS

PART IV: WILL GENOCIDE EVER END?

EPILOGUE

APPENDICES 207

ILLUSTRATIONS

PREFACE

Genocide develops over a period of time. There are always warning signs, but after the failure of the international community to respond to the warning signs of genocide in former Yugoslavia and Rwanda, talk about such things sounds hollow, indeed. "Future generations and the writing of history will one day judge those of us in a position to act on how we respond to the cycle of systematic mass murder that is a growing feature of the modern world," wrote Stephen and James Smith in May 2000. It summarizes their rationale for founding Aegis, a UK-based genocide prevention initiative.

The Smith brothers began Aegis to promote a fundamental change in the response of the international community to genocidal situations and to encourage a movement away from reactive measures to policies and practices of prevention. *Will Genocide Ever End?* is a collection of short essays – "think pieces," really – intended to encourage college and university students, politicians, activists, and citizens alike to reconsider how they do business. Each essay was written by a practitioner or scholar, chosen because of his or her ability to state his or her position clearly and succinctly on one of the following questions: *What is genocide? What are the causes and mechanisms of genocide? What can be done about genocide? Will genocide ever end?*

Like Aegis itself, which recognizes that no one organization alone can accomplish the task of genocide prevention, we recognize that this book could not have come to life through the efforts of one person alone. We are immensely indebted to all the writers who so generously responded to our invitation to write an essay for *Will Genocide Ever End?*

Our thanks go to Paragon House and to Gordon Anderson who provided encouragement and editorial guidance. We thank Wendy Whitworth, who graciously managed so many practical and editorial tasks, Glen Powell, who designed our book and worked with us every step of the way, and Jerry Fowler, who provided invaluable counsel. We thank Lawrence Serrano, a Claremont McKenna College student, who helped us when we began our work. Finally, we thank the Smith family and the staff at the Beth Shalom Holocaust Memorial Centre, Laxton, England, for their commitment to "remembering for the future." We hope *Will Genocide Ever End?* complements your extraordinary work for humanity.

The soldiers above were in German South West Africa (later Namibia) when 80 percent of that colony's indigenous Hereros were slaughtered in 1904-1905 during one of the twentieth century's first genocides.

Photo © Getty Images/Hulton

INTRODUCTION

Stephen D. Smith

Although the term "genocide" is relatively recent, its occurrence is not new. Mass slaughter has been used as a means of asserting dominance, imposing ideology, and altering the status quo for millennia. It has been implemented over and over again as a tool of fear, as a means of pillage, of changing ethnic balance, of creating space, and of subjugating the weak for the benefit of the strong. From the deaths of thousands of slaves in Egypt disposed under the foundations of the pyramids to Joshua's conquest of the town of Ai;[1] from the millions wiped out by Genghis Khan[2] to the destruction of Central and South American populations by the Conquistadors,[3] the search for dominance and the propensity to waste life has left genocide's countless victims scattered throughout virtually every chapter of human history.

The twentieth century opened as a century of promise, but by the time it ended, an estimated 200 million civilian deaths[4] littered the global landscape, the result of the deadly policies of a spectrum of political ideologies. There has also been a tragic shift in expectations. At the beginning of the last century, the expectation was that adult males wearing uniforms and carrying weapons would be the likely victims of warfare. By the end of the twentieth century, however, something quite different was true. Not adult males wearing uniforms – soldiers – but civilians – the majority of them women and children – were the victims.

This is where cause for concern lies. Genocide, mass death, and ethnic cleansing are not on the decline, either in incidence or scale. Our ability to predict the occurrence of genocide may be markedly more sophisticated today than it was in the past, but our ability to prevent genocide does not seem to be more effective today than it was in the past. The struggle for power, the subjugation of vulnerable groups and the creation of conflict is part of the current social reality and seems set to continue for the foreseeable future. The question is: In what ways can the actions of *genocidaires*-in-waiting be stopped or mitigated, prior to the implementation of their deadly campaigns?

1

STEPHEN D. SMITH

At a time when the International Criminal Court (ICC) has just received the final signatures ratifying its permanent existence, when the government of Rwanda is about to institute the *Gacaca* courts to try the perpetrators of genocide, and when Slobodan Milosevic is standing trial for the crime of genocide in The Hague, can there be any better moment than this to ask what human beings have learned from past genocides? This book is not about the solution to genocide, but about some of its complexities. It focuses on genocide's persistence in human history, and it tries to explain its presence, and observe its mechanisms. Most significantly, it begins to ask in what ways the recurrence of genocide might be halted.

Why is the murder of the weak such an important weapon of the powerful? How does the act of mass murder find legitimacy within any given ideology and its associated political system? How do past precedents of genocide help us to predict its potential in the present? How do the perpetrators justify the evil act they commit, while maintaining moral legitimacy? What kind of deterrents might work to persuade the potential killers to desist? These are some of the questions asked in this book.

The victims of genocide deserve more than any short essay can deliver. The perpetrators are more complex than a few thousand words can describe. The mechanisms of death are too varied to explain in simplified form. The challenge of prevention is too fraught with difficulty to begin to answer in a single volume, and yet, we must try to do so because most people will never take up the challenge of reading a long, complicated treatise on genocide.

Will Genocide Ever End? contains short essays and comments by experts working on the cutting edge of some of the most difficult territory of human social interaction. The contributors come from a variety of disciplines, experiences and areas of professional expertise, but they share one personal concern that brings them together. Over many years, all have observed genocide and its dark dimensions, and more than anything, they hope their expertise will never again be necessary.

Notes

1. Joshua 8: 2-25, *The Holy Bible*, New International Version.
2. See www.freedomsnest.com/rummel_pre20a.html#mongols.
3. William M. Brinton, *An Abridged History of the United States*, 1996, www.ushistory.info.
4. R.J. Rummel estimates that over 169 million people were killed by governments between 1900 and 1987, excluding casualties of war. See further www.hawaii.edu/powerkills/20TH.HTM.

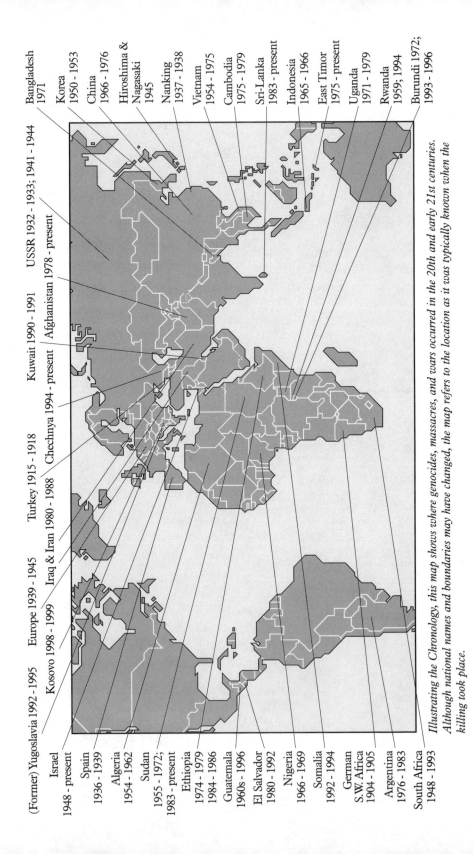

(Former) Yugoslavia 1992 - 1995   Europe 1939 - 1945   Turkey 1915 - 1918   Kuwait 1990 - 1991   USSR 1932 - 1933; 1941 - 1944   Bangladesh 1971

Israel 1948 - present   Kosovo 1998 - 1999   Iraq & Iran 1980 - 1988   Chechnya 1994 - present   Afghanistan 1978 - present   Korea 1950 - 1953

Spain 1936 - 1939   China 1966 - 1976

Algeria 1954 - 1962   Hiroshima & Nagasaki 1945

Sudan 1955 - 1972; 1983 - present   Nanking 1937 - 1938

Ethiopia 1974 - 1979   Vietnam 1954 - 1975

1984 - 1986   Cambodia 1975 - 1979

Guatemala 1960s - 1996   Sri-Lanka 1983 - present

El Salvador 1980 - 1992   Indonesia 1965 - 1966

Nigeria 1966 - 1969   East Timor 1975 - present

Somalia 1992 - 1994   Uganda 1971 - 1979

German S.W. Africa 1904 - 1905   Rwanda 1959; 1994

Argentina 1976 - 1983   Burundi 1972; 1993 - 1996

South Africa 1948 - 1993

Illustrating the Chronology, this map shows where genocides, massacres, and wars occurred in the 20th and early 21st centuries. Although national names and boundaries may have changed, the map refers to the location as it was typically known when the killing took place.

CHRONOLOGY

Carol Rittner, John K. Roth, and James M. Smith

No Chronology can be complete or exhaustive. This one simply tries to provide readers with a broad context for the essays that follow.

DATE	EVENT
1904–1905	Slaughter of the Hereros in German Southwest Africa [Namibia] by German troops. According to the UN Whitaker Commission (1985), the slaughter of the Hereros was one of the first genocides of the twentieth century.
1914–1918	World War I.
1915–1918	In the Ottoman Empire, the Young Turk regime tries to destroy its Armenian population. By 1918, an estimated one million Armenians were dead.
November 1917	Bolsheviks [Communists] seize power in Russia.
June 28, 1919	The Versailles Treaty is signed.
1924	Belgium accepts the mandate of the League of Nations to administer Rwanda and Burundi.
1926	Belgian colonial authorities in Rwanda and Burundi introduce a system of ethnic identity cards to help them differentiate Hutus and Tutsis.
August 27, 1928	The Kellogg-Briand Pact is signed. It condemns "recourse to war for the solution of international controversies."
1932–1933	In the Union of Soviet Socialist Republics (USSR), between five and seven million peasants – most of

them Ukrainians living in Ukraine and the traditional Cossack territories of the North Caucasus – starve to death because the government, under the leadership of Joseph Stalin, seizes the 1932 crop and foodstuffs from the population.

January 30, 1933 President Paul von Hindenburg appoints Adolf Hitler Chancellor of Germany.

1936–1939 Following a military revolt against the Republican government of Spain, a bloody civil war, fought with great ferocity on both sides, ensues. The Nationalists, as the rebels are called, receive aid from fascist Italy and Nazi Germany. The Republicans receive aid from the USSR, as well as from International Brigades, composed of volunteers from Europe and the United States.

December 1937– January 1938 During the Sino-Japanese war (1937-1945), the Imperial Japanese Army overruns Nanking, China's capital city. For seven weeks, Japanese soldiers sack the city, execute thousands of soldiers, slaughter and rape tens of thousands of civilians, all in contravention of the rules of war. This incident becomes known as "the Rape of Nanking."

September 1, 1939 Nazi Germany invades Poland; two days later, Britain and France declare war on Germany; World War II begins.

1939–1945 During World War II and the Holocaust, the Nazis and their collaborators murder six million Jews; millions of others also are swept into the Nazi net of death.

1941–1944 On the territory of the USSR, whole nationality groups, including Volga Germans, Balkars, Chechens, Crimean Tatars, Ingushi, Karachai, Kalmyks, and Meskhetians, are deported and resettled in remote areas (e.g., Central Asia and Siberia) to work in mines, labor camps, factories, and farms. Estimates of the loss of life are not exact, but in the worst case (Crimean Tartars), the loss of life is about 50%.

December 7, 1941 Japanese aircraft bomb Pearl Harbor, an American naval base in the Pacific; the next day, the US, Great Britain, Australia, and New Zealand declare war on Japan. Three days later, December 11, 1941, Germany and Italy declare war on the United States. World War II expands to the Pacific.

November 1, 1943 In the Moscow Declaration, the US, Great Britain, and the USSR announce that individuals guilty of "atrocities, massacres and cold-blooded mass executions" will be held criminally responsible.

1944 Raphael Lemkin's book, *Axis Rule in Occupied Europe: Laws of Occupation, Analysis of Government, Proposals for Redress* (Washington, D.C.: Carnegie Endowment for International Peace) is published. Lemkin coins the word "genocide" to describe "the destruction of essential foundations of the life of national groups, with the aim of annihilating the groups themselves."

May 8, 1945 Nazi Germany surrenders; World War II ends in Europe.

August 6, 1945 An American B-29 airplane drops an atom bomb on Hiroshima, Japan. The combined heat and blast pulverize everything in the explosion's immediate vicinity, generate spontaneous fires that burn out almost 4.4 square miles and kill between 70,000 and 80,000 people, besides injuring more than 70,000 others.

August 8, 1945 In the London Agreement, representatives from the US, Great Britain, the USSR, and the provisional government of France sign an agreement that includes a Charter for an International Military Tribunal to conduct trials of major Axis war criminals.

August 9, 1945 An American B-29 airplane drops a second atomic bomb on Nagasaki, Japan, killing between 35,000 and 40,000 people, injuring a like number, and devastating 1.8 square miles.

September 2, 1945 Japan surrenders; World War II ends.

November 20, 1945 The Nuremberg War Crimes Trials begin. Suspects are charged with, and tried for, crimes against peace, crimes against humanity, and war crimes.

January 10, 1946   The United Nations (UN) General Assembly meets for the first time, in London. One week later, January 17, the first session of the UN Security Council is held.

April 18, 1946   Inauguration of the International Court of Justice (ICJ) – the *World Court* – established in 1945 by the San Francisco Conference, which also created the UN. The seat of the ICJ is at The Hague, but sessions may be held elsewhere when the court thinks it is necessary. The court's primary function is to pass judgment upon disputes between sovereign states.

May 3, 1946   The International Military Tribunal for the Far East (Tokyo War Crimes Tribunal) convenes in Tokyo to prosecute Class A war criminals. They are charged with, and tried for, crimes against peace, crimes against humanity, and war crimes.

October 1, 1946   At the international trial of major German war criminals held in Nuremberg, verdicts are announced for the defendants. Those condemned to death are executed, then cremated.

May 14, 1948 – present   Following the UN-mandated partition of Palestine, Israel declares independence; wars and conflict with Arab nations and the PLO continue into the present.

December 9, 1948   The UN General Assembly adopts the Convention on the Prevention and Punishment of the Crime of Genocide.

December 10, 1948   The UN General Assembly adopts the Universal Declaration of Human Rights.

1948–1993   The National Party comes to power in South Africa. Racial segregation, sanctioned by law, is widely practiced; the National Party extends the policy and gives it the name *apartheid* – literally "apartness."

June 25, 1950–   On the Korean peninsula, a bloody war is fought

July 27, 1953	between North and South Korea. The UN, with the US as the principal participant, comes to the aid of South Korea; the People's Republic of China comes to the aid of North Korea.
1954–1962	In 1962, following a brutal war for independence lasting nearly eight years, Algeria gains its independence from France.
1954–1975	In Southeast Asia, the "Second Indochina War" grows out of a protracted conflict between France and the Vietnamese. After the Battle of Dien Bien Phu (1954), France withdraws from her Indochinese colonies. The US becomes increasingly involved in Vietnam, drawn into what becomes known in the West as the Vietnam War.
1955–1972	Conflict between the government in Sudan, dominated by Arabic-speaking, Islamic northerners, and rebels in the African, largely non-Muslim south, results in the deaths of an estimated 500,000 southern Sudanese.
1959	After a bloody Hutu revolt, during which 20,000 Tutsis are slaughtered, Belgium places Rwanda under military rule. Thousands of Tutsis flee to Uganda.
May 23, 1960	In Argentina, agents of the Israeli Secret Service (*Mossad*) capture Adolf Eichmann, a Nazi German war criminal.
1961	British lawyer Peter Benenson launches the non-governmental human rights organization, Amnesty International.
April 11– August 14, 1961	The State of Israel tries Adolf Eichmann for crimes against the Jewish people for his role in implementing the Nazi Final Solution. He is found guilty, sentenced to death, and during the night of May 31, 1962 is hanged.
1961–1962	Rwanda and Burundi gain their independence.
1960s–1996	In Guatemala, during a protracted civil war, more than 200,000 people lose their lives; most are Mayan

civilians. A UN-sponsored truth commission, the Historical Clarification Commission, created after the war ended in 1996, documented unspeakable atrocities: murder, mutilation, rape, and torture, and held the Guatemalan state responsible for acts of genocide against Mayan communities.

October 1965–
March 1966

In Indonesia, conservative forces, including the army and Muslim militias, kill at least 100,000 people as part of a sustained campaign against left-wing forces. An overwhelming number of the victims are members of the Indonesian Communist Party (PKI), or those suspected of supporting the Communists. They are killed in hundreds of local massacres.

1966–1969

In response to Biafra's attempted secession, the Nigerian government crushes the resistance of the Ibos. Particularly horrifying is the government's use of the politics and strategy of starvation. Between 600,000 and 1,000,000 Ibos are killed in battles and massacres, or die of famine and disease.

1966–1976

In 1966, Chinese Communist Party Chairman Mao Zedong tightens his control on the reins of power. He launches the *Great Proletarian Cultural Revolution*. Radical students organize themselves into paramilitary groups known as *Red Guards*. They attack "old" ideas, "old" culture, "old" customs, and "old" habits. Upheaval, violence, and death follow in the wake of these attacks.

March 18, 1969

The war in Vietnam spills over into Cambodia, as the US Air Force secretly begins bombing North Vietnamese sanctuaries in rural Cambodia. Between 1970–1973, some 150,000 Cambodians are killed by the American bombardments.

1971

Bangladesh (former East Pakistan) achieves independence from Pakistan. During a nine-month long war, Pakistani troops kill between 1,000,000 and 3,000,000 people and rape an estimated 250,000 girls and women. India intervenes and the West Pakistani Army capitulates on December 16, 1971. The Bangladeshi Army and Bengali settlers begin killing non-Bengali tribal peoples of the Chittagong Hill Tracts of south-eastern Bangladesh. More than 200,000 are wiped out.

1971–1979 In Uganda, Idi Amin overthrows Milton Obote in a *coup*. He and his government are responsible for the deaths of an estimated 300,000 of their own people. During the Amin years, there are reports of rapes of women, beheadings of men, women, and children, and cannibalism.

1972 In Burundi, three attempted *coups* (1965, 1969, and 1972) against the Tutsi-dominated government lead to severe reprisals against Hutu civilians, including massacres in 1972 labeled genocide by some experts.

1974 In Paraguay, the government is blamed for allowing the slaughter, torture, and enslavement of the Guayaki Aché Indians by hunters and slave traders, effectively wiping out the tribe.

September 1974–1979 After seizing political control in Ethiopia, the Provisional Military Administrative Council (PMAC) institutes a policy of threats, arrests, torture, and extra-judicial killing to repress any opposition to it. The government kills, tortures, or jails so many members and supporters of the Ethiopian People's Revolutionary Party (EPRP) that it is practically eliminated as a political force.

1975–present In an effort to prevent the island of East Timor, a former Portuguese colony, from declaring itself independent, Indonesia invades it, imprisoning, torturing, and slaughtering opponents. Between 1975–1978, an estimated 200,000 people, out of a population of 600,000, die. Many are killed, others die as the result of disease and human-made famine. A new outbreak of violence after an August 30, 2000 referendum approving East Timorese independence precipitates international intervention.

April 1975–
January 1979

Pol Pot and his Khmer Rouge forces overthrow the American-backed Lon Nol government. They rename Cambodia Democratic Kampuchea and subject the people to the world's most radical political, social, and economic revolution. An estimated 1,500,000 million of its people are massacred or starved to death; foreign and minority languages are banned, and neighboring countries are attacked by Khmer Rouge forces. The Khmer Rouge are dislodged only after Vietnam's army intervenes.

August 1, 1975

Signing of the Helsinki Accords at the conclusion of the first Conference on Security and Cooperation in Europe (CSCE). The Helsinki Accords were primarily an effort to reduce tension between the Soviet and Western blocs by securing their common acceptance of the post-World War II status quo in Europe. This major diplomatic agreement stimulates the proliferation of human rights groups throughout the world.

1976–1983

After a military junta seizes control of Argentina on March 26, 1976, thousands of people are forcibly "disappeared" by security forces. It becomes known as the Argentine "'Dirty War' of Disappearances."

1978

Helsinki Watch (in 1988, renamed Human Rights Watch), a non-governmental human rights organization, is established. Other "Watch" committees are established in various parts of the world.

1978–present

In Afghanistan, a Communist regime seizes power in 1978, with the assistance of the USSR. The Afghan government terrorizes the non-Communist educated class. In 18 months, 32,000 are executed. When the USSR itself invades Afghanistan in December 1979, the Soviets use terror, including chemical weapons, gruesome atrocities, the destruction of crops, orchards, animals, food supplies, and water sources, in their war against the Muslim resistance. After the Soviets withdraw in 1989, killings continue to be carried out by the puppet regime, which collapses in 1992. Following the withdrawal of Soviet troops in the mid-1990s, and after some years of internal conflict, the Taliban, an ultra-conservative Muslim political and religious fundamentalist faction, emerges and takes control of the government. They perpetrate their own horrors, torturing and killing thousands until the Taliban-controlled government is toppled by American military power, following the September 11, 2001 attack on the World Trade Center in New York City.

1980–1992   During 12 years of civil war in El Salvador, approximately 70,000 people lose their lives in killing and bombing raids waged against civilians throughout the Salvadoran countryside.

1980–1988   Iran and Iraq wage war against each other; casualty figures are highly uncertain, though estimates suggest more than 1,500,000 casualties; an estimated 1,000,000 are dead.

1983–present   In Sudan, an estimated 2,000,000 people, mostly civilians, have died as the result of civil war. The present government, which seized power in 1989, has used famine as a weapon of war, causing untold suffering and death. Principal victims include the Dinka and Nuer peoples in southern Sudan and the Nuba of central Sudan.

1983–present   In Sri Lanka, an ongoing civil war pits the Sri Lankan government against the so-called "Tamil Tigers." An estimated 60,000 people have lost their lives thus far.

1984–1986   The Ethiopian government forcibly resettles hundreds of thousands of peasants from arid environments to more fertile areas. An estimated 700,000 people, including the sick and the elderly, are seized on streets, from farms and market places, and forcibly resettled. Conflicts erupt between those indigenous to an area and those resettled. Overall, the result is what some scholars have called "genocidal killing by resettlement."

February 19, 1986   After President Ronald Reagan puts his support behind ratification, the US Senate finally authorizes ratification of the United Nations Genocide Convention. The Convention is ratified in 1988.

January–June 1987   The Iranian attack on Basra begins. By the time the battle for the town grinds to a halt, analysts estimate 40,000 Iranians and 25,000 Iraqis are killed, making it the bloodiest battle in the bloodiest war since World War II.

May 1987–1988   Under the leadership of Saddam Hussein, Iraq becomes the first country ever to attack its own citizens with chemical weapons. The Iraqi government launches a campaign against its Kurdish population. In 1987-1988, Hussein's forces destroyed several thousand Iraqi Kurdish villages and hamlets and killed close to 100,000 Iraqi Kurds, nearly all of whom were unarmed, and many of whom were women and children.

August1990–March 1991   In response to Saddam Hussein's invasion of Kuwait on August 2, 1990, the UN Security Council authorizes the use of "all means necessary" to eject Iraq from Kuwait. A US-led coalition attacks Iraqi forces. By the time the Persian Gulf War ends and Iraq accepts ceasefire terms, an estimated 20,000 Iraqi military and 2,500 Iraqi civilians are dead.

1992–1995   Yugoslavia disintegrates in a bloody, vicious civil war. Croats, Muslims, and Serbs all commit atrocities against each other, although according to an American CIA report, Croats and Muslims committed "discrete" atrocities, "but theirs lacked 'the sustained intensity, orchestration, and scale of the Bosnian Serbs' efforts.'" Backed by Yugoslav President Slobodan Milosevic, Serbian military and paramilitary forces expel Muslims from territory under their control, set up concentration camps, rape thousands of women and girls and kill tens of thousands of civilians.

April 6, 1992   Bosnia-Herzegovina, after World War II, one of six constituent republics of Yugoslavia, becomes an internationally recognized independent state.

August 15, 1992-   "Operation Provide Relief," a UN humanitarian effort,
March 31, 1994   begins in Somalia. President George Bush commits 25,000 US combat troops to help. In October 1993, 18 US soldiers are killed and 84 wounded in a gun battle. As a result, President Bill Clinton, Bush's successor, orders US troops to withdraw from Somalia. The Somalia experience will have profound impact on future US involvements around the world.

1993–1996   In Burundi on October 31, 1993, a group of Tutsi army officers kidnap and kill Burundi's first Hutu president. Mass violence, instigated by both Tutsi and Hutu extremists over the next three years, leaves an estimated 200,000 civilians dead.

May 25, 1993   The UN Security Council creates the International Criminal Tribunal for Former Yugoslavia (ICTY). It is empowered to try individuals for genocide, crimes against humanity and war crimes. It is seated in The Hague, Netherlands.

1994–1999   On December 11, 1994, Russian troops invade Chechnya. Augmented Russian forces totaling perhaps 40,000 troops manage to take Grozny in March 1995, but at the cost of heavy civilian casualties; Chechen guerrilla resistance continues in other areas of the republic. Both sides commit atrocities, although the far larger Russian military is guilty of the worse excesses. A provisional peace treaty is signed. Russian troops soon withdraw from the territory but return in late 1999, after which heavy fighting resumes. An estimated 100,000 people die and more than 600,000 people are forced to flee their homes during the 1990s.

April 6, 1994–   On April 6, President Juvenal Habyarimana of

July 1994   Rwanda and President Cyprien Ntaryamira of
Burundi are killed when their plane is shot down by
a missile. The killing of Tutsis begins 30 minutes
later. More than 800,000 Tutsis and moderate Hutus
are slaughtered by the Hutu-dominated government
and by Hutu extremists over a period of three months.

November 8, 1994 The UN Security Council creates an ad hoc tribunal
for Rwanda. The tribunal is known as the International
Criminal Tribunal for Rwanda (ICTR) and is empowered to try individuals for genocide, crimes against
humanity and war crimes. The tribunal is seated in
Arusha, Tanzania.

July 1995   In Bosnia, Bosnian Serb forces seize the UN-protected
safe area of Srebrenica, home to 40,000 Muslim men,
women, and children. The Bosnian Serb Army, under
the command of General Ratko Mladic, slaughters
some 7,000 Muslims, the largest massacre in Europe
in fifty years.

June 1997   In Cambodia, Pol Pot surrenders to Khmer Rouge
rebels.

July 1997   Pol Pot is charged with treason by his former Khmer
Rouge colleagues and tried by a people's tribunal.

April 15, 1998   Pol Pot dies, apparently of natural causes.

July 17, 1998   A diplomatic conference in Rome adopts the Statute
of the International Criminal Court (ICC), a perma-
nent international forum to prosecute genocide,
crimes against humanity, and serious war crimes. The
Court will be headquartered in The Hague.

September 2, 1998 Jean-Paul Akayesu, a Hutu and former government
official in Rwanda, is convicted in the first genocide
case prosecuted before an international tribunal.
The conviction is also historic because it establishes
that mass rape, when committed with intent to
destroy a group, in whole or in part, can amount to
genocide.

Winter 1998–   Serb police and militia loyal to Serb President

Spring 1999 Slobodan Milosevic commit atrocities in Kosovo. In an effort to stop the atrocities, the North Atlantic Treaty Organization (NATO) bombs Serbia.

May 24, 1999 The UN War Crimes Tribunal (ICTY) indicts Slobodan Milosevic, President of Yugoslavia, for crimes against humanity and war crimes committed in Kosovo.

September 30, 1999 –present A massive Russian military force enters Chechnya in response to alleged terrorist bombings in Moscow and in response to the incursion of Chechen militias into the neighboring Russian Republic of Dagestan. Chechnya is devastated and its capital, Grozny, is almost totally obliterated.

May 2000 The United States Holocaust Memorial Council's Committee on Conscience places Chechnya on its genocide watch list.

Fall 2000 The US Holocaust Memorial Museum's Committee on Conscience issues a genocide warning for Sudan.

March 2001 Slobodan Milosevic, former President of Yugoslavia, is arrested.

June 2001 Former president Milosevic is surrendered to the ICTY in The Hague, where he has been indicted and will stand trial for crimes against humanity in Kosovo. The prosecutor ultimately files two additional indictments covering events in Bosnia and Croatia. The Bosnia indictment includes the charge of genocide.

August 2001 The ICTY finds former Bosnian Serb General Radislav Krstic guilty of genocide. He is the first person convicted of genocide by an international tribunal in Europe.

February 2002 Slobodan Milosevic's trial begins before the ICTY in The Hague.

May 6, 2002 The administration of President George W. Bush, flouting the advice of major allies and outraging human rights organizations, renounces any obligation to cooperate with the new International Criminal Court.

July 1, 2002 The Rome Statute to create a permanent International Criminal Court (ICC) with jurisdiction over crimes against humanity and genocide comes into force.

SOURCES USED TO COMPILE THE CHRONOLOGY

Chalk, Frank and Kurt Jonassohn. *The History and Sociology of Genocide.* New Haven, CT: Yale University Press, 1990.

Charny, Israel, ed. *Encyclopedia of Genocide.* Vols. 1 and 2. Santa Barbara, CA: ABC-Clio, 1999.

Gutman, Roy and David Rieff, eds. *Crimes of War: What the Public Should Know.* New York: W. W. Norton & Company, 1999.

Horowitz, Irving Louis. *Taking Lives: Genocide and State Power.* New Brunswick, NJ: Transaction Publishers, 1997. 4th ed.

Kuper, Leo. *The Prevention of Genocide.* New Haven: Yale University Press, 1985.

Naimark, Norman M. *Fires of Hatred: Ethnic Cleansing in Twentieth-Century Europe.* Cambridge, MA: Harvard University Press, 2001.

Niewyk, Donald and Francis Nicosia. *The Columbia Guide to The Holocaust.* New York: Columbia University Press, 2000.

Power, Samantha. *"A Problem from Hell" : America and the Age of Genocide,* New York: Basic Books, 2002.

Public Broadcasting System Website: www.pbs.org

Roth, John K. et al. *The Holocaust Chronicle.* Lincolnwood, IL: Publications International, Ltd., 2000.

Social Education, February 1991. Vol. 55 #2.

Totten, Samuel, William S. Parsons, and Israel W. Charny, eds. *Century of Genocide: Eyewitness Accounts and Critical Views.* New York: Garland Publishing, Inc. 1997.

Starved or shot after being marched into the desert, these women and children were among more than a million Armenians killed in Turkey during the Armenian genocide, 1915-1918.

Photo Armin T. Wegner © Gomidas Institute UK

PART I
WHAT IS GENOCIDE?

The capital of the United States is a museum city. Ranging from the multiple venues of the Smithsonian Institution to the United States Holocaust Memorial Museum, whose more than two million annual visitors learn about what is arguably the twentieth century's best known genocide, scores of sites in Washington, D.C., evoke memory and try to keep forgetting at bay. A new museum will open its Washington doors in 2007. Strategically situated two blocks from the White House, the Armenian Genocide Museum and Memorial will focus its attention on the mass destruction of Armenian life and culture carried out by the Ottoman Turkish regime in 1915.

At that time, the term genocide did not exist. Almost thirty years would pass until Raphael Lemkin coined it. Subsequently, the United Nations agreed to its 1948 Convention on the Prevention and Punishment of the Crime of Genocide. Not only for these reasons, however, does fierce political controversy still rage about whether the Armenians' fate at the hands of the Turks should be openly and universally acknowledged as genocide. Fearing reparations claims, as well as stains on national honor, the government of post-Ottoman Turkey persistently and tenaciously denies – massive evidence to the contrary notwithstanding – that the Armenians suffered genocide. For their part, American presidents have regularly issued statements coinciding with the April 24 observance of Armenian Memorial Day, which mourns the 1915 slaughter. Taking care not to offend Turkey, a NATO ally presently regarded as crucial in the United States' war on terrorism, those presidential pronouncements have yet to use the word genocide in reference to the mass deportation and murder of Armenians perpetrated by the Turks.

Few questions are more deceptive than "What is genocide?" At first glance, that question appears to be simple and straightforward. Primarily, it appears to call for the definition of a term. The appearance, however, is not reality. Yes, the question does call for a definition, and definitions of genocide have been given. Unfortunately, as illustrated by Armenian history and also as shown by the essays in this book's first part, the definition of genocide is an

21

issue that is full of problems and pitfalls. Far from being conceptual alone, those problems and pitfalls point to cases of life and death for millions. Before the killing begins and long after it ends, the issues surrounding genocide – the term and the reality to which it points – affect the present and the future as well as our understanding of the past.

How genocide is defined affects global politics. Calling – or refusing to call – acts of violence genocidal can make a huge difference in international relations, humanitarian intervention, early warning that might prevent disaster, and historical memory and its legacies. Mapping genocide's blood-stained terrain and the issues it poses for another question – Will genocide ever end? – rightly begins with exploration of the far-from-simple question, one loaded with decisive implications for humankind: What is genocide?

1

THE POLITICS OF DEFINITION

John K. Roth

"New conceptions require new terms."
Raphael Lemkin,
Axis Rule in Occupied Europe

In 1994, the political scientist R. J. Rummel, a demographer of what he called democide, published an important book called *Death by Government.* Writing before he could have taken account of the late twentieth-century atrocities in Bosnia, Rwanda, or Kosovo, Rummel estimated that "the human cost of war and democide" – he defines *democide* as "the murder of any person or people by a government, including genocide, politicide, and mass murder" – is more than "203 million people in this [twentieth] century."[1]

"If one were to sit at a table," Rummel went on to say, "and have this many people come in one door, walk at three miles per hour across the room with three feet between them (assume generously that each person is also one foot thick, navel to spine), and exit an opposite door, it would take over *five years and nine months* for them all to pass, twenty-four hours a day, 365 days a year. If these dead were laid out head to toe, assuming each to be an average of 5 feet tall, they would reach from Honolulu, Hawaii, across the vast Pacific and then the huge continental United States to Washington D.C. on the East coast, *and then back again almost twenty times.*"[2]

While Rummel may have thought that such calculations would make the abstraction of huge numbers more concrete, it is not clear that he even convinced himself, for he placed an endnote number at his calculation's conclusion. Note 14 reads as follows: "Back and forth, over 4,838 miles one way, near twenty times? This is so incredible that I would not believe the calculation and had to redo it several times."[3]

It All Depends

The point of starting with Rummel's demography is not to dwell primarily on his statistics, devastating though they are, but instead to focus on the concepts he employs, a task that represents a variation on Raphael Lemkin's theme that "new conceptions require new terms."[4] In Rummel's vocabulary, *democide* includes many, but perhaps not all, cases of genocide. It all depends on how *genocide* is defined. For Rummel, the key defining issue would be the part that killing plays.

Here is how Rummel defines genocide: It is, "among other things, the killing of people by a government because of their indelible group membership (race, ethnicity, religion, language)."[5] His qualification "among other things" is important, for it indicates that the genocidal destruction of a group is not restricted to outright killing. The destruction, Rummel observes, can take place *"by other means*, such as by preventing births in the group or by causing mental harm." In a word, "genocide does *not* necessarily have to include killing."[6]

Genocide involves killing – one-sided killing, it is important to add – but not killing necessarily or always.[7] More extreme than the violation of individual human rights, although it always includes such violations, genocide, which often but not always takes place in war time, connotes the destruction of a group. Still, we might ask, what is meant by a *group*, and, we might add, how is *destruction* to be understood? These questions, and by no means do they exhaust genocide's puzzles, are crucial because what I am calling "the politics of definition" makes issues about prevention, intervention, and prosecution of genocide's perpetrators pivot around them.

Notice next that the problem is not that there is a lack of responses, if not answers, to the questions I have identified. Since Lemkin's coining of the term *genocide* during World War II as the Nazi annihilation of European Jewry raged, numerous attempts to define genocide have been made. Nevertheless, for various reasons – political and philosophical – the question "What is genocide?" remains vexing and unsettled. The results include a paradox: There is widespread agreement both that genocide has taken place and that its threats plague the present and the future, and yet the definition of genocide is still contested. Genocide scholars share insights about genocide's nature, but they do not agree on every detail. Governments, whose interests are not likely to coincide with those of scholars – at least not completely – may accept formulaic definitions, but when it comes to applying those definitions to concrete cases, the interpretations are likely to diverge as national interests dictate.

A Multitude of Sins

Issues about how genocide should be defined and understood are part of the Holocaust's legacy, for the Third Reich's destruction of European Jewry was genocide or nothing could be. With Nazi Germany's annihilation of the Jews in mind, Raphael Lemkin, a Jewish lawyer who fled from Poland during the Holocaust, first defined genocide to mean "the destruction of a nation or of an ethnic group," observing that genocide denoted "an old practice in its modern development."[8] Lemkin saw that the plight of the Jews under Hitler was not a simple repetition of past historical patterns. Yet precisely what was new and unprecedented in those circumstances? Far from resolving that issue to everyone's satisfaction, Lemkin's discussion initiated a continuing debate.

One problem with Lemkin's early definition, and it has never gone away, is that genocide covers a multitude of sins. The destruction of a nation or of an ethnic group can happen, for example, through deprivation of the means to live and procreate or through killing targeted people outright. In short, the methods of genocide can be diverse. Even killing can be slow and indirect – starvation, for instance – as well as quick and immediate. The destruction process, moreover, can be as subtle as it is prolonged. Procedures to curtail birth rates and to increase mortality can have a genocidal effect over time. Eventually a people can also disappear if their culture is decimated by eliminating intellectual leadership, dismantling institutions, and suppressing literacy.

Owing considerably to Lemkin's influence, the United Nations established a post-Holocaust "multitude-of-sins" understanding of genocide when it adopted the 1948 Convention on the Prevention and Punishment of the Crime of Genocide. The document defined genocide as "any of the following acts committed with intent to destroy, in whole or in part, a national, ethnical, racial, or religious group, as such: a. Killing members of the group; b. Causing serious bodily or mental harm to members of the group; c. Deliberately inflicting on the group conditions of life calculated to bring about its physical destruction in whole or in part; d. Imposing measures intended to prevent births within the group; e. Forcibly transferring children of the group to another group." In addition, the UN Convention provided that punishable acts should include not only genocide itself but also "conspiracy to commit genocide; direct and public incitement to genocide; attempt to commit genocide; complicity in genocide."

Despite their apparent aims, neither Lemkin's nor the UN's definitions made the identification of genocide an easy matter.[9] The reasons include the following: First, the identification of genocide depends on determining intent, which can be hard to do before it is too late. Arguably, nothing makes the concept of genocide more ambiguous than the emphasis on intent that seems unavoidably to be built into it. On the other hand, if intent is not included in the meaning of words such as *genocide* or *genocidal*, it would be hard to understand how one would account for the very thing that genocide turns out to be: namely, the targeting for destruction, in whole or in part, of some specific group of people.

Without intention to single people out, no such targeting is likely or even possible. However, it does not follow that attacks on specific groups of people are necessarily genocidal. Immense harm can be inflicted on a group, and yet it may not be the case that genocide is being attempted or that it has taken place, for genocide requires intention. Otherwise, the concept becomes so vague as to be of very little help. That said, intention to commit genocide remains devilishly hard to prove until things have gone so far that annihilation of a group is virtually unmistakable. By that point, intervention or prosecution will be right and good, but also too late for genocide's victims.

Sadly, there is a sense in which those who perpetrate genocide tend to have a crucial advantage. Those who intervene or prosecute after the fact usually arrive too late. Early warning procedures have tried to make up for this disadvantage, but the definitions of genocide – coupled with the problems of intervening before the worst has begun – make the application of such warning systems problematic, too.

Second, as already indicated, the UN definitions acknowledge that the methods of genocide can be diverse. Those methods are not restricted to outright killing and mass murder, and they may take a long time to do their work. Such factors complicate the problem of stating when genocide is under way, at least they do so if the goal is to intervene before it is too late.

Third, the definitions of genocide allow for more or less extreme cases of depopulation – destruction of a group "in whole or in part" – and it can be complicated to determine when a group is being functionally, if not totally destroyed. To amplify this third point, there is a difference between genocide understood as the annihilation of a national, religious, or ethnic identity, and a more radical form that makes no exceptions for the giving up of such identity through assimilation or conversion, and thus aims at the utter annihilation of everyone who embodies the targeted identity. The difference is that between seeing the potential victim of genocide as having a fixed and immutable nature versus one that could be altered by choice or acculturation. In the latter case, genocide might spare individuals more easily than in the former.

The standard definitions are less than adequate – at least they are if clear international understanding aimed at prevention or intervention against genocide is the goal. One challenge – if it can be met, which is itself a serious problem – is to find definitions that are not, on the one hand, so broad as to trivialize genocide and to render uses of the term frivolous or, on the other hand, so narrow that cases of mass death are unreasonably excluded from the category of genocide. Another challenge is to establish credible international law based on sound definitions of genocide. Still other challenges include the establishment of potent sanctions and persuasive early warning systems against genocide. All of these tasks remain works in progress.

What to Do?

"I beg you / do something / learn a dance step / something to justify your existence / something that gives you the right / to be dressed in your skin in your body hair / learn to walk and to laugh / because it would be too senseless / after all / for so many to have died / while you live / doing nothing with your life."[10] The author of those words, Charlotte Delbo, was not Jewish, but her arrest for resisting the Nazi occupation of her native France made her experience the Holocaust when she was deported to Auschwitz in January 1943. Delbo survived the Nazi onslaught. In 1946, she began to write the trilogy that came to be called *Auschwitz and After*. Her work's anguished visual descriptions, profound reflections on memory, and diverse writing styles make it an unrivaled Holocaust testimony. As the trilogy draws to a close, Delbo writes, "I do not know / if you can still / make something of me / If you have the courage to try . . ."[11]

As a non-Jewish survivor of the Holocaust, Charlotte Delbo witnessed genocide, even if at the time she did not know the word, let alone possess a fully adequate definition of the concept. Our situation is vastly different from hers, and yet it is not completely so. We, too, have witnessed genocide. We also have the word, but, as yet, we do not possess a fully adequate definition of the concept, at least if we expect universal agreement about its meaning and about how to apply its meaning to the particularities of political circumstances.

Raphael Lemkin was right when he said that "new conceptions require new terms." It is just that the "terms" have to be understood in terms of practice as much as in terms of theory and conceptualization. The likelihood is that we will never possess a fully adequate definition of genocide, at least if we expect universal agreement about its meaning and about how to apply its meaning to the particularities of political circumstances. If so, a key question becomes "What to do?"

One part of the answer to that question, I believe, is that the struggle to prevent genocide, to intervene against it, to prosecute its perpetrators will have to go on without the luxury of settled definitions. Such work will be daunting, for those who commit genocide will take advantage of the ambiguities that always give genocide room to hide. No doubt work will continue to refine genocide's definition, but "it would be too senseless" to be hesitant to act while genocide's toll rises, as it is likely to do in the twenty-first century. Facing the question, "What is genocide?" we are apparently left to say: We must be "dis-illusioned"; we probably cannot define it once and for all to everyone's satisfaction. Nevertheless, we have seen enough to know that genocide is real and that it deserves no more victories.

Like so much else in human experience, more than half the battle depends on the force of will to say, in spite of imperfect definitions, that genocide is taking place *there* and it must be stopped or that genocide is likely to take place *here* and it must be prevented. Failing such determination, the answer to the question "What is genocide?" is likely to be, in a word, *unending*.

Notes

1. R. J. Rummel, *Death by Government* (New Brunswick, NJ: Transaction Publishers, 1997), 13, 31. Yehuda Bauer's observations about Rummel's data are worth noting: "Rummel has been criticized for exaggerating the losses. Even if the criticisms were valid, a figure lower by 10 or 20 or even 30 percent would make absolutely no difference to the general conclusions that Rummel draws." See Yehuda Bauer, *Rethinking the Holocaust* (New Haven, Conn: Yale University Press, 2001), 12-13, 277 n.17.

2. Rummel, *Death by Government*, 13, 31.

3. Ibid., 28.

4. Raphael Lemkin, *Axis Rule in Occupied Europe* (Washington, D.C.: Carnegie Endowment for International Peace, 1944), 79.

5. Rummel, *Death by Government*, 31. Further issues surround Rummel's use of the term indelible. Apparently it refers to qualities that are permanent or to characteristics that cannot be removed. It is arguable whether a person's religion or language fits that description, even though Rummel includes religion and language in the examples he lists to illustrate indelible group membership. Even nationality, ethnicity, or "racial" identity might be less than crystal clear in that sense. Of course, much usually hinges on how genocide's perpetrators identify their targets. That fact means that hard and fast lines are hard to draw, if they can be drawn at all, between what potential victims can or cannot do to alter identities that would leave them trapped within or allow them to elude a particular genocidal web.

Yehuda Bauer argues that only national, ethnic, or racial groups should be considered targets for genocide. He would deny that status to religious or political groups. The difference, he claims, is that in the first three cases a potential target of genocide cannot change those identities; only the decision of a potential perpetrator could do so. On the other hand, he contends, membership in religious and political groups is a matter of choice. Unfortunately, Bauer's analysis is neater than genocide's realities turn out to be. Perpetrators may decide that religious and political identities are not always matters of choice. Likewise, their understandings of ethnicity, nationality, and even race may leave open, at least to some extent, an individual's self-determination of identity. Rather than putting too fine a point on the matter, it may be well to leave open the nature of a potential victim group, taking seriously that genocidal perpetrators will reserve to themselves the dubious prerogative of defining a victim group as they will. On these points see Bauer, *Rethinking the Holocaust*, 10-13, and Frank Chalk and Kurt Jonassohn, *The History and Sociology of Genocide: Analyses and Case Studies* (New Haven, Conn: Yale University Press, 1990), 25-26.

6. Rummel, *Death by Government*, 33. The italics are Rummel's.

7. Genocide is not about reciprocal killing. It is the perpetrator's aim to wipe out the victim group, but the victim group does not have such plans for the perpetrator, let alone the means to carry them out. See Chalk and Jonassohn, *The History and Sociology of Genocide*, 23.

8. Lemkin, *Axis Rule in Occupied Europe*, 79.

9. I use the word "apparent" advisedly. The point would not apply to Lemkin, who definitely wanted genocide to be identifiable and checked, but it is worth noting that a consequence of the UN Convention – intended or unintended, as the case may be, by some of the parties to it – is that agreement about when genocide is actually taking place, let alone in the offing, is much more difficult than it might seem to be at first glance.

10. Charlotte Delbo, *Auschwitz and After*, trans. Rosette C. Lamont (New Haven, Conn: Yale University Press, 1995), 230.

11. Ibid.

2

AS OLD AS HISTORY

Roger W. Smith

What today we call "genocide" is as old as history. One of the earliest and most explicit accounts dates from the twelfth century B.C.E.[1] and is replete with slaughter, ideological justification, the transfer of children to the group of the perpetrator, and the enslavement of the victims not executed. The Assyrians, Greeks, Romans, Mongols, and many other peoples prior to the modern world committed genocide, but it would never have occurred to them that they were engaged in some kind of crime, least of all a crime against humankind. Rulers actually boasted of how many thousands they had killed, how many peoples they had eliminated. In the modern age of colonization in the Americas, Australia, and Africa there developed new rationalizations for the mass destruction of human groups, especially the idea of "development." What this meant in practice was that some humans must die so that others could live well.

Yet there were moral objections that began to have force by the nineteenth century and even the beginnings of a human rights movement with the exposure of King Leopold's horrific exploitation of Africans in the Congo. Still, it was not until 1944 that the term "genocide" was used to describe the destruction of whole peoples, and it was not until 1948 that the United Nations declared genocide a crime against international law. The Convention on the Prevention and Punishment of the Crime of Genocide, after a sufficient number of ratifications, went into force on January 12, 1951.

The term "genocide" was coined by the jurist Raphael Lemkin in his study of *Axis Rule in Occupied Europe*[2] to signify the destruction of a nation or an ethnic group. He created the term from the ancient Greek *genos* (race, tribe) and the Latin *cide* (killing) to correspond to such terms as tyrannicide and homicide. But we should note that the parallel with homicide is faulty: homicide can be justifiable (self-defense), but can there ever be a justifiable genocide? Also, genocide is an all or nothing crime; it does not allow of degrees of criminality as homicide does (murder, manslaughter, criminal negligence). Some scholars have proposed that we revise this view in order to conform to the law of homicide, but this would seem to undermine the very notion of genocide as an *intentional, non-accidental* crime against an entire group. To find a person guilty of genocide, however, does not in itself settle the question of the degree and type of punishment.

Lemkin was the driving force to create the Convention on Genocide. It is not clear, however, that his vision of genocide is embodied in the Convention. Lemkin writes in 1944 that genocide signifies "a coordinated plan of different actions aiming at the destruction of essential foundations of the life of national groups, with the aim of annihilating the groups themselves." Some of this might fit within the concept of ethnocide, the destruction of a culture, rather than the physical elimination of a group.

Genocide is today almost universally recognized as a crime against international law. The Convention on Genocide defines the crime of genocide as follows:

In the present Convention, genocide means any of the following acts committed with intent to destroy, in whole or in part, a national, ethnical, racial or religious group, as such:

  (a) Killing members of the group;

  (b) Causing serious bodily or mental harm to members of the group;

  (c) Deliberately inflicting on the group conditions of life calculated to bring about its physical destruction in whole or in part;

  (d) Imposing measures intended to prevent births within the group;

  (e) Forcibly transferring children of the group to another group.

The first convictions have come fifty years after approval of the UN Convention: by the International Tribunal for Rwanda and subsequently by the court for the Former Yugoslavia.

Criticisms of the Convention's definition abound. It is ambiguous, it excludes political groups from the list of victims subject to genocide, and with its requirement for specific intent, a perpetrator can argue (as Brazil did) that its killing of indigenous peoples was not because of their ethnicity but to possess their lands.

Scholars have devised their own definitions of genocide. Some want to get rid of the notion of intention altogether, others to include political groups, still others to include all groups as potential victims of genocide. A few would say that genocide is only genocide when the intention is to eliminate every member of a group, others accept the idea of partial genocide. A few distinguish between "genocide" and "politicide" on the basis of the groups and the motivation for violence. Many, though, are concerned with what might be called the moral, as opposed to legal, conception of genocide: the genocidal rather than genocide, with saving lives, rather than punishing perpetrators.

Another approach is to see genocide as a concept with blurred edges, and thus not easily defined, but whose core is actions that tend to destroy a group as a functioning body. What is emphasized here is the family relationships between a variety of acts, motivations, and consequences. At the same time, family differences come into play: war, sporadic killings, political repression, and ethnic cleansing would in most instances be described as something other than genocide. For example, although war was in ancient times usually genocidal, and in modern times kills an enormous number of civilians, today most scholars would regard it as genocide only if the killing continued on a large scale after one side had surrendered. Nuclear war, however, could lead to "omnicide," the destruction of all life on earth, the ultimate (and final) genocide. Finally, there is often a close relationship between war, revolution, and genocide, with one leading to the others.

What genocide is can be described in many different ways. It is a crime against humankind committed on the body of a particular people. Its inherent potential is to distort and alter the very meaning of "humankind," erasing for all time particular biological and cultural possibilities. Furthermore, for a particular group to claim for itself a right to determine what groups are, in effect, human, possessing the right to life, is a threat to the existence of all other humans. All humans thus have a stake in preventing genocide.

Genocide requires a notion of collective guilt pushed to the extreme; though often passed off as "punishment" for rebellious behavior or subversion, genocide is a form of total war. And although philosophers have often treated evil as a "mistaken idea of the good," genocide would seem to be an example of willed evil, filled with rituals of degradation, as well as unimaginable pain.

But in the modern world those who initiate, or otherwise participate in genocide, typically deny that the events took place, that they bear any responsibility for the destruction, or that the term "genocide" is applicable to what occurred. Denial is the last stage of genocide, bringing it into the present; a kind of double killing in which the victims are first murdered, then memory of the deed is itself destroyed.

Genocide is also a set of stories and voices, those of victims, perpetrators, bystanders, rescuers, and those who summon us to action or later attempt to understand the events. Some accounts, such as that of the American Ambassador Henry Morgenthau of the Armenian Genocide[3] and the caravans of death moving toward the Syrian desert in 1915, reveal genocide for the radical evil it is:

> In a few days, what had been a procession of normal human beings became a stumbling horde of dust-covered skeletons, ravenously looking for scraps of food, eating any offal that came their way... sick with all the diseases that accompany such hardships and privations, but still prodded on and on by the whips and clubs and bayonets of their executioners. And thus, as the exiles moved, they left behind another caravan – that of dead and unburied bodies, of old men and women dying in the last stages of typhus, dysentery, and cholera, of little children lying on their backs and setting up their last piteous wails for food and water.

In conclusion, I would point out that, although we often hear genocide described as actions of the mad, primitive, or bestial, it is ordinary human beings who have enacted most of the mass killing of other groups throughout history. Genocide is committed only by humans; it is made possible, not by the animal in us, but the human; by our capacity for abstraction, rationalization, objectification, and organization. Since 1945 more persons have died through genocide and state-sponsored massacres than have been killed by all international or civil wars during the period. Today we recognize genocide as a crime, yet many of us go on killing. And we are the being created in the image of God.

Notes

1. Numbers 31.
2. Raphael Lemkin, *Axis Rule in Occupied Europe: Laws of Occupation, Analysis of Government, Proposals for Redress* (Washington, D.C.: Carnegie Endowment for International Peace, 1944).
3. *Ambassador Morgenthau's Story* (Garden City New York: Doubleday, Page & Company, 1918).

3

THE UN CONVENTION

Steven L. Jacobs

On December 9, 1948, the United Nations passed the "Convention on the Prevention and Punishment of the Crime of Genocide," objectively and ultimately, the final result of the indefatigable and Herculean efforts of one man who pleaded, cajoled, argued, and harassed the members of the General Assembly, including the Security Council, to do that which was morally and ethically responsible in the aftermath of the revelations of the Holocaust/*Shoah* of the Second World War. That man was Polish Jewish jurist, professor of law at Duke and Yale Universities, advisor to the International Military Tribunal at Nuremberg, Germany, and refugee to the United States from the carnage and destruction of Nazified Europe, Dr. Raphael Lemkin (1900-1959). Though his own "journey to genocide" actually began in his youth after first reading Polish Nobel Laureate Henryk Sienkiewicz's 1904 novel *Quo Vadis*, and is reflected in his own 1944 masterwork *Axis Rule in Occupied Europe: Laws of Occupation, Analysis of Government, and Proposals for Redress,*[1] his over-riding commitment to preventing a repetition of such events within the framework of international law remains his own fitting tribute to the forty-nine members of his own family, including his parents, who perished at the hands of the Nazis. (Somewhat ironically, his adopted and beloved country did not ratify the "Genocide Convention," as it has come to be called, until 1988, almost three decades after his death, largely because of the patient work of then-Wisconsin Senator William Proxmire and the political machinations of then-President Ronald Reagan over against its opponents, principally Senator Jesse Helms of North Carolina.)

Though controversies and debates, sometimes acrimonious, continue to exist regarding not only the wording of specific sections of the Convention and issues of implementation and punishment – even in the aftermath of both Rwanda and Bosnia – it remains the *only* legal document internationally affirmed, and, truthfully, laid the groundwork for both the International

Criminal Tribunal for Yugoslavia (ICTY) and the International Criminal Tribunal for Rwanda (ICTR).

Even before commenting on the specifics of the text itself, simply put, *genocide is that act by a group, with or without governmental support and/or sanction, to eliminate from the polity, either in whole or in part, another group*. Thus, realistically, the first question which arises in any discussion of genocide is a sociological one: what constitutes a group? Sensitive to this very issue, and always the lawyer aware of the need for consensus, Lemkin was able to win definitional support for any "national, ethnical, racial or religious group" (Article II); he was unsuccessful, however, in his efforts to have *political groups* retained in the United Nations document. Thus, the issue of political groups remains a sticking point even today.

Turning to the actual Convention itself, specifically Article II, even before its five sub-sections, two other definitional issues were addressed and remain in the document: those of *intentionality* and *whole and/or partial group elimination*. Given the reality of intra-group conflicts, and the horrendous spectacles of mass-killings and massacres of unparalleled atrocity to which the human community has been witness in the nineteenth and twentieth centuries (e.g. the Turkish genocide of the Armenians and the Nazi genocide of the Jews, in addition to Bosnia and Rwanda), do or do not such acts, therefore, constitute *genocidal intent*? The scholarly and legal pursuit of documentary and evidential support of such intent thus becomes not only a legal but a moral necessity.

Within this same Article II, activities constituting genocide are all-too-briefly enumerated, though specific examples are not given, again, raising the problematic specter of definitional divisiveness even among advocates and proponents: (1) killing; (2) bodily or mental harm; (3) "conditions of life" leading to genocide; (4) preventative birth measures (abortion? forced contraception? sterilization?); and (5) forcible transfer of children. Despite total specificity, here, however, the "intent," at least, is clear: the ultimate physical and numerical diminishing of a group leading ultimately to its demise, if not immediately, then within one or two generations. What is not addressed, however, is the distinctive cultural nature of any group within any larger society, and whether or not the destruction of such distinctiveness – outside of those four groups already mentioned – equally constitutes genocide. It was, however, an issue with which Lemkin himself was concerned. In his as-yet-unpublished autobiography *Unofficial Man: The Autobiography of Raphael Lemkin*, he refers specifically to the contributions made by various cultural groups both historically and contemporarily then in existence.

Article III further enumerates those *acts* which are punishable offenses under the Genocide Convention: (1) genocide itself, as problematically defined in Article II; (2) conspiracy to commit; (3) public incitement of such acts (Here, the role of the public radio in the case of the Rwandan genocide, for example, comes immediately to mind.); (4) attempt to commit; and (5) complicity in such acts. Equally, it *does* call for tribunals, either in those nation-states where such acts of genocide have taken place, or "international penal tribunals" agreed to by the contracting parties to the Convention. (It was this latter possibility which was at the root of the United States' reluctance to ratify the Genocide Convention: the fear that this country, too, could, conceivably, be brought before the "bar of justice" because of its enslavement of Africans during the nineteenth century or its treatment of Native Americans even earlier and conterminous with its treatment of Blacks in both the nineteenth and the twentieth centuries.) Likewise, the Genocide Convention does not, however, spell out in any detail whatsoever, the juridical principles by which either tribunal is to be constituted or those mandates and/or powers of enforcement by which it is to act.

What has not been addressed in this all-too-brief discussion thus far, nor in the Genocide Convention itself, is the foundational issue which has been realistically and pragmatically affirmed – *after* World War II in the case of the Jews, and in the cases of Cambodia/Kampuchea, Bosnia and Rwanda – *despite* the 1648 Treaty of Westphalia which clearly defined the sovereign territorial and legal integrity of any nation-state, and set the stage for almost four centuries of Western and non-Western thinking: that of the willingness of the international community to over-ride invasively the integrity of any nation-state, under the umbrella auspices of its primary international body the United Nations, where consensus affirms that genocide is being practiced. What is even more complex, and not fully addressed in the search for preliminary and causative factors leading to genocide, however, is the willingness of this same international community to invade where the threat is there but the act has not yet taken place. The IMT (International Military Tribunal), ICTY, and ICTR are all *post-genocidal* responses, as was the combined international air strike in the case of Bosnia and the bureaucratically delayed response in the case of Rwanda (i.e. the eighteen-month hesitancy of the United States State Department to label what was occurring in Rwanda a genocide, coupled with the consistent bureaucratic hesitancy of the United Nations' leadership to heed the advice of its own military leaders). Adding further to this nightmare is the growing realization that, unlike Hitler's twofold agenda of military conquest and global elimination of the world's Jews, genocide does not require external war for its implementation, and not all civil wars amongst groups, even with governmental sanction, equate with genocide.

As the world grows increasingly smaller, and the human community increasingly interconnected, it can ill afford repeated expressions of genocide. As it continues to look towards legal solutions, not only of definition but of prevention and punishment as well, the pioneering work of Dr. Raphael Lemkin more than fifty years ago comes ever closer to bearing fruit.

Notes
1.   Washington, D.C.: Carnegie Endowment for International Peace, 1944.

4

UNDERSTANDING THE "G" WORD[1]

Stephen C. Feinstein

The "G" word, Genocide, became exceedingly popular and important during the last years of the twentieth century. This was not an accident, but a unique confluence of memory and a legal classification for mass murder. Raphael Lemkin's great contribution to humanity was a word that described civilization's worst characteristic, its intent and ability to commit mass murder. Now, genocide is being used and misused to identify events of destruction. The misuse is often not intentional, but comes from misunderstandings between Holocaust, spelled with either a large or small "h," ethnic cleansing, small-scale versus large-scale massacre, and the like. Similarly, the word genocide, through historical analysis, has been imposed as a measuring device on previous massacres and slaughter of native populations. This includes massacres and deportations of Native Americans in the Western Hemisphere and Australia, and the massacre of 1.5 million Armenians by the Ottoman Turks between 1915 and 1922. Such historical conclusions have immense legal implications. Governments that are successors to regimes that carried out genocide usually have strong objections to the use of the word, as it implies the legal need for restitution in some form. A consequence of the avoidance of the use of the word genocide has been denial of genocide, most visible in the case of the Turkish Republic *vis-à-vis* its Ottoman predecessors regarding Armenia.

By the end of the nineteenth century, the horror of human suffering has magnified. The concentration camp apparently made its appearance in Cuba in 1898. Imperialism took a high toll of native African peoples due to simple technological advantages by Europeans. Differences between the fighting front in battle and the home front became non-existent in World War I and probably had merged many times before the first air raids of 1915. The Polish émigré writer Joseph Conrad undoubtedly had a good sense of what was happening to humanity because of imperialism. In *Heart of Darkness*, he suggested that the negativity associated with human behavior might go even further in the direction of increased atrocity.

Since the end of the event now called the Holocaust or *Shoah*, defined as the extermination of European Jewry by Nazi Germany, there has been a logical attempt to establish the comparability of certain terrible events. Words of memory have often been discovered or invented to convey the burdens of memory and ongoing trauma felt by subsequent generations. Thus, for the Roma and Sinti, "Holocaust" may be a convenient entry point for convincing the public that the "gypsies" as well as the Jews were targets of racial extermination. However, the word *Porrajmos* (the abyss) has greater appeal among the Roma and Sinti as it is specific to their tragedy. Indeed, the use of the word genocide appears to be a search for a universal word to label crimes which are of high proportions and for which conventional words like catastrophe, massacre, slaughter have insufficient meaning.

Raphael Lemkin invented the word genocide in 1944 and since then, what appeared to be a relatively precise legal term has become a word subject to debate. While Holocaust, *Shoah* or *Porrajmos* may be words related to memory, genocide is legalistic. Lemkin's original definition was: "By 'geno-cide,' we mean the destruction of a nation or of an ethnic group.... Generally speaking, genocide does not necessarily mean the immediate destruction of a nation, except when accomplished by mass killings of all members of a nation."[2] Lemkin's initial definition included destruction of language and culture. But as Lemkin noted, "Genocide is directed against the national group as an entity, but manifestations of genocide impact individuals."[3]

Lemkin's definition of genocide suggests it can be either a short-term event or something of longer duration, resulting in "the imposition of the national pattern of the oppressor,"[4] that results ultimately in "biological superiority."[5] This definition, however, which possesses a much wider meaning than in the UN Convention on the Prevention and Punishment of Genocide, provides the capacity to interpret imposed policies by national states and policies of domination during the immediate "civilized" past as "genocide." Lemkin clearly did not mean the ancient past when slavery and mass destruction were often assumed to be a consequence of military defeat. Rather, his focus was more on "modern" states' systems that developed since the age of colonialism. Lemkin's important focus regarding cultural geno-cide (imposition of the language of the oppressor and destruction of lan-guage and artistic values of those under domination), destruction of an exist-ing economic order, "biological genocide" (which encourages depopulation of "non-related blood" and increase in the birthrate of the dominant group[6]), as well as "physical" genocide (through killing, racial discrimination in feeding, negative health policies) were directly reflective of German policies in occupied Europe, but contained universal messages for all societies. Implied in his definition is the idea that genocide can be a slow process. Most significantly, the idea of prevention of genocide depends upon the institution of new levels of international law that recognizes the universality of the human community.

Lemkin's wide-ranging definition of genocide, however, was not accepted into the final version of the United Nations Convention in 1948. Article II of the Convention defined genocide with some precision but also removed the element of political genocide:

Any of the following acts with intent to destroy, in whole or in part, a national, ethnical, racial or religious group, as such:

a. Killing members of the group;

b. Causing serious bodily or mental harm to members of the group;

c. Deliberately inflicting on the group conditions of life calculated to bring about its physical destruction in whole or in part;

d. Imposing measures intended to prevent births within a group;

e. Forcibly transferring children of this group to another group.

Leo Kuper has noted that at the end of World War II, the Charter for the Nuremberg tribunal (August 8, 1945) of the Allies established "crimes against peace," "war crimes," and "crimes against humanity." The understanding seems to have been that genocide could be either a crime against humanity or a war crime.[7] However, in the debate on the Convention, the Soviet delegation argued "that the inclusion of political groups was not in conformity 'with the scientific definition of genocide and would, in practice, distort the perspective in which the crime should be viewed and impair the efficacy of the Convention.'"[8] Indeed, one can easily comprehend Soviet objections to "political genocide" as well as religious and cultural genocide as forms of genocide, since Soviet ideology and practice had destroyed both opposition political groups as well as having maintained a concerted attack on religion from 1917. In addition, many nationalities of the USSR, such as Crimean Tatars and Chechens, were deported from their homelands, which may be viewed as a form of "ethnic cleansing," or cultural genocide, because of implications for culture when people are removed from their native territories.

Above all, however, the most controversial aspect of the UN Convention is the issue of *intent*. The idea of intentionality came from the Holocaust and was easily discernible in Nazi ideology and Hitler's speeches even if a document about *Endlösung* has never been found. If Nazi Germany left a long paper trail about its intent *vis-à-vis* the Jews and Roma/Sinti, other regimes in the present as well as the immediate past were not so eager to leave such information. Thus, while most scholars recognize the Armenian massacres of 1915-1922 as a "genocide," a debate about intent still exists despite documents from the Ittihadist /Young Turk Party of the Ottoman Empire. The debate also has potency in the debate about the fate of Native peoples in the New World, especially Natives of the Great Plains at the hands of the government of the United States and the Aboriginal peoples at the hands of the Australian government in Australasia. In both of the latter cases, a pattern of policies, difficult to label as genocide under the Convention, occurred which had a "genocidal effect": extermination of tribes, curtailment of births, loss of language, the taking of children into special schools, and exposure to diseases.

Thus, without a clear case of intent, genocide is difficult to prove. The records of the United Nations and the International Criminal Tribunal for crimes in the Former Yugoslavia at The Hague seem to prove this. The Holocaust and the extermination of 800,000 Tutsis by Hutus in Rwanda (in 1994) have been the only two "true genocides," although it appears that the destruction of Cambodia's own people by the Khmer Rouge during the 1970s may eventually be recognized as an "autogenocide." The Armenian Genocide arguments, by contrast, focus on recognition of an event by a current regime, the Turkish Republic, of the sins of its predecessor, the Ottoman Empire. Using the Holocaust and Rwanda as models, it appears that only a total military defeat of a genocidal regime, along with immediate trial of surviving leadership and perpetrators, can insure a recognition of genocide and retributive measures. Kuper has written that "Genocide is pre-eminently a government crime and governments can hardly be expected to plead guilty."[9] While genocide is a government crime that requires intent, The Hague court on Bosnian atrocities has convicted Serbian commanders of both crimes against humanity and genocide. Dusko Tadic, for example, whose trial began on May 7, 1996, was convicted of crimes against humanity (Article 5 of the Statute – persecution on political, racial and/or religious grounds; murder; inhumane acts), grave breaches of the 1949 Geneva Conventions (Article 2 – wilful killing; torture or inhuman treatment; wilfully causing great suffering or serious injury to body or health), violations of the laws or customs of war (Article 3 – cruel treatment; murder), but not genocide. This 1997 decision was important, nevertheless, as it was the first case since World War II when an individual was found guilty of these crimes, while the government of Serbia had not been charged with such crimes. In August 2001, Radislav Krstic was found guilty on the charge of genocide and sentenced to 46 years in prison. In September 2001, a United Nations court has ruled that Serbian troops did not carry out genocide against ethnic Albanians during Slobodan Milosevic's campaign in Kosovo from 1998 to 1999. Tribunals in Rwanda have convicted eight people on charges of genocide as of the time this paper was written. The interesting question that runs through these cases is whether an individual can be convicted of genocide when the government he represents is not? The events in former Yugoslavia have yet to qualify as a genocide.

One of the results of the failure of the UN Convention to have a capability of rapidly defining genocide (the failed and frustrating debate over Rwanda in the Security Council during 1994 will suffice as an example) is a disconnect between the legal definition of genocide and the memory of it within the afflicted community. Thus while both Jews and Germans (and now Europeans) commemorate the negative memory of the Holocaust, they do so on different days. The Jewish commemorative day, *Yom HaShoah*, has been established for the 27th of the Jewish month of Nissan, roughly around the time of the Warsaw Ghetto uprising in 1943, but also between the Jewish holiday of Passover and the Israeli commemorations for fallen soldiers and Israeli independence. However, as other victims of Nazism have embraced January 27, which is the anniversary date of the liberation of Auschwitz by Soviet troops, will those who were still being killed and mutilated after January 27 adhere to such a commemoration? Discourse about memory has focused more precisely on May 8, the commemoration of the final collapse of National Socialism and the end of the war. In the case of commemorating the Armenian genocide, however, the Armenians commemorate the date on April 24, while the other side denies the event happened. Such disconnections on several levels raise important questions about the popularization of the word "genocide" and the legal definition through the UN Convention, which is quite different. The Vatican has become involved, during the years 2000 and 2001, in the question of recognition of the Armenian genocide. On November 9, 2000, Pope John Paul II recognized the Armenian destruction as "genocide" in a joint statement with his Armenian counterpart, Catholicos Karekin II. On September 27, 2001, in a short speech at the Genocide memorial in Yerevan, the Pope referred to "The horrible violence that was brought onto the Armenians, repels us." He referred later to the event as *Medz Yeghern*, the Armenian language equivalent of "genocide," similar to how the Hebrew word *Shoah* means Holocaust. The Turkish government was not inflamed by the use of *Medz Yeghern*, as it was not, in their eyes, the "G-word," genocide.

Nevertheless, progress toward recognition of the "G-word" as genocide will remain complex unless a new understanding of international law and the human community emerges. This was well-stated by Michael Ignatieff, who, at a lecture at the United States Holocaust Museum in December 2000, noted a frightening scene of Claude Lanzmann's *Shoah*, when a Polish peasant was asked how he felt about the destruction of the Jews. Quoting the text of the film, Ignatieff noted the peasant as saying: "When I cut my finger, I feel it. When you cut your finger, you feel it." Ignatieff, it appears, has focused us on the essence of the "G-question," when he wrote: "Because we do have to ask why, exactly, genocide is a crime against humanity? Why is a crime against Jews, or any other human group, a crime against those who don't belong to that group?" When we figure out the answer to this, we will undoubtedly have an answer to the question of exactly what "genocide" is and how the human community deals with it.

Notes

1. The use of the phrase "G-Word" was suggested to me in a review by Mark Mazower entitled "The G-Word," *The London Review of Books*, Vol.23, No. 3, 8 February 2001.
2. Raphael Lemkin, *Axis Rule in Occupied Europe: Laws of Occupation, Analysis of Government, Proposals for Redress* (Washington D.C.: Carnegie Endowment for International Peace, 1944), 79.
3. Ibid., 80.
4. Ibid., 79-80.
5. Ibid., 81.
6. Ibid., 86.
7. Leo Kuper, *Genocide* (New Haven: Yale University Press, 1981), 21-22.
8. Ibid., 25.
9. Ibid., 113.

5

STATES OF GENOCIDE AND OTHER STATES

Helen Fein

Genocide in the second half of the twentieth century defied the hopes of the post-Second World War era expressed (after the 1946 international trials of Nazi war criminals at Nuremberg) by the passage of the United Nations Genocide Convention by the General Assembly in 1948. Many believed that the mass murder of people simply because of who they were would never again be allowed to happen undeterred or unpunished.

Genocide continues, despite the decline of communism and fascism. In fact, since 1945, it has spread in Africa, Asia, and Latin and Central America, and has reappeared in Europe as well. In the twentieth century, state killings of civilians are estimated to have taken 169 million lives, which is four times the total number of war victims, according to R. J. Rummel.[1]

Why Do Genocides Occur?

Chalk and Jonassohn have distinguished four major reasons why genocide occurs: "1. To eliminate a real or potential threat; 2. To spread terror among real or potential enemies; 3. To acquire economic wealth; or 4. To implement a belief, ideology or theory."[2] Other scholars identified similar patterns which I label as types of genocide: ideological, retributive, developmental and despotic. These are ideal-types or constructs and actual cases may overlap categories as the motives and rewards of genocide are mixed.

Developmental or utilitarian genocides are probably the least well-documented because they occur in interior and less visible areas – also areas less reported by the media. For this reason, we cannot be sure how prevalent they are. Most genocides are retributive state responses preceded by threats to the state or élite in power. But the accusation of a threat may be a construction of the perpetrator as in the Armenian genocide and the Holocaust – ideological genocides. In other cases, the state provoked the threat.

Although genocide has its roots in antiquity and is associated with warring states, empires and colonization, its use within the state for radical demographic reformation in the twentieth century is new. Both World War 1 and II were the backdrop for warring powers eliminating minorities: the Armenians in the Ottoman Empire in World War 1 and the Jews and Roma in Nazi-controlled and allied Europe in World War II. Its practice increased in the latter part of the twentieth century, an era of decolonization. Although genocide can and has appeared on all continents, in recent decades it has been more prevalent among newer states than among older ones. Reviewing genocide in Asia, Africa, and the Middle East after 1945, I found the use of genocide during conflicts within states in these regions between 1968-88 was three times that between the years 1948-1968.[3] States of terror can become states of genocide when rulers detect members of a distinctive ethnic group challenging the state, as in Guatemala (Mayan Indians) and Iraq (Kurds).

In the post-World War II era, genocide was most often a response by dominant ethnoclasses (i.e., groups holding a monopoly of power based on their ethnic identity) to rebellions by suppressed ethnoclasses. Unfree, authoritarian and one-party communist states (in ascending order) were most apt to use genocide. Such regimes often resorted to genocidal actions more than once. In fact, genocide and genocidal massacres occurred so often in conflicts in these areas that they could be considered the norm (in a statistical sense).[4]

States involved in wars were most apt to use genocide. In some cases, genocide triggered war; in most cases, war was a cover for genocide. There are several reasons for this: wars justify aggression, and victims of genocide may be viewed as enemies or related to enemies outside state borders. Some genocides and war can be linked to movements spurred by resentment over wars lost in the past.

In virtually all cases, war masks the crime of genocide, which is a premeditated and rational crime. In other words, genocide is rational in view of the ends the *genocidaires* intend to accomplish. Genocide is a response to two problems of the state by the élite who control – or who want to control – the state: Who rules? Who belongs? This pattern is most evident in the case of ideological genocide.

In such genocides, the *genocidaires* devise a "political formula" regarding what constitutes the greater good and who are the "real" state people.[5] This excludes the group who do not fit their definition: for example, so-called non-Aryans in Germany, non-Turks in the Ottoman Empire, and non-

Hutus in Rwanda, leaving these groups vulnerable to elimination if the *genocidaires* come to power and other circumstances are right.

During the nineteenth century, many political philosophers believed the state was created to represent the people. Out of this assumption the idea arose, rooted in democratic liberal nationalism, that a people could remove or overthrow the state and change the government. In the twentieth century, many non-democratic states believed that the state could remove the people using genocide and ethnic cleansing (often leading to genocide). Totalitarian (and some authoritarian) states proceeded to eliminate the people who did not fit the state's political formula or were seen as a threat.

Threat is defined in the view of the men in power. The victims may be seen as a real or a symbolic threat. Sometimes, the victims are groups which rebel or do not accept their place, and the perpetrators choose to eliminate them rather than share power with them. Sometimes, the threat is symbolic, as was the "Jewish threat" in Germany. The Jews were loyal Germans, making no claims except to be equal citizens, and were no material, political or military threat. The Jewish threat was a product of centuries of Christian religious and racial antisemitism, a fantasy which led to the Nazi re-definition of the Jews in Germany as outside the German people (*Volk*) and nation, aliens and enemies.

There are several necessary preconditions for genocide:

1. The exclusion of the victim from the universe of obligation of the collective conscience.[6] This is indicated by direct statements, media propaganda and legislation or discriminatory enforcement of laws. Such statements and depiction charge that the victim is alien and does not belong, demonize and stigmatize the group as non-human, applying animal, insect, germ and viral metaphors. Legal definition and discrimination deny the victims protection under the law and may affix ethnic identity cards, signs and marked passports to separate them and prevent their escape.

2. There is a problem attributed to the victim – the "Jewish problem," "Armenian problem," "Tutsi problem," etc. – or an opportunity seen to be impeded by them, such as expansion in the hinterlands and economic development; and

3. There is the lack of internal checks or external checks on the perpetrator. Dictatorships and totalitarian states lack internal checks. This leads to a calculated decision on the part of the perpetrators that they can get away with genocide.

4. They (usually correctly) anticipate there will be no checks – reprisal, intervention, sanctions or even recognition – from major powers and other patrons.

War is a facilitating condition as it generally provides immunity from oversight and intervention by hostile powers. It enables other states to avoid recognizing events as genocide. They are apt to frame the ongoing murders just as part of war, "ethnic conflict" or "age-old hatred" to avoid any responsibility to stop them.

While communist and fascist states are the major *genocidaires* and mass murderers, other major and regional powers have committed genocide or overlooked genocides and genocidal massacres by their client-states in the past. The *genocidaires'* awareness that there have been (until recently) no sanctions against previous users of genocide reinforces their readiness to commit genocide.

Implications

The United Nations Convention on the Prevention and Punishment of the Crime of Genocide has two aims, but until recently the international community ignored both. We note that two preconditions preparatory to waging genocide (3 and 4 above) can be changed by major states making it clear that the potential *genocidaires* will not get away with it. When deterrence (which can be backed by diplomatic, economic, and military sanctions) does not work, intervention is necessary. But western states still prefer to promise post-war retribution (in Bosnia and Rwanda as they threatened in World Wars 1 and II) rather than promptly to recognize and intervene to stop genocide. Retribution or judgment seems cost-free in comparison to deterrence or intervention which is costly, but this is not so.

It is now evident that the failure to deter is not only a political and moral failure but a threat to international security and development – an economic black hole. For example, the failure to deter genocide in Rwanda and promptly to arrest the fleeing *genocidaires* has caused greater massacres in the Congo, civil and international war that has cost the lives of hundreds of thousands directly and indirectly and perpetuated the cycle of fear and terror. It has been reliably estimated that it would have cost one dollar for early prevention to every twenty dollars (maximally) spent on emergency relief and trials (billions of dollars in all) and the meter is still ticking.[7] Rwanda, a poor country to begin with, has dropped towards the bottom ranking of all states in social and economic development.[8]

Studies have shown both that social scientists can predict genocide and recognize it in the making and that the American public wants to stop it with multilateral intervention if needed.[9] Political leaders and non-governmental organizations are on the cusp of what could be a turning point in the twenty-first century. We can no longer say "Never again" when we are the people enabling genocide to reoccur again and again and again.

Notes

1. R. J. Rummel, *Death by Government* (Rutgers, NJ: Rutgers University Press, 1991), 11.

2. Frank Chalk and Kurt Jonassohn, *The History and Sociology of Genocide* (New Haven: Yale University Press, 1990), 29.

3. Helen Fein, "Accounting for Genocide after 1945: Theories and Some Findings," *International Journal of Group Rights* I (1993): 79-106.

4. Ibid.

5. Gaetano Mosca, *The Ruling Class*, trans. Hannah D. Kahn, ed. and rev. by Arthur Livingston (New York: McGraw-Hill, 1939), 70-72.

6. Helen Fein, *Imperial Crime and Punishment* (Honolulu: The University Press of Hawaii, 1977). Chapter 1 revises and expands the concept of the common or collective conscience in Emile Durkheim, *The Division of Labor in Society*, trans. George Simpson (New York: Free Press, 1933).

7. Helen Fein, "The Three P's of Genocide Prevention: With Application to a Genocide Foretold – Rwanda" in *Protection Against Genocide–Mission Impossible?* ed Neal Riemer (Westport, CT: Praeger, 2000), 59.

8. Rwanda dropped from 149 (of 173 states) on the Human Development Index reported in 1993 by the United Nations Development Programme [UNDP] *Human Development Report* (New York: Oxford University Press, 1993) to 174 (of 175 states) in 1997, see *Human Development Report* (New York: Oxford University Press, 1997).

9. Helen Fein, "The Three P's of Genocide Prevention," 59-62; and Barbara Harff and T. R. Gurr, "Genocide and Politicide in Global Perspective: The Historical Record and Future Risks," in Stan Windass, ed., *Just War and Genocide* (London: Palgrave, 2002).

HUMANITARIAN INTERVENTION AND THE SCOPE OF THE DUTY TO PREVENT GENOCIDE

What then are the legal rights and duties of states in intervening against the crime of genocide? Pursuant to Article I of the Genocide Convention (1948), contracting parties undertake to "prevent and punish" the crime of genocide. The legal scope of this obligation was first raised before the International Court of Justice in the Case Concerning Application of the Genocide Convention, initiated by Bosnia-Herzegovina against the Federal Republic of Yugoslavia in 1993, though not yet adjudicated on the merits. In his instructive Separate Opinion, Judge Sir Elihu Lauterpacht, examined, among other issues, the essential question of whether "every party is under an obligation individually and actively to intervene to prevent genocide outside its territory when committed by or under the authority of some other party." His dispassionate assessment was that the "limited reaction of the parties to the Genocide Convention in relation to [various] episodes [of genocide] may represent a practice suggesting the permissibility of inactivity."

At first sight, the conspicuous failure to intervene against the 1994 genocide in Rwanda, despite ample prior knowledge and opportunity to act, is an instance of state practice supporting this restrictive interpretation of the duty to prevent. However, it is intriguing to consider the widespread assumption that defining the atrocities as "genocide" would somehow trigger an obligation to intervene. For example, the Washington Post *observed in 1994 that the "Clinton administration deliberately stopped short of saying the tribal slaughter [in Rwanda constitutes] genocide – a declaration that would require US and other foreign intervention under a 1948 international convention."*

Ultimately, legal debates as to whether such a duty to prevent exists or not revolve around the internalization of civilized mores that we deem befitting in the international community. To move from cynicism and empty platitudes to a condition of genuine empathy and resolve to prevent genocide, there is but one option: to embrace the inextricable oneness and indivisibility of humankind, not merely as a vague and pious aspiration, but as an inescapable reality in an increasingly interdependent Global Village. In the eternal words of the Persian mystic Sa'adi, "all people are limbs of one body," and a limb in distress may only be disregarded to the detriment of the whole body.

Payam Akhavan (USA)
Former Legal Advisor to the International Criminal Tribunals
for the former Yugoslavia and Rwanda

6

ETHNIC CLEANSING

Paul Mojzes

The word "genocide" suggests a horrendous attempted or successful extermination of an entire people. It is the worst category of human violence – aside perhaps of omnicide, the destruction of the entire world. The word itself is apparently the product of the mid-twentieth century and, therefore, some have concluded that genocide is of modern making. However, history abounds with genocidal actions. We know from the Hebrew Bible alone of the destruction of entire tribes or urban populations as well as large-scale exiles of entire populations, enslaved and forcibly transferred to a totally alien territory (e.g. the Assyrian exile of Israelites and the Babylonian exile of Judeans). A tremendously large number of peoples from the past no longer exist. Under the criteria of the United Nations Genocide Convention, we would conclude that genocides took place. For instance, many would say Europeans carried out genocide over Native American Indian populations and some argue that the process continues.

For over a century there have been numerous attempts to root out entire people by modern means such as efficient bureaucracies, transportation, propaganda, and technology of mass murder. Part of an intensified ideology of intolerance that appears to learn from previously carried out genocides suggests that entire people have to be killed off or that they have to be removed from a territory and separated out of mixed areas where they have previously lived alongside each other. Examples come readily to mind, the Armenian genocide by Turks, the Holocaust of the Jewish population in Europe, the genocide of Crimean Tartars and Chechens by the order of Stalin, the Balkan wars at the beginning, middle, and end of the twentieth century, Pol Pot's Cambodian genocide, Rwanda and Burundi, and so forth.

So terrible are the individual cases of genocide and so large their number that the United Nations criminalized genocide. The Convention for the Prevention and Punishment of the Crime of Genocide was adopted by Resolution 260 (III) A of the UN General Assembly on December 9, 1948, and entered into force on January 12, 1950. The Convention states that genocide is a crime that should be deterred or punished whether carried out in war or peace. "(T)he following acts committed with the intent to destroy, in whole or in part, a national, ethnical, racial or religious group" are regarded as genocidal:

(a) Killing members of the group;

(b) Causing serious bodily or mental harm to members of the group;

(c) Deliberately inflicting on the group conditions of life calculated to bring about its physical destruction in whole or in part;

(d) Imposing measures intended to prevent births within the group;

(e) Forcibly transferring children of the group to another group."

In recent years claims that genocide is being carried out over the members of one's group have greatly proliferated. Even ethnic or racial groups that are rapidly increasing in numbers have complained of genocide, for instance, when they felt that birth control was advocated or actually applied manipulatively or forcibly, even if only over a small number of people of that group. Some have suggested that adoption of some children of one group by members of another group amounts to genocide. Or else that the exiling of people of an ethnic group from one place, even though the larger ethnic group is not threatened by such an act, also constitutes genocide.

The frequency of claims of genocide weakens the impact of the word. If genocides were a commonplace, then they would seem not to deserve such overwhelming concern. The climate of widespread claims of genocidal victimization is, ironically, supported by the vague wording of the Genocide Convention itself. The problem, in my opinion, is the words "in part" and "mental harm." How large or small is "in part?" We know of massacres of certain groups, which may well be war crimes but not the crime of genocide. There have been extremely savage expulsions of populations from a territory, e.g., Greeks from Anatolia and Turks from Greece in the early 1920s, but were these genocidal acts? If the Chinese population in a location in Indonesia is killed and driven out, does it constitute genocide of the Chinese? Would Stalin's policies of forced collectivization, which caused massive famines resulting in the death of about nine million Ukrainians, be considered genocide or was it something else?

The charge of genocide should be used sparingly lest it loses its force to horrify, though it does not mean that pogroms, massacres, concentration encampment, mass rape, and expulsions are not horrendous evils. But they are lesser evils than genocide. Real genocide, namely the real intent to destroy a people, is one the world's greatest evils, as it threatens not merely a large number of people but an entire unit of people. Thus one may freely conclude that the "Final Solution of the Jewish Question," as envisioned by the Wannsee conference of Nazi leaders in January 1942, as well as its precursors, led to genocide. Nazis carried out genocides not only over Jews, but also over a number of captive nations. So did some of their puppet regimes.

In the Balkans someone invented a formula for dealing with a rival group: "Kill one third, expel one third, and convert one third." More than one ethnic group in the Balkans subscribed to this idea and one may certainly consider it genocidal. The wars in the Balkans in the last decade of the twentieth century introduced into our vocabulary the term "ethnic cleansing." At first it was attributed solely to Serbs, as they wanted to remove all Croats and/or Muslims from certain areas in Croatia and Bosnia-Herzegovina. Many in the West still think that it was only Serbs who practiced ethnic cleansing. A closer examination of the wars from 1991-1995 indicates that Croats and Muslims also carried out ethnic cleansing, though not on as wide a scale.

Thus some have concluded that the term "ethnic cleansing" is of the most recent vintage. However, already in the 1970s and 1980s, Serbs claimed – and such views were confirmed by Western media – that they were being ethnically cleansed by Albanians from Kosovo. Such claims have receded from Western awareness as we learned of Slobodan Milosevic's "ethnic cleansing" of Albanians in Kosovo (on the heels of ethnic cleansing in Croatia and Bosnia-Herzegovina), which was actually a case of "counter-ethnic cleansing." When NATO occupied Kosovo, Albanian extremists carried out a "counter-counter ethnic cleansing," the most successful of all because it has practically eliminated Serbs from their own province.

But the history of this term goes much further back. In the epic poem "Mountain Wreath" written by Montenegrin Orthodox Bishop Petar Petrovic II-Njegos in 1847, he describes a campaign in the late eighteenth century by Montenegrin Christians against the Turks and Turkized (Muslim) Montenegrins who were the overlords. During the campaign Muslims were massacred by most violent means, not sparing anyone; for this he used the term "cleansing."

Is "ethnic cleansing" simply a euphemism for genocide, which makes genocide more acceptable, more sterilized? That depends on a number of factors. In most wars there is forcible removal of populations. Not every case qualifies as genocidal. When large number of Mexicans were driven out of territories occupied by the USA, was that genocide or ethnic cleansing? When Jews were forbidden to live in England, was it genocide or ethnic cleansing? In my opinion while every genocide is ethnic cleansing, not every ethnic cleansing is genocide. If an ethnic cleansing does not genuinely threaten the existence of a group, it would not qualify as genocide.

In the vast majority of cases, both genocides and ethnic cleansing are carried out during and immediately after wars. They are generally characterized by greater barbarity and brutality than most wars, because the purpose of the brutality is to so threaten and scare the victim population as to make them abandon an area by fleeing or by being expelled. Genocides are not spontaneous mob actions, though they may appear so. Rather they are the product of the organized propaganda to demonize the victim group. Usually genocides are deliberate actions planned by some leaders of the perpetrating group who consciously exaggerate the rivalry, threat, difference, alienation, and need for elimination of the "other." Under modern conditions the instigators of genocide usually do not personally participate in the brutalities, but they ideologically justify it, organize it, command it to either regular armed forces or paramilitary units, and incite the potential perpetrators to a level of bloodthirstiness that then easily controls the conscience of people who otherwise might not even approve of such action, much less engage in it. In most cases criminal elements (psychopaths and sociopaths) of the perpetrating population are let loose to carry out cold-blooded horrors that defy our imagination. Once such actions have taken place, it is hard to reverse the process because the level of mutual hatred is so high that the perpetrators feel they have to finish the job lest in some future generation the descendants of the victims carry out retribution.

On some level it is hard to analyze the reasons for genocide; yet on another level they are fairly easy to locate. It is part of the sinful human condition to hate (and much has been written as to what causes hatred). A basic impulse of hatred is to wish the disappearance of the one whom we hate. Combine this fact with a collectivist mentality in time of crisis and one gets the precondition for genocide. Human beings do have a herding instinct and seek safety among those who resemble them, no matter how flimsy that likeness may be (e.g. blood relation, racial or national affinity, sexual orientation, or religious identity). When a group feels threatened, real or imaginary, it seeks to defend itself against threats. Those threats are often impersonal and complex. Genocidal leaders seek a scapegoat to focus the defensive mechanism of the group against a victim people who can be relatively easily distinguished and against which there may have been grievances which are now vastly exaggerated. Once the perpetrating population buys into the oversimplified logic of "us or them," the conditions for genocide have been created. Obviously genocide is greatly promoted by an imbalance in armament; usually a well-armed group carries out genocide over a population that is unarmed and little prepared for defense, though from time to time ethnic cleansing is carried out under conditions of civil wars or within the scope of a larger war, when one group decides to settle scores with a rival group (e.g., the Croat genocide over Serbs in Croatia and Bosnia during World War II, or the attempted extermination of Roma (Gypsies) in many parts of Europe during the same time period).

There is no easy or quick normalization of relations between the victim and perpetrator group after genocide. Much time needs to pass to heal the most open wounds so that some of the memory of horrors is dulled. Locating and punishing the inciters and organizers of genocide by some recognized judicial means, such as a domestic or international war crimes court, is a precondition for normalization, as is some willingness for reparations or atonement if the genocide did not happen too long ago. There has to be a willingness by responsible leaders of the perpetrator people to ask forgiveness, though it is not clear whether survivors of a genocide are "authorized" to grant forgiveness on behalf of those who did not survive. Processes of reconciliation, including penitent actions by descendants of perpetrators or mediation by third party groups, can help the process of moving beyond the greatly aggravated conditions that make coexistence nearly impossible. At times separation of two groups may be the most effective way of dealing with the impossible tension (e.g., the expulsion of Germans from Poland, Czechoslovakia, and Yugoslavia after World War II or the exchange of population between Greece and Turkey in the 1920s).

Obviously preventing genocide is both easier and more fruitful than dealing with its after-effects. A conscious effort of preventing demagogues from coming to power and manipulating people is the best solution, but this is particularly difficult in unstable transitional crisis periods, as was well illustrated by the rise of Milosevic, Tudjman, and Karadzic – not to mention Hitler and Stalin. In societies where different peoples live next to each other, it is insufficient simply to coexist in uneasy toleration. Conscious efforts need to be made by both government and civil and religious groups for people of these groups to intermingle, get to know each other, deal openly with mutual grievances, build confidence, and – watch their language. The American principle of unlimited freedom of speech and press, including hate speech, is, frankly, dangerous. Demagogic language is incendiary and can easily lead to great damage; it is almost always a prelude to genocide. The constitutional prohibition of hate language in countries such as

Germany and Austria that have experienced the power of Nazi propaganda, appears to be a better defense against genocide than the US constitutional provisions.

One of the best defenses against genocide would be the sure knowledge that organizers would definitely be punished, as the UN Convention stipulates, but with the proviso that leaders of great powers who incite genocide or ethnic cleansing are prosecuted in the same way as leaders of small states are. For the time being this is a utopian idea, but in the beginning of this century no one imagined that the community of nations would at least verbally, though somewhat ineffectively, turn against perpetrators of genocide. It has been said that prior to attacking Poland in 1939, Hitler said: "Who, after all, speaks today of the annihilation of the Armenians?" Obviously, many of us do – and not just Armenians – and many of us have committed ourselves to do everything in our power to prevent future attempts at annihilation.

7

POPULATION ELIMINATION

Richard L. Rubenstein

There have been many attempts to define genocide since World War II. In 1944 Raphael Lemkin, an international lawyer, offered the first, defining it as "the coordinated and planned annihilation of a national, religious, or racial group by a variety of actions aimed at undermining the foundations essential to the survival of a group as a group."[1] Lemkin also noted that genocide is a "form of one-sided killing" in which the perpetrators intend to eliminate their victims who by contrast have no comparable intention. Lemkin's definition was followed by many others such as the 1946 UN Resolution that defined genocide as "the denial of the right to exist of entire human groups, as homicide is denial of the right to live of individual human beings..."[2]

I would like to propose an alternative definition: genocide can best be understood as *the most radical method of implementing a state or communally-sponsored program of population elimination.* I believe that this definition facilitates an understanding of the larger historical conditions under which populations have been targeted for elimination.[3] Genocide can be understood as the last stop on a journey of destruction that starts with the least harsh form of population elimination, namely, emigration schemes in which unwanted individuals are provided with transportation from their home community to a foreign destination, but not the means to return. For example, in the early decades of the nineteenth century, a number of English parishes sent their paupers and other "undesirables" with only a few pounds sterling to North America where they were expected to fend for themselves.[4]

Compulsory expulsion is a harsher method of population elimination. Jews were expelled from England in 1290 and from most of France in 1306. On March 31, 1492, Spain's Catholic monarchs, Ferdinand and Isabella, promulgated the Edict of Expulsion by which all Jews who had not or would not become Christian were compelled to leave Spain. There have been many large-scale population expulsions in the twentieth century. When Germany attacked Poland in 1939, western Poland was incorporated into the Reich as the Warthegau. Almost immediately, the Nazis began a monumental program of expulsion and resettlement. Ethnic Germans from the Baltic countries were "resettled" to the Warthegau and Jews were either expelled or forcibly confined to miserably overcrowded ghettos. After the war, it was the Germans' turn. More than 12 million ethnic Germans were expelled from Eastern Europe and settled largely in a truncated West Germany. There was, however, a fundamental difference. Most expelled Germans were eventually able to start new lives; the expulsion of the Jews was a prelude to genocide.

Although they seldom, if ever, succeed completely, perpetrators of genocide seek the total elimination of the target population. The Nazis expressed this succinctly in the term "Final Solution of the Jewish Problem." The Turks expressed their genocidal intentions with even greater frankness. On September 15, 1915, Taalat Bey, a member of the ruling triumvirate of the Turkish government, sent a telegram to the Police Office in Aleppo, Syria, announcing that the Government had

> ...determined completely to exterminate the Armenians living in Turkey... Regardless of the women, children and invalids, and however deplorable the methods of destruction may seem an end is to be put to their existence without paying any heed to feeling or conscience.[5]

Between 600,000 and 1,000,000 Christian Armenians were killed. The exact number cannot be determined. Whatever the number, there is a scholarly consensus that the Armenian genocide anticipated the Holocaust. Nevertheless, here again there was a fundamental difference. The Turkish genocide was aimed primarily at inhabitants of Turkish Armenia, a region that straddled the border between Turkey and Tsarist Russia. Unlike the Nazis, the Turks had no interest in hunting down *all* Armenians. Nazi Germany aimed eventually to exterminate *all* the world's Jews. A genocide of such universal scope had never before been attempted.

No combination of conditions will *necessarily* lead to genocide but there are some conditions that are likely to foster state-sponsored genocide. The most fundamental condition is *population redundancy*. A governing authority is far less likely to consider a program of population elimination where there is a labor shortage. For example, after World War II, with millions of German soldiers held as prisoners of war in the Soviet Union, Germany encouraged the immigration of "guest workers" from Muslim countries, especially Turkey, to help restart its economy. This action constituted an historic reversal of Europe's traditional policy toward Muslim immigration. The trend continues to some extent at present because of Europe's aging indigenous population and the need for a youthful labor force to supply the productivity necessary to finance Europe's health insurance and old age pension systems. Elsewhere, this writer has argued that, as a result of the modernization of Europe's economy in the nineteenth and early twentieth centuries, Europe had a crisis of overpopulation.[6] A diminishing number of Europe's exploding population was required for agriculture. Much of this population was absorbed by the continent's growing manufacturing base, but by no means all. Emigration and imperialist colonization provided Europe with a demographic safety valve for its population surplus. As a result, unemployment did not become a dangerous social problem until the twentieth century. During the Great Depression of the 1930s, the demographic safety valve was largely unavailable.

The terms "redundant" or "surplus" population are not absolute. Whether a society has such a population depends on how it is organized. The Nazis classified Germans of all ages with debilitating diseases as "useless eaters." As such, they were considered surplus and were targeted for extermination. Pre-modern societies with protective extended families as their fundamental units were less likely to have surplus populations than modern societies that value productive efficiency and economic rationality, although the rootless foot soldiers of the Crusades are an indication that Europe was beginning to develop a surplus population as early as the twelfth century. Nevertheless, mass redundant populations are largely a by-product of modernity.

Yet another reason why genocide has been more likely to develop in the modern period has been the organization of the world into states with well-defined borders and bureaucracies capable of limiting immigration. The borders of most countries were largely closed to European Jews during the 1930s, including the United States, the United Kingdom and British-controlled Palestine. The Nazis correctly concluded that there would be no practical impediment to the extermination of those who remained in their hands.

Nevertheless, even under conditions of a population surplus, no government is likely willingly to perpetrate large-scale mass murder unless its leaders are convinced that their actions are beneficial to those members of their own community whom they value. Put differently, no government will enter upon a program of mass murder absent some form of religious or moral legitimation. That was true even of the Nazis.[7] Such legitimation requires the *radical demonization* of the target group and its depiction as capable of inflicting significant harm on the perpetrator community. In the case of the Jews, a religious legitimation was ready at hand in the accusation that by their disbelief the Jews were collectively in every generation the murderers of God and, as such, in league with Satan. The demonization was further intensified by the identification of the Jews with Judas, the disciple who betrays Christ with a kiss. Because these identifications were inextricably woven into the heart of the Christian story, they operated at the level of pre-theoretical consciousness and were normally opaque to critical scrutiny. The congeries of demonizing accusations carried with them the implicit warning that Jews would use the powers that had allegedly enabled them to "murder" God to destroy the enemies in whose midst they dwelt. At bottom, there was a fear component in Nazi antisemitism.

In the case of the Armenians, the Turks were convinced that their Christian minority would betray them to Christian Russia, their wartime and hereditary enemy, and had to be exterminated. In the early thirteenth century, Pope Innocent III regarded the Cathars, the advocates of the Albigensian heresy, as mortal enemies of the Catholic Church. When the Pope became convinced that the Cathars could not be persuaded to return to the Church, he wrote to King Phillip Augustus of France admonishing him that such an alien body within Christendom could only be cured by the knife.[8] Although it took several decades, all of the Cathars were either killed or compelled to return to the Church.

However, demonization alone will not lead to genocide. The Jews were held in contempt for almost two thousand years before they became the target of outright genocide. In addition to demonizing a target group, a perpetrating community is likely to experience radical socio-economic and/or political stress and upheaval before embarking on such a program. Such stress may be caused by a humiliating defeat in war for which the target community is blamed. Against all rational calculation, the German right was convinced that the Jews were responsible for their country's defeat in World War I and, if left unchecked, would plot Germany's destruction in World War II. Turkey was defeated in the First Balkan War of 1912 by a coalition of Christian Balkan states aided by Russia and lost all of its remaining possessions in the Balkan Peninsula. As a result, its leaders were convinced that the presence of a large Christian population, the Armenians, on both sides of the Turkish-Russian frontier constituted a radical danger during World War I.

Another example of destabilizing stress was the victory of the radically anti-Christian Bolshevik Regime in Russia in 1917. The revolution was a catastrophic upheaval and was perceived with considerable justice as a major threat to European civilization. Unfortunately, right-wing propaganda throughout Europe identified Jews with Bolshevism and portrayed them as seeking to use Bolshevism to destroy civilization. In spite of the opposition of the overwhelming majority of Jews to Communism, the highly visible presence of a few Jews among the Bolshevik leaders rendered the right-wing accusations credible to all too many Europeans.

A final ingredient necessary for the perpetration of genocide is the *cover of war*. Killing the enemy is considered legitimate in wartime and, if one can identify the target population as the enemy, there are few, if any, scruples left to prevent the project from proceeding.

In conclusion, I would like to suggest that many of the same conditions are also likely to foster programs of terrorism on the part of non-governmental groups. Non-state terrorism is not likely to flourish absent a redundant population with angry males who lack either vocational slots or regard the available slots as beneath their training, competence or dignity. Like genocide, terrorism requires moral and/or religious legitimation which in turn requires the demonization of the target community. Like genocide, terrorist groups seek the disruption and ultimate destruction of the target community. There are, of course, differences; genocide cannot be successfully implemented by non-government organizations; terrorism can. Governments usually sponsor terrorist activities surreptitiously when overt military strikes carry too great a risk of punishing retaliation. Finally, although both genocide and terrorism have been practiced for many centuries, the era of high technology and globalization is especially conducive to such activities and requires heightened, sophisticated vigilance among those who seek to diminish or eliminate them entirely.

Notes

1. Raphael Lemkin, *Axis Rule in Occupied Europe* (Washington, DC: Carnegie Endowment for International Peace, 1944), 92.

2. Frank Chalk and Kurt Jonassohn, *The History and Sociology of Genocide* (Yale University Press: 1990), 9. See Leo Kuper, *Genocide: Its Political Use in the Twentieth Century* (New York: Penguin Books, 1981), 23.

3. For an elaboration of this theme, see Richard L. Rubenstein, *The Cunning of History: Mass Death and the American Future* (New York: Harper and Row, 1975) and *The Age of Triage: Fear and Hope in an Overcrowded World* (Boston: Beacon Press, 1983).

4. Cumberland was one such parish. It provided its "undesirables" with transportation to North America and £3. See Stanley C. Johnson, *A History of Emigration: From the United Kingdom to North America, 1762-1812*, 1st ed. 1912

(London: Frank Cass, 1966), 66.

5. The telegram is quoted in Manuel Sarkisyanz, *A Modern History of Transcaucasian Armenia* (Nagpur, India: Udyam Commercial Press, [Distributed by E. J. Brill, Leiden], 1975), 196.

6. See *The Cunning of History* and *The Age of Triage*.

7. This point is made effectively by Peter J. Haas, *Morality After Auschwitz: The Radical Challenge of the Nazi Ethic* (Philadelphia: Fortress Press, 1988).

8. The letter was written November 17, 1207. The text is found in Jonathan and Louise Riley-Smith, *The Crusades: Idea and Reality* (London: 1981), 78-80.

Forced to dig their own graves, these eastern European Jews were soon shot to death by members of Nazi murder squadrons (Einsatzgruppen), which took the lives of more than one million Jews and Gypsies within a few months after Hitler's army invaded the Soviet Union on June 22, 1941.

Photo © Yad Vashem

PART II

WHAT ARE THE CAUSES
AND MECHANISMS OF
GENOCIDE?

On April 16, 2002, the Dutch government headed by Prime Minister Wim Kok submitted its resignation to Queen Beatrix. Parliamentary governments have resigned before, and arguably Kok's gesture did not have much practical impact because national elections were but a month away. Nevertheless, this resignation was unprecedented. As Samantha Power, author of *"A Problem from Hell": America and the Age of Genocide*, put the point in the *Washington Post*, "for the first time in history, a Western government resigned because it was a bystander to genocide."

What moved Kok to act? A 7,600-page report commissioned by the Dutch government and compiled over six years by the Netherlands Institute for War Documentation found that a Dutch peacekeeping unit – admittedly too small, insufficiently armed, inadequately mandated and supported by the United Nations – had allowed the Bosnia Serbs to have their way in a ten-day onslaught against Bosnian Muslims who were supposedly under the protection of the UN-backed Dutch force in the so-called "safe area" of Srebrenica in July 1995. By no means do the Dutch alone bear responsibility for what happened to Srebrenica's Muslims during this most brutal chapter of the 1992-95 war in Bosnia, which unleashed the worst mass murder in Europe since the Holocaust. More forceful international intervention could have spared Srebrenica, but the responsibility for this slaughter lies first and foremost with the Bosnian Serb general, Ratko Mladic, and his followers.

When Mladic and his company took over Srebrenica, they separated the Muslim women and then took the men and boys to the woods nearby and murdered them. At the time of this writing, Srebrenica, whose pre-war population of 36,000 was mostly Muslim, has been ethnically "cleansed." Its population of 8,000 is now mostly Serbian. Meanwhile, wanted by international courts on genocide charges, Mladic and Radovan Karadzic, the former Bosnian Serb president, remained at large in 2002.

How does genocide happen? What are its causes? What mechanisms drive it? The essays in this book's second part explore those questions and respond to them. They show that no two genocides are exactly alike; they also reveal that all genocides share features in common. Although not identical, steps to isolate and separate people take place. The means and duration of murder are not the same, but most genocides, if not all, involve mass killing. The perpetrators are always particular people, such as Mladic and his Serbian followers. The victims are always specific, such as the Bosnian Muslims in Srebrenica. But whatever their ethnicity or group identity may be, there are perpetrators and victims in every genocide. There are also bystanders. Without them, neither the causes nor the mechanisms of genocide would have their way so easily.

8

A TWENTIETH-CENTURY PHENOMENON?

Mark Levene

The prevalence of genocide in the twentieth century was not some sort of aberration peculiar only to societies with an unusual cultural disposition, or the product of societies that, perhaps due to some misfortune of historical circumstance, took a special path in their development. Nor was genocide the product of societies afflicted by the undemocratic rule of highly ideological or authoritarian regimes. These aspects may tell us something about the phenomenon but they do not address its wellsprings. In my view, genocide is a by-product of very general drives toward what is referred to in German as a *Wille zu Macht*, a drive to power.

There is nothing new about such tendencies in the human condition. The only thing that provides a twentieth-century distinction is the framework within which genocide occurs. The drive to political power in contemporary history can only effectively succeed through control of modernized or at least modernizing nation-states operating within a global community of such states. While today we may accept this situation as both normal and normative, it is important to recall that this international inter-connected community, or more accurately system of states, only came to fruition during the last century when circumstances – in terms of power distribution – singularly favored regimes that had arrived there first, a century or more earlier. As such, to view genocide as the misfortune of God-forsaken societies "out there" which otherwise have nothing to do with ourselves, is entirely mistaken. Genocide is as much a state response to extrinsic realities as to intrinsic ones. In other words to a global political economy, which we, in the liberal west, to a significant degree have determined, shaped, and dominated.

Not only do genocides, or at least the modern variant of them, have a large number of common ingredients, but also looked at as a whole, there are connecting threads among them. We can discern a pattern which we urgently need to understand, not least because there have been approximately fifty genocides since 1945. They have taken place in all hemispheres and in all types of societies. Indeed, the frequency and scale of genocide intensified in the post-communist last ten years of the twentieth century.

What makes genocide? Raphael Lemkin considered it a form of state-organized warfare, one directed exclusively at a communal group or groups, rather than at other states. The intention of this warfare, he thought, is to annihilate the group(s) partially or totally. Thus, Lemkin stressed actions aimed at the disintegration of the biological structure of a group. He thought of genocide as a phenomenon that did not discriminate on the basis of gender or age. Perpetrators sought to destroy all members of the group, whether they were young virile men, their aged grandparents, pregnant women, or babies.

Two particularly salient questions immediately arise: First, how do we recognize a communal group? To which I would reply, we don't. The group may identify itself as such in ethnic, religious, or social terms, but for the purposes of genocide, it is wholly identified or, perhaps more to the point, *misidentified* by the perpetrators. When, for example, the Nazi leadership determined to kill the Jews, they did not consult leading rabbinic scholars about Jewish identity. The Nazis themselves decided who was and was not a Jew. If the perpetrators decide they want to kill an aggregate population because they think that population constitutes a group, they will do so, whatever best authority tells them to the contrary. A second and more critical question is Why? Why do people find themselves labeled not just as different, but in such a way that the state, at some point, determines that the only available course of action is to eliminate them collectively?

Part of an answer must be to remind ourselves that any blithe assumption that we have shuffled off the most irrational, savage and ugly characteristics of the human condition, only reveals the enormous gap between what we propose humanity to be and what it actually is. This gap does not mean we are forever trapped by our most basic, visceral fears, or by the tendency to lash out when we cannot control them. However, it does suggest that what we have been trying to achieve as a species, particularly in the accelerated process of development of the last two hundred years, does contain within it the potential for genocide.

Implicit in this last statement is the possible key to why genocide is so particularly modern. The phenomenon is intrinsically bound up with state-led projects of social engineering, which try to transform traditional societies – often very rapidly in revolutionary leaps "forward" – and with what happens when, in the face of the sheer magnitude of the tasks which states set themselves, these efforts go drastically wrong. It is no accident that the victims of genocide are those who find themselves in the way of, or actively dissent from, or have cultural belief-systems which question the plausibility of such projects. Meanwhile, genocide is rarely the result of simple, one-dimensional matters of ethnicity, religion or social status. It is not an accident that the first authentically modern genocides can be traced back to the seventeenth, eighteenth, and early nineteenth centuries, to societies which were at the forefront of the drive toward nation-statehood. Revolutionary France in the Vendée, Britain in the Americas and Antipodes, the United States in its drive to trans-continental hegemony – these powers in their determination to brook no obstacles in the way of their crisis-ridden paths to modernity provided many of the prototypal ground-rules for genocide. What they did *en route* to global power, latter-day states and nation-state builders would seek to emulate.

The greater the drive to transcend the limitations of modern political and economic realities, the greater is the potentiality and scope for genocide. True as that statement may be, however, it is too simplistic. Not every society in the twentieth century has taken a genocidal route. The leading western liberal states have been notable in putting aside their former genocidal selves, at least in their own domestic situations, while one can think of scores of other, newer nation-states, whose emergence, while often turbulent, crisis-ridden and even bloody, has not resulted in anything we can specifically denote as genocide.

If my argument affirms that all modern states have at least some potentiality to commit genocide, there still remains the question: What, specifically, do Germany, Russia, China, Turkey, Iraq, Cambodia, Indonesia, Pakistan, Bangladesh, Burma, Ethiopia, Rwanda, Burundi, Sudan and Guatemala – to name some notable offenders – have in common? Superficially, one would have to concede, not a great deal. The range of this group in terms of wealth and power, not to say political and cultural background, hardly offers firm grounds for comparison, while any attempt to suggest ideological proclivities or totalitarian systems as the connecting thread would either stretch the point to the ridiculous or demand comparison with other ideologically hard-line or authoritarian-prone regimes who have not been notable offenders. Put most starkly: How would we propose to make a connection between the genocides committed by Nazi Germany and Hutu-Power Rwanda? In other words, what is shared by modern Germany, a leading, modern industrial giant with an authentic civil society and roots deep in the Enlightenment project, and Rwanda, an underdeveloped, stunningly poor, post-colonial backwater?

Three elements make for a greater tendency towards genocide in the case of both Germany and Rwanda. Two of them are closely linked. I would call both Germany and Rwanda *old-new states* and *weak-strong states*. By this I mean that if one looks at the history of Rwanda, for example, one finds a state that drastically reformulated itself to engage and survive in the modern world. One also finds a state that from its own cultural and political perspective could quite justifiably look back to an earlier pre-colonial era in which it had not only a political and territorial coherence, but also a sense of its own power.

Rwandans, for example, are acutely aware that in the past their state counted in regional terms. Others looked to it with respect. Once people have that idea, the opportunities for inflating such a narrative into a national myth of a golden age become almost endless. Indeed, modernity has provided a very special tool – history – with which to play this game and to inculcate its teachings into generations of classroom children. Consider Germany, this time: after its modern political creation in 1871, no one would have proposed that it was anything other than very strong, and for many Germans in the period up to World War I, this is exactly how it felt. Following World War I, however, Germany began to feel that somehow she had been denied her due, held back, and kept from her rightful place in the world.

What we have here are the seeds of self-doubt, but rarely is that mindset articulated in this way. More likely it will be articulated as follows: There is something preventing the good, sound part of "our" society from breaking through, something that contaminates its health, takes away its virtue, emasculates and debilitates its wholeness and virility. Such fear is what we find over and over again in genocide's background. Whether the group is Tutsi, Jewish, or Armenian, it is portrayed as a foreign body, which not only does not fit into the national whole but whose very existence upsets the desirable equilibrium. But there is even more: the group is assumed to be actively malevolent, collectively working from within to sabotage "our" forward advance, conspiring with foreign enemies, ruining "our" chances, and ultimately destroying "our" people.

We need to understand critically the context in which a possibly long-term and nasty interaction between a communal group and state, even where that is founded on a whole set of misconceptions or confabulations, crystallizes into something much more dangerous and ultimately genocidal. Again using Rwanda as an example, let me illustrate what I mean.

We cannot understand the Rwandan genocide in 1994 without knowing what happened there between 1959 and 1963. Rwanda was a state emerging from colonialism in which there was a genuine dynamic between two sets of élites – one predominantly Tutsi, representing those who had traditionally held power within Rwanda, the other Hutu, representing the vast majority of the population who traditionally had not shared in the power. The Hutu élite won, making this victory not only a revolutionary landmark in the history of the country, but also providing them with an opportunity to present to their population and the world a particular Hutu version of Rwanda, both historic and actual. While the Tutsi élite clearly were overthrown, they did not accept their defeat, thus ensuring a prolonged period of crisis in which large numbers of their followers attempted to destabilize the regime from neighboring countries to which they had fled. As a result, the people whose position became really vulnerable were the Tutsi who remained in Rwanda. Whether they identified with the exiled opposition or saw themselves as entirely loyal to the new regime, it was inevitable that every time over the next thirty years when there were rumors of another Tutsi invasion, or of massacres of Hutu in neighboring Tutsi-run Burundi, the Tutsis in Rwanda were the ones most likely to suffer.

In sum, then, here is my point: When the children of the Tutsi exiles did invade in 1990, thus precipitating a genuine crisis, the children of the 1959 Hutu victors recalled these earlier times as they sized up what was happening. Once again, they thought, the nation was in danger; the gains of the revolution were threatened with nullification. This time, however, the most radical Hutus promised themselves that there would be no repeat of the mistake their fathers had made. This time, there would be a complete and utter Tutsi *nettoyage*.

Many people are familiar with the term "Never Again" as used by Holocaust memorialists as an invocation that there should be no more genocides. With the Hutu-Power radicals who seized power in 1994, however, we have an insight into what I would call the perpetrators' "Never Again" syndrome, and with it, we have the third element that marks off the potentiality, as opposed to its actuality, of genocide in all modern states. The major genocides of our last century have all occurred when the radical leaderships of *old-new, weak-strong* states have perceived that the integrity of their state, usually combined with some agenda they have set themselves, is threatened by forces they associate with some other similar moment of crisis in the recent or mythic past. As Hitler lurched into "the Final Solution" in the summer of 1941, when his war against Russia was no longer moving as planned, it was the "Never Again" memory of November 1918, the moment of Germany's defeat in the First World War, that came to the fore. The notion that it was revolutionary Jews on the streets of German cities who were responsible for the mythic "stab in the back" speaks volumes, of course, not only about Hitler's state of mind but also about that of millions of ordinary Germans unable to face up to the reality of a self-inflicted trauma and catastrophe. The same sort of pattern informed the 1915 Ittihadist onslaught on its Armenians. On this occasion their "Never Again" memory was one of alleged Armenian plots in the 1890s intended to subvert and destroy the Ottoman state.

History tells a great deal about the lengths to which state leaderships will go under wholly desperate conditions, even and perhaps especially if those conditions are largely self-inflicted. So often genocide has taken place under conditions of general war or the threat of war, not simply because war provides a convenient cover under which a mass exterminatory program can be carried out, but because the targeted group within are seen by the *genocidaires* as an extension of the enemy without. In the extreme case of the Holocaust, this relationship was actually reversed. The so-called western plutocracies and Communist Russians supposedly were doing the bidding of the all-powerful, world-manipulating Jews.

Blaming the victims as the proxies and stooges of foreign powers intent on the destruction of nation and state not only provides at least a partial explanation of the process whereby antipathy against a group can under conditions of acute crisis trigger a genocidal response, but it also dramatically brings us to more current events. We tend to think of what happened in Kosovo in 2000 as a genocide averted by western-led international action. But, more worrying, it contained the classic elements of a genocide about to be triggered and in which the pretext, albeit unwittingly, was provided in the form of the ultimatums made upon Serbia at Rambouillet by the very same leaders of the international community.

This analysis brings me back to the paradox at the heart of genocide. Recent genocides are the actions of desperate regimes in societies whose transition to the modern world has been particularly problematic. Such regimes have suffered – or they think they have suffered – some major collective trauma or traumas. Owing to deep-seated frustration or embitterment, usually shared by élites and widespread segments of the larger population, there is a potent discrepancy between the world as they see it and the world as they believe it ought to be. It is for this reason that highly ideological or militarized regimes are usually able to take power and hold it, often with a substantial degree of popular backing, and then to implement radical, even idiosyncratic programs for development, even where these programs may fly in the face of the international rule-book, let alone reality.

Does Kosovo prove that we have advanced, that we can look forward to a twenty-first century not only in terms of a new liberal world order, but in terms of one policed so that the very idea of any state's entertaining genocide becomes an impossibility? Implicitly, if not explicitly, I have argued against the likelihood of such scenarios. Genocide is a dysfunction not just of particular societies but of our entire global community and of the political economy that goes with it. Wish-fulfillment may lead us to think of the United Nations as a body of equally sovereign and independent nation-states. Nevertheless, ours is a world so unequal in its distribution of power that the goal to surmount this obstacle and thus to realize a genuinely unfettered independence – a realization of the unrealizable – remains a potent one. In the increasing inequality of world society at the beginning of the twenty-first century lies genocide's greatest future potential.

Military Intervention in Genocide

Firstly, there is absolutely no way that we will find effective and lasting solutions to these conflicts if we work from different plans. Unless we move to one integrated plan of the political, the humanitarian, the military, the security, the economics, the nation-building, the sustainable capabilities, with all these components working together with different emphases at different times depending on the scenario, we will continue to be wrapped up in classic warfare and classic responses.

Secondly, no plan will be of any value if we continue to put in the very short milestones that we impose. If we are going into conflict resolution using military or whatever other force, if we are trying to solve something as profound as genocide can be, we have to consider not years, but decades. So we should not go in unless we have an integrated plan and we are prepared to invest and sustain it for decades.

And thirdly, the essence of the intervention, or stopping of such acts as genocide, is to create a secure atmosphere, a state of mind even within the population and leadership, that will permit moderates safely to come to the fore and grasp the initiative. We have spent fifty years of Cold War defining the policy of "to attack, to defend, to withdraw." We haven't spent one minute defining "create an atmosphere of security."

Lt. Gen. (ret.) Romeo Dallaire (Canada)
Commander of the UN Assistance Mission,
Rwanda, 1993-1994

9

CIRCUMSTANCES OF MODERN GENOCIDE[1]

Robert Melson

In April 1994 the world was flooded by grisly images of piles of murdered men, women, and children from Rwanda. Some of the bodies were discovered in mass graves, some in churches that had become catacombs for the victims and some floating along rivers and rotting in lakes. The slaughter was so extensive that the bodies threatened to clog the rivers and pollute the lakes. It soon became clear that the world community was once more confronted with genocide. Indeed, what happened in Rwanda was no limited massacre or even what the United Nations calls a "genocide-in-part." This was the real thing: more than a half-million Tutsi murdered – three quarters of the population – and the attempt by the Rwandese state and the Hutu majority to exterminate every last Tutsi. Like the Holocaust and the Armenian genocide, the destruction in Rwanda fits the category of "total domestic genocide," what the UN calls a genocide-in-whole.[2] The Rwandan genocide is the most recent instance of state-sponsored mass-murder driven by ideology in a context of revolution and war that has been a hallmark of our modern era.

The Rwandan genocide was an instance of modern genocide among which the Holocaust, the Armenian genocide, and the Cambodian genocide are prime examples. What links all of these instances and makes them "modern" are the role of ideology and the circumstances of revolution and war. No doubt the intentions of the killers, as expressed in their ideological pronouncements, are essential for an understanding of the causes of genocide. Indeed, how could we begin to understand the Holocaust without an analysis of Nazism, or the Armenian genocide without Pan Turkism, or the Cambodian genocide without Maoism, or indeed, the Rwandan genocide without the "Hamitic Hypothesis," which claimed that the Tutsi were foreign invaders and usurpers whose provenance was not Rwanda but

Ethiopia.[3] However, in any society, including liberal peaceful democracies, there are people who harbor murderous thoughts against national, ethnic, religious, racial, and other groups, but since they do not have the power to act on their intentions, their murderous projects are mostly still-born. The question therefore arises: *What are the circumstances under which genocidal killers might be able to gain power in order to act on their intentions?* In some important cases, the circumstances of revolution and war made it possible for genocidal killers to come to power and to implement their policies.

The Nazis came to power in 1933 after the destruction of the old regime of Imperial Germany and the collapse of the Weimar Republic. They put into effect their "Final Solution" under the circumstances of the Second World War. The Young Turks came to power in a disintegrating Ottoman Empire in 1908. They tried to implement radical changes, and started the deportations of the Armenians under the circumstances of the First World War. The Khmer Rouge came to power on April 17, 1975, after years of struggling first against the Sihanouk and then the Lon Nol regimes under the circumstances of the wider war for the former Indochina. Having seized power, the revolutionaries destroyed the Khmer middle and upper classes, and committed genocide against the Chams and the Vietnamese. And the Rwandan genocide was a product both of the revolution of 1959 and the war against the RPF (Rwandese Patriotic Front) that the revolution spawned. In these four instances, all of which are culturally and historically independent, the revolutionary regime was governed by an ideology that identified certain groups as the enemies of society; it was at war with foreign and domestic enemies – some of them of its own making – and, under those circumstances, it sought to destroy what it called "the enemies of the revolution."

Why do some revolutions lead to genocide? When revolutionary vanguards come to power in a situation where most institutions have been undermined and the identity of the political community is in question, they need to reconstruct society, revitalize support for the state by way of a new system of legitimation, and forge new identities. Under revolutionary circumstances they will redefine the identity of a subset of the political community as "the people," "the nation," "the race," "the religion," or "the class." These are the group or groups that are celebrated by the ideology of the revolutionaries and from whom they hope to draw their support. In Germany it was the "Aryans," in Turkey it was the Muslim Turks, in Cambodia it was the Khmer peasantry, and in Rwanda it was the Hutu. However, groups that are not included and are singled out as racial, national, religious, or class enemies, run the danger of being defined as "the enemies of the revolution and the people." And it is such groups that may become the victims of repression or genocide. In Germany it was the Jews, in Turkey it was the Armenians, in Cambodia it was the Khmer middle and upper classes as well as the Chams and the Vietnamese, and in Rwanda it was the Tutsis.

At its founding, a revolutionary regime seeks not only to reshape the domestic social structure and redefine the identity of its people, it also aims to alter the state's international situation. Indeed, for many revolutionaries it was their country's relative weakness in the international arena that prompted them to challenge the old regime in the first place. Thus revolutions are often the products of war and lead to further war. It is under the circumstances of revolution that leads to war that genocide is most likely to be committed. The Holocaust occurred in the midst of World War II, the Armenian genocide in World War I, the Cambodian genocide in a war over Indochina, and the Rwandan genocide in a war against the RPF.

There are three ways in which revolutionary war is closely linked to genocide: First, it gives rise to feelings of vulnerability and to paranoid fears that link supposed domestic "enemies" to external aggressors. The victims of all of the major modern genocides were said to be in league in a nefarious plot with the enemies of the revolutionary state: the Jews with the Bolsheviks, the Armenians with the Russians, the Khmer upper classes with the American imperialists, and the Rwandese Tutsis with the Rwandese Patriotic Front (RPF) – the armed forces of the Tutsi resistance. Second, war increases the autonomy of the state from internal social forces, including public opinion, public opposition and its moral constraints. Third, war closes off other policy options of dealing with "internal enemies." The expulsion of "internal enemies" may not be possible, while their assimilation and/or segregation may take too long and may not be feasible in a wartime situation. Thus it is that revolutions, and especially revolutions that lead to wars, can provide the circumstances for genocide.

This is not to suggest that all revolutions lead to genocide, nor that all genocides are the products of revolution. Indeed, the British and the American revolutions did not lead to genocide; moreover, invasions, colonialism, and religious revivals are among some of the other circumstances that can promote genocide. What is essential as well is the ideology of the revolutionaries, as discussed above.

Finally, the Rwandan genocide was a total domestic genocide, what the UN would call a "genocide-in-whole" as against a "genocide-in-part," and as such it was the African version of the Holocaust. There are some apparent similarities to the Holocaust, among which an official racism and the hier-archically-organized dictatorial state stand out. There are also some features which are unique to the Rwandan genocide, most notably the scale of popular participation in the killing. Never before was an overwhelming majority of a population mobilized by the state to become the "willing exe-cutioners" of a minority. Millions of ordinary Hutu men, women, and chil-dren followed the dictates and orders of about 100,000 government func-tionaries and managed to slaughter hundreds of thousands of Tutsis at a rate much faster than the Holocaust.[4]

Scholars of genocide are now left to ponder not only the extraordinary features of the Holocaust but those of the Rwandan genocide as well. Why did the Nazis truly believe that there was a World Jewish Conspiracy aimed at the German people and that Jews the world over were their enemies? How was it possible for so many ordinary Rwandans to respond to the appeals of Hutu Power, and, seizing any weapon at hand, go forth to murder their Tutsi neighbors with whom they had lived in peace for centuries? Such are some of the insights and questions raised by the Rwandan genocide.

Notes

1.   Some of the following discussion derives from my article, "Revolution, War, and Genocide," in *The Encyclopedia of Genocide*, ed. Israel Charny (Santa Barbara: ABC-CLIO, 1999), 499-501, and from a forthcoming contribution "Modern Genocide in Rwanda: Ideology, Revolution, War and Mass Murder in an African State" in *Genocide in the Modern World* (New York and Oxford: Oxford University Press, forthcoming) edited by Ben Kiernan and Robert Gellately.

2.   According to the widely accepted UN definition formulated in 1948, genocide means actions "committed with intent to destroy in whole or in part a national, ethnical, racial or religious group as such." By implication the UN recognizes the distinction between the destruction of a group as a "whole" (genocide-in-whole) from the destruction of its "part" (genocide-in-part), although it uses the same term for both phenomena. I have emphasized that distinction to differentiate "total" (genocide-in-whole), like the Holocaust, the Armenian genocide and Rwanda, from "partial" genocide, like Biafra, Bosnia, and Kosovo. The significant point here is that the Rwandan genocide was an instance of a "total" genocide or extermination, which makes it comparable to the Holocaust and the Armenian genocide. See *Yearbook of the United Nations, 1948-49* (New York, 1949), 959-60. For a more detailed discussion of these terms see my *Revolution and Genocide: On the Origins of the Armenian Genocide and the Holocaust* (Chicago: University of Chicago Press, 1992), 22-30.

3.   Gerard Prunier, *The Rwanda Crisis: History of a Genocide* (New York: Columbia University Press, 1995), 7-8.

4.   See Christian P. Scherrer, *Genocide and Crisis in Central Africa* (Westport, Conn: Praeger, 2001), 125.

10

PSYCHOLOGICAL FOUNDATIONS

Clark McCauley

Genocide has come to refer to any large-scale killing in which victims are targeted for their membership in a social category. Most commonly these categories are defined by ethnicity (e.g., Jews in Nazi Germany) or social class (e.g., "landlords" and "rich peasants" in Communist China). The killing is indiscriminate in the sense that all members of the target category are at risk: men and women, children, and old people. People are killed, not for anything they have done, but for who they are as group members.

Ethnic riots can kill people in this indiscriminate categorical way[1] but riots are not usually considered a form of genocide because riots are usually brief (days or at most weeks in duration) and usually kill relatively small numbers of people (dozens, hundreds, at most a few thousand). Similarly terrorist attacks such as that on the World Trade Center on September 11, 2001 are not usually considered genocide because such attacks are usually episodic and usually kill only hundreds or at most thousands of people.

Genocide, then, refers to systematic, long-term, and large-scale killing that targets all members of an ethnic or class category. This paper will explore some of the basic facts of genocide and some of the basic psychology behind these facts.

Genocide is Government Business

The first and most obvious fact about genocide is that government – the state – is the indispensable perpetrator. Large-scale killing requires organization. Victims have to be identified; bodies have to be disposed of. Killers have to be transported to the victims (Rwanda), or victims have to be transported into killing camps (Nazi Germany, Maoist China, Soviet Union), or killed in the displacement from their homes (Armenians in Turkey). Big killing is a big job that cannot be left to the vagaries of emotional arousal. As a motivation for killing, anger is too individual, too uncoordinated, too unreliable. Organization replaces individual motivation with organizational routine and bureaucratic incentives.

Thus genocide cannot be understood as an emotional outburst – the boiling up of hate and rage against the target group. Smaller and episodic killing, as in ethnic riots, may be an expression of anger and outrage,[2] but big killing requires organization and government is the big killer. In *Death by Government*, Rummel estimates 34 million battle-related deaths in the twentieth century, and 170 million unarmed civilians killed by government.[3] The victims are usually killed by their own government, or, more accurately, by the government of the state in which the victims live. Stalin, Mao, Hitler, Chiang Kai-shek, Lenin, Tojo, and Pol Pot killed by class and politics as much as by ethnicity, but all killed with the power of government. Big killing in Cambodia, Rwanda, and East Timor was government-organized killing.

With organization and the monopoly of violence enjoyed by the state, big killing does not require large numbers of killers. In Rwanda, a very low-tech genocide involving more machetes than machine guns, the percent of Hutu actually involved in killing Tutsi probably did not exceed five percent.[4] In higher-tech genocides such as the Holocaust, the percentage of killers is likely to be smaller yet. Probably fewer than one percent of adults in Nazi Germany were directly involved in killing Jews.

Genocidal Killers Are Not Crazy

Though relatively few, the killers are not abnormal. Big killing cannot depend on recruiting psychopaths and other unreliables; big killing depends on recruiting normal people to kill and to kill indiscriminately. The killers may have a criminal record, may be drunk, may enjoy violence – but they do not suffer from any psychosis or character disorder recognized in the *Diagnostic and Statistical Manual* of the American Psychiatric Association.

An easy way to recognize the normality of those involved in government-sponsored killing is to reflect on the better-than-average American boys who dropped fire bombs on Dresden, Hamburg, and Tokyo, and dropped nuclear bombs on Hiroshima and Nagasaki. Most men of military age had been mobilized out of these cities, leaving mostly women, children, and old people as the predictable victims of the bombing.

Genocidal Killing is a Product of Normal Psychology

How are normal people brought to genocidal killing? The psychology of killing has to do with individual-level mechanisms of desensitization and dehumanization, and with a perceived threat that makes killing by category morally acceptable and even necessary.

Desensitization

Desensitization can occur at a purely perceptual level. Having killed one person, killing another looks smaller. Germans killing Jews, for instance, often found the work disgusting at first, but became less disturbed about it as the killing was routinized.[5]

Another kind of desensitization is more motivational. We tend to find reasons for what we do. In social psychology, the literature on dissonance theory gives evidence of the power of this tendency. Behavior contrary to our beliefs or values – behavior that might loosely be called "stupid" or "sleazy" – is a threat to our self-esteem; we are motivated to develop new beliefs that justify and make sense of the behavior.[6] In the psychology of commitment, our own bad behavior becomes the cause of reasons for more and more extreme bad behavior. (Happily this same psychology can also lead to rationalizing and extending good behavior, but that is not the focus here.)

The power of commitment is evident in many forms,[7] not least in the obedience paradigm made famous by Milgram.[8] The surprise in Milgram's paradigm is that most normal individuals will escalate shocks to "another subject" in a "learning experiment," from a negligible 15 volt shock for the first wrong answer all the way to 450 volts – labeled "Danger – Strong Shock" – if the experimenter asks them to. Equally surprising is a less-known variation of Milgram's paradigm, in which the experimenter is called away and it is a supposed fellow-subject who comes up with the idea of raising the shock one level for each mistake. In this variation, 20% of subjects go all the way to the maximum 450 volts.

The authority of the experimenter cannot explain the 20%; rather it seems to be the progressive commitment of the subject that is important. There is no reason not to give the first shock, 15 volts is nothing. If 15 volts is nothing, why not 30 volts? If 30 volts is ok, why not 45? And so on. The slow escalation in shock levels is a slippery slope on which the best reason to give the next shock level is that the subject has already been given the last level; if there is something wrong with the next level, there must have been something already wrong with the last level.

Self-justification is a powerful source of desensitization; the rationalization of initial violence supports increasing violence against the same target group. The rationalization is likely to take the form of perceiving the target group as increasingly bad and threatening, and increasingly deserving of retribution and pre-emptive violence.

De-humanization

Killing by category requires a particular kind of categorization. Killing by category can be justified, perhaps can only be justified, by a belief that all members of the category are equally guilty or equally threatening. A common belief of this kind is that all members of a group share a common "essence" – an invisible something that distinguishes the group from other groups and leads to common group characteristics, or at least the tendency to develop these characteristics.

The idea of essence appears to be very basic in human cognition. We seem to be born with a tendency to make sense of the world of living things in terms of essence. A tiger is a tiger because it has the essence of a tiger. A three-legged and albino tiger is still a tiger because it still has the tiger essence. If the essence of tigers makes them threatening, all tigers are threatening – old ones, young ones, sick ones – all of them. If cockroaches are disgusting, all cockroaches are disgusting – big ones, little ones, brown ones, black ones – all of them.

It appears that both children[9] and adults[10] often understand the human world, like the rest of the living world, in terms of essences. Hirschfeld believes that racial categories depend upon a biologically-based cognitive module that prepares human children and even adults to interpret the world of human differences in terms of essences. This human-kind-creating mechanism interacts with culture to produce essentialized categories such as gender and race. Gil-White believes that ethnic groups are commonly understood as having different essences, and suggests that the human-kind-creating mechanism was selected for in evolution because it facilitated generalization of inferences from one member of an ethnic group to all the other members of that group. The savings in learning about a whole ethnic group from encounter with one member of the group is arguably similar to the savings in learning about tigers from encounter with one tiger.

An essentialized category combines immutability (essence expressed in physical characteristics or tendencies that cannot be changed in an individual's lifetime), discrimination (not all characteristics differ by essence), and heritability (essence-related characteristics fixed at birth). Racial and gender categories are near-universal outcomes of the human-kind-creating module, and kinship categories are likewise commonly essentialized. Nazi Germans essentialized Jews in the Holocaust, and both Germans and Jews currently essentialize their own people in the "right of return" laws in both Germany and Israel.

Research on essentializing social groups is only beginning, but enough is available to suggest that the idea of essence is an important part of dehumanizing an enemy. If they are all alike in essence, they are all alike in threat and must be killed.

The Cause

Genocide requires a cause that justifies categorical killing, a cause more important than life. Such a cause is the culture, way of life, or world-view that gives meaning to life and meaning to death.

Terror-management theory[11] begins from the idea that humans are the only animals that know they are to die. Fear of death is potentially a paralyzing terror that can interfere with individual adaptation, social relations, and, ultimately, with reproductive success. The answer to fear of death is culture: all the ways in which humans are different from other animals, from the most everyday and thoughtless rituals to the most profound interpretations of the meaning of life. Existential terror is managed by allegiance to a cultural world-view that includes both standards of value and the individual self-esteem that comes from meeting cultural standards.

Thus US students made to think about their own death show increased allegiance to cultural standards: higher evaluation of the US, those who praise the US, and those who exemplify US cultural values; lower evaluation of foreigners, those who criticize the US, and those who violate cultural values. In addition, McGregor et al[12] show that mortality salience increases aggression against those who threaten the cultural world-view.

Terror management theory suggests that the power of a group over its members is the extent to which the group answers the human problem of mortality. Membership in a tennis club does not offer much promise of immortality. Similarly a neighborhood, a team, a union, or an economic class may offer little promise of immortality. But a race, an ethnic group, a nation, a religion – these do offer participation in a group seen to have a long past and an unlimited future. If one of these mortality-buffering groups is seen as threatened, especially if the continued existence of the group is seen as threatened, then the members of the threatened group may be willing to give their own lives for their group and even more willing to kill members of the threatening group.

Conclusion

Taken together, essentialism and terror-management offer a deadly combination. If our group is threatened by another group, particularly if the very existence of our group is threatened, then we are justified in killing them to preserve the culture that is more important to us than life. If in addition the threatening group is seen as essentially bad and essentially hostile, then we are justified in killing all of them. Indeed their different essence means that they are not quite human, and we can slaughter them the same way we would slaughter diseased animals. Finally, the killing capacity of the individual killers is multiplied by the psychology of desensitization, especially the rationalization of initial killing with reasons for more killing. It is this combination of psychological elements that supports large-scale, systematic killing by category, and these elements may be collectively necessary for genocide to occur.

Notes

1. D. L. Horowitz, *The Deadly Ethnic Riot* (Berkeley, CA: University of California Press, 2001).

2. Ibid.

3. R. J. Rummel, *Death by Government* (New Brunswick, NJ: Transaction, 1994).

4. D. N. Smith, "The Psychocultural Roots of Genocide: Legitimacy and Crisis in Rwanda," *American Psychologist*, 53 (1998), 743-753.

5. C. R. Browning, *Ordinary Men* (New York: Harper Collins, 1992).

6. J. Sabini, *Social Psychology*, 2nd edition (New York: Norton, 1992).

7. R. B. Cialdini, *Influence: Science and Practice*, 2nd edition (Glenview, IL: Scott, Foresman, 1988).

8. S. Milgram, *Obedience to Authority* (New York: Harper & Row, 1974).

9. L. A. Hirschfeld, *Race in the Making: Cognition, Culture, and the Child's Construction of Human Kinds* (Cambridge, MA: MIT Press, 1996).

10. F. J. Gil-White, "Are Ethnic Groups 'Species' to the Human Brain?: Essentialism in our Cognition of some Social Categories," *Current Anthropology*, 42 (2001, in press).

11. T. Pyszcznski, J. Greenberg & S. Solomon, "Why Do We Need What We Need? A Terror Management Perspective on the Roots of Human Social Motivation," *Psychological Inquiry*, 8 (1997), 1-20.

12. H. A. McGregor, J. D. Lieberman, J. Greenberg, S. Solomon, J. Arndt, L. Simon, & T. Pyszczynski, "Terror Management and Aggression: Evidence that Mortality Salience Motivates Aggression against Worldview-threatening Others," *Journal of Personality and Social Psychology*, 74 (3) (1998), 590-605.

11

MECHANISMS OF GENOCIDE

Eric Markusen

Genocide – the intentional destruction of a human group, in whole or in significant part – is a complex phenomenon and process that requires contributions from a range of individuals, institutions, and organizations. Therefore, the title suggested for this essay by the editors, "Mechanisms of Genocide," is appropriate, as one of the meanings of "mechanism," according to the *Oxford Universal Dictionary*, is "a system of mutually adapted parts working together."

In suggesting this chapter, the editors also posed two key questions:
- How do *genocidaires* carry out genocide?
- What methods, so-to-speak, do they use?

In order to answer these questions, this essay first examines how the mind-set necessary to engage in genocide is created in leaders, élites, and citizens of the genocidal regime. Then it discusses the establishment of genocidal institutions and organizations, and the recruiting and training of perpetrators. Next, a number of methods of group destruction are identified and illustrated with examples from past genocides.

Creation of a Genocidal Mentality

In order for genocide to take place, a sufficient number of individuals within the genocidal regime must be willing to engage directly in, or support, the killing and other forms of destruction of large numbers of human beings. The mind-set that justifies such atrocities may be called a "genocidal mentality." Even when top leaders, like Hitler, possess such a genocidal mentality, it is necessary for their regimes to create such attitudes among members of élites and ordinary citizens alike.

Robert Jay Lifton, a psychiatrist, has done pioneering research on the genocidal mentality, notably in his 1986 book, *The Nazi Doctors: Medical Killing and the Psychology of Genocide*,[1] and later, in his 1990 book, written with me, *The Genocidal Mentality: Nazi Holocaust and Nuclear Threat*.[2] Both books expose a social and psychological dynamic whereby periods of extreme economic, political, and social disruption make people susceptible to the ideologies of leaders who blame the problems on one or more groups within the society and lead an escalating campaign of discrimination, disenfranchisement, and ultimately violence against the members of the targeted groups.

The vast majority of genocides have emerged during periods of social stress and threat. Since war is among the most common and powerful forms of social disruption, it is often associated with genocide. Helen Fein, one of the founders of the field of genocide studies, states in her article, "Civil Wars and Genocides: Paths and Circles," "Genocide almost always occurs within a context of war, and sometimes triggers war or the renewal of war."[3]

Under such circumstances, leaders may begin to blame one or more ethnic, racial, religious, political, or other groups for the troubles in the society and develop an ideology that both accuses them of causing the problems and proposes their removal as a means of solving the problems.

A universal element in the genocidal ideology is dehumanization of the victims: regarding them as less than fully human and therefore not meriting empathy or mercy. Thus, the Nazis routinely referred to their Jewish victims as "vermin" and "lice," and the Hutu killers in Rwanda called their Tutsi and other victims "cockroaches." In past centuries, colonists from all over Europe who destroyed millions of indigenous peoples in the Americas, Asia, and Africa employed animal imagery when describing their victims and justifying their slaughter.

In modern genocides, propaganda is an important means of promulgating the genocidal mentality among the populace. The Nazis used print media, radio, newsreels, and films to promote their image of the German master-race polluted and threatened by the Jews, Slavs, and other "racial inferiors." Even German schools were used as propaganda outlets, as so-called "scientific racism" that justified persecution of the Jews was a mandatory part of the curriculum from primary school through the university. Numerous scholars who have studied the genocidal wars that ravaged the former Yugoslavia between 1991 and 1995 emphasize the powerful role of the media – especially television – to create fear and incite anger against the "others," be they Croat, Muslim, or Serb.

Establishment of Genocidal Institutions and Organizations

The vast majority of governments that commit genocide are not democratic, which means that their leaders have tremendous power to exploit political, military, economic, and other resources for their genocidal projects. In his landmark three-volume history of the Holocaust, *The Destruction of the European Jews*, Raul Hilberg noted that, "If we were to enumerate the public and private agencies that may be called the 'German government' and those agencies that may be called the 'machinery of destruction,' we would discover that we are dealing with identical offices."[4]

Since genocides are planned and organized by the highest government officials and their aides and assistants, contribution to the genocide may be regarded as patriotic duty, and the violations of normal standards against killing innocent men, women, and children seen as legitimate, since they have been authorized by the government.

The military and police play crucial roles in many genocides, as they have the training and the means to implement the various policies that begin with identification and persecution of the victim group and culminate in the planned effort to destroy the group. In most societies, the genocide victims have very little power, virtually no weapons, and no means of effectively organizing escape or resistance against such overwhelmingly better-equipped perpetrators.

Academics, too, make important contributions to the decision to commit genocide and the actual implementation of it. They often play a key role in the ideological rationalization for genocide, using their scholarly credentials and influence to support the accusations against the victim group and to justify discrimination and persecution based on race, religion, or some other group characteristic. Advanced education and professional codes of ethics have not prevented many individuals – including professors, doctors, lawyers, and ministers – from participating directly in the actual killing, torture, and other forms of atrocity.

Bureaucratic organization is an important mechanism in modern genocide. The Nazis are often seen as the epitome of a vast bureaucratic operation that killed millions of people from many nations over a period of several years. But all modern genocides utilize some of the features of bureaucracy to increase the efficiency of the killing project. Even the Cambodian genocide of 1975-1978, which employed relatively low-technology killing methods, relied upon a careful bureaucratic organization that generated massive amounts of memos and other documentation, much of which was captured when the Khmer Rouge perpetrators were ousted by Vietnamese military forces.

And certain features of bureaucratic organization – the hierarchical authority structure, compartmentalization of tasks and division of labor, and a disinclination to allow moral concerns to intrude on matters of procedure and efficiency – make it easier for functionaries within the organization to ignore or repress uncomfortable thoughts about what they and their organization are doing.

Recruiting and Training of Perpetrators

For genocide to occur, individuals able and willing to carry out the destruction of the targeted group must be recruited and trained for their tasks. It is important to note that the majority of men and women responsible for genocides have not been sadistic or psychotic. In *The Nazi Doctors*, Lifton called attention to "the disturbing psychological truth that participation in mass murder need not require emotions as extreme or demonic as would seem appropriate for such a malignant project. Or to put the matter another way, ordinary people can commit demonic acts."[5]

It is also important to note that involvement in killing projects can assume many forms and degrees of complicity. *Bystanders*, who witness the evolving genocidal project, but who play no direct, active role in it, are the most numerous. Beyond the tacit support of bystanders, genocidal projects also require the participation of many *accomplices*, who never "get their hands dirty" or even witness the actual killings, but who nonetheless make indispensable contributions. Such contributions include the articulation, rationalization, and promulgation of a victimizing ideology. A second type of contribution by accomplices involves formulation and administration of laws, policies, and practices that persecute a targeted group. Other accomplices serve the killing project by designing, creating, and servicing the technology needed to organize and carry out the actual killing.

Finally, the *perpetrators* are those directly involved in the actual killing process. It is common for the killers to be carefully indoctrinated with the genocidal ideology, told repeatedly that they are serving the highest national purposes of defending the nation against whatever threats are attributed to the victim group, and systematically trained – often through exposure to violence – to cause massive suffering and death to members of the group. In his important new book, *Masters of Death: The SS-Einsatzgruppen and the Invention of the Holocaust*,[6] Richard Rhodes shows in detail how men sent out into Russia and the Baltics to slaughter masses of Jews were exposed, as part of their training, to escalating levels of violence which had the effect of progressively brutalizing them and desensitizing them to the suffering of their victims.

Not surprisingly, genocidal killers are often recruited from the ranks of soldiers, many of whom have been in combat, and the police, whose daily work often entails using force and violence. The Nazis were not alone in releasing violent criminals from prison in order that they might serve in the genocide as killers and guards. However, women, and even children, have been employed in killing projects, including the Holocaust and the Cambodian genocide of 1975-1978, respectively.

Methods of Group Destruction

Once the genocidal mentality has sufficiently pervaded a society, institutional and organizational arrangements made, and perpetrators prepared for the task ahead, the process of group destruction can begin. Human ingenuity has invented a mind-numbing array of means by which human groups, and their individual members, have been destroyed.

One attempt to identify methods of group destruction was made by the United Nations in the Convention on the Prevention and Punishment of the Crime of Genocide (UNGC) – its very first human rights legislation, passed unanimously on December 8, 1948. The UNGC, and the United Nations itself, was a response by the international community to the horrors of the Second World War in general, and the Nazi genocide against the Jews and others in particular.

In the UNGC five types of actions that can result in the destruction of a human group, in whole or in significant part, were identified and prohibited. Each is discussed in turn, with some illustrations from cases of genocide.

Killing Members of the Group

Mass killing of members of the victim group – not because of anything they have done as individuals, but simply because they are members of a group targeted for destruction – is perhaps what most people think of when they hear the word "genocide." And with good reason, as direct mass killing is a key feature of all genocides. A very incomplete listing of direct killing techniques includes burying alive, burning, drowning, clubbing, stabbing, slashing, deliberate infection with disease, shooting (individually and *en masse*), and gassing (in both mobile and stationary gas chambers). In many genocides, a variety of killing methods is used. The Nazis, for example, used the ancient method of forcibly rounding up victims and then massacring them, as well as the more "modern" method of gassing. The largest gas chambers at Auschwitz could hold up to 2,000 people at one time, and were operated by hundreds of personnel, including inmates, around the clock.

Causing Serious Bodily or Mental Harm to Members of the Group

Many members of targeted groups are forcibly removed from their homes, forced to give up their jobs, prohibited from being in public and from interaction with members of other groups – all of which cause extreme stress. Many others are imprisoned in concentration camps, where they are tortured and mentally terrorized. Rape and other forms of sexual assault are often employed.

Deliberately Inflicting on the Group Conditions Calculated to Bring about Its Physical Destruction

Deprivation of food is a common means of destroying groups. At times, it occurs within concentration camps or ghettos or other places where large numbers of captive people are held at the complete mercy of the genocidal regime. In other cases, such as the 1933 famine in the Ukraine, which killed as many as six million, people starve to death on their own land, when crops are destroyed or confiscated, or relief supplies are not allowed to reach the victims.

Imposing Measures to Prevent Births Within the Group

The Nazis experimented with several means of mass sterilization, including rapid castration of men with no anesthetic, and exposure of women to high amounts of radiation. Forced sterilization was also used against members of indigenous peoples in North America. Widespread rape of women, in some cases resulting in pregnancy, also had the effect of preventing births since many of the raped women would be so severely stigmatized that their chances of marrying and having more children were significantly reduced.

Forcibly Transferring Children of the Group to Another Group

In colonial genocides against indigenous peoples, taking children from their parents and giving them to other families or placing them in special boarding schools, was a common practice. During the Armenian genocide of 1915, the Turkish perpetrators, and their helpers, often seized children from the long lines of people being marched to their death in the desert and sold the children into slavery. The Nazis had a special program, *Lebensborn*, that involved taking the Polish children who met Nazi race standards from their parents and giving them to German couples to rear.

Ethnocide

The methods identified by the UNGC by no means exhaust the ways in which groups can be destroyed. One of these other means – "ethnocide," or the deliberate destruction of a group's culture – was listed in an early draft of the Convention, but was later removed. However, such policies as suppression of a group's language, prohibition of cultural rituals and practices, defilement of cemeteries, forcible removal from ancestral lands, and destruction of cultural monuments like churches and mosques, libraries, and museums all can contribute to the eventual disappearance of a human group. This is particularly true if they are accompanied by one or more of the methods of group destruction discussed above.

Concluding Comment

Once the mechanisms of genocide have started to operate, it is extremely unlikely that either the designated victims or ordinary citizens of the genocidal regime can stop them. Individual escapes and rescues do occur. But, without intervention from the outside – usually involving the military defeat of the regime – genocide tends to continue until the degree of group destruction sought by the perpetrators has been achieved.

Notes

1. Robert Jay Lifton, *The Nazi Doctors: Medical Killing and the Psychology of Genocide* (New York: Basic Books, 1986).

2. Robert Jay Lifton and Eric Markusen, *The Genocidal Mentality: Nazi Holocaust and Nuclear Threat* (New York: Basic Books, 1990).

3. Helen Fein, "Civil Wars and Genocide: Paths and Circles," *Human Rights Review*, Vol. 1, No. 3 (April-June 2000): 49.

4. Raul Hilberg, *The Destruction of the European Jews* (New York: Holmes & Meier, 1985), 55.

5. Lifton, *The Nazi Doctors*, 5.

6. Richard Rhodes, *Masters of Death: The SS-Einsatzgruppen and the Invention of the Holocaust* (New York: Alfred Knopf, 2002).

12

USING RAPE AS A WEAPON OF GENOCIDE

Carol Rittner

> **"Genocidal rape:** a military policy of rape
> for the purpose of genocide..."
> — Beverly Allen,
> *Rape Warfare*

There is nothing unprecedented about rape during wartime. According to Susan Brownmiller, women are raped in war "as casually, or as frenetically, as a village is looted or gratuitously destroyed."[1] Perhaps this is why rape often is dismissed by military and political leaders as a private crime committed by undisciplined soldiers who have momentarily lost control. It also may be why so much scholarly analysis has failed to take note of "the role of systematic rape and sexual assault in the destruction of a group... despite its centrality to women's experience of genocidal violence."[2]

Rape, "unlawful sexual intercourse with a female without her consent,"[3] flourishes during war. It respects neither nationality nor geographic location. It has accompanied wars of religion and wars of revolution. It rears its ugly head when soldiers want to relieve tension, banish boredom, or assert *machismo*. Rape has nothing to do with sex and everything to do with power and dominance. Both sides – *all sides* – use rape as a weapon of terror and an instrument of revenge. Rape, according to Amnesty International, is a form of torture. It is an act perpetrated by men against women, although not exclusively so.[4]

Why do men rape women during war-making? Here is what Rita Nakashima Brock and Susan Brooks Thistlewaite have to say about this:

> In the eyes of the world's "higher" religions, women are only derivative human beings. They are regarded as vehicles and not

persons in their own right. As objects and not subjects, women symbolize the connection between the human and the land, the familial construction of community and the generation of life. These are all perspectives that support the logic of rape in war or terror. In war or terror, those to be subdued or conquered are not full persons, they no longer control their community boundaries and have lost their capacity for self-direction. Rape is a form of violence against women, but in war and terror, it is *directed* against the whole community and especially against the males who formerly controlled sexual access to these same women.[5]

For centuries, rape was considered a war crime, but the history of the twentieth century reveals how little the "laws of war have been observed – and how rarely they have been enforced."[6] Anne Llewellyn Barstow called rape "war's dirty secret,"[7] because very often rape committed during war was neither documented nor discussed in standard history books. Consequently, once a war ended, rape, whether perpetrated by one's enemy or by one's ally, slid to the margins of history, or faded into oblivion. It was there, but not there, so-to-speak.

We see this, for example, following World War II. Not even the founding statute of the International Military Tribunal (IMT) at Nuremberg made any specific reference to rape. Neither did its companion tribunal in Tokyo,[8] although the IMT for the Far East did prosecute General Iwane Matsui, the man in charge of the Japanese troops at the time of the "Rape of Nanking" (which actually happened at the end of 1937 and beginning of 1938). Matsui was sentenced to death, but not one woman who was raped by soldiers under his command was ever called to testify.[9] We also can "hear" the silence around the issue of rape in the United Nations Genocide Convention, which did not include any specific mention of rape, even though men have been making women's bodies their battlefields since the beginning of recorded history, and longer. These days, however, it is not possible to remain quiet about rape and sexual violence during war. This was no more evident than during the last ten years of the twentieth century.

Roy Gutman, an American reporter who was foreign correspondent for *Newsday*, an American daily newspaper, covered the breakup of former Yugoslavia in the early 1990s after Croatia, Macedonia, and Slovenia declared their independence. "The war that began in April 1992 was predictable. What no one could have imagined was the atrocities against Muslim and Croat civilians for which the Serbs invented the euphemism 'ethnic cleansing.'"[10]   It was a new term added to the world's lexicon of terror, and it meant "rendering an area ethnically homogenous by using force or intimidation to remove persons of given groups from the area."[11]   It was complemented by a new weapon added to the world's arsenal of horror: *genocidal rape* – "a military policy of rape for the purpose of genocide."[12]

During the late summer of 1992, Gutman wrote numerous stories about Muslim women who had been raped by Serb civilians, soldiers, and para-military irregulars.   He heard so many stories about sexual violence and rape that he said analysts were beginning to think it was a deliberate part of what was already a brutal Serb military policy.   "Serb forces in northern Bosnia," he wrote in one dispatch, "systematically raped 40 young Muslim women of a town they captured early this summer, telling some of their victims they were under orders to do so, the young women say.   Statements by victims of the assault, describing their ordeal in chilling detail, bear out reports that the Serb conquerors of Bosnia have raped Muslim women, not as a by-product of the war but as a principal tactic of the war."[13]   Gutman goes on to quote Dr. Melika Kreitmayer, leader of a gynecological team who examined many of the women.   This was not simply an example of "male instinct" gone amok.   Rather, these women "were raped because it was the goal of the war."   Kreitmayer believed "that someone had an order to rape the girls."[14]

Bosnian Muslim women were raped and sexually violated because they were part of the unwanted ethnic "other."   They were raped because the Serbs wanted to drive them away; they wanted to "cleanse" *their* territory of all non-Serbs.   The Serbs raped these women because they wanted to inter-rupt the ethno-continuity of the victim group.[15]   Rape was used to further the Serb policy of *ethnic cleansing*, and it was "practiced in Bosnia-Herzegovina and Croatia by members of the Yugoslav Army, the Bosnian Serb forces, Serb militias in Croatia and Bosnia-Herzegovina, the irregular Serb forces known as Chetniks, and Serb civilians."[16]   It should be noted as well that rapes were not exclusive to the Serb forces in Bosnia.   There were examples of "rape warfare" on a smaller scale by the other national groups. According to international relief workers and human rights analysts, "the Serbs set the pattern in 1992 – organizing the conquest to achieve a Greater Serbia, setting up concentration camps and practicing systematic rape." Bosnian Croats adopted the same tactic in Spring 1993 as they tried to estab-lish their own territory.   Likewise, forces of the largely Muslim government in Bosnia also raped and caused mayhem, "but not as a tool of government policy."[17]

As the war in former Yugoslavia exhausted itself, Rwanda, a tiny country in Africa, erupted in a paroxysm of ethnic violence. Far from being a "spontaneous" eruption, however, it had been carefully planned. People around the world watched in horror as images of death, thanks to CNN, cascaded across their television screens. In Rwanda, between April and July 1994, an estimated 800,000 men, women, and children, the overwhelming majority Tutsis, were savagely slaughtered by their Hutu neighbors, after a plane carrying the Rwandan President, Juvenal Habyarimana, was shot down, some believe, by extremist members of his own Hutu party. "Habyarimana's death served as the pretext to launch the genocide. Rwanda's national radio as well as a number of private stations relayed instructions to the death squads, the so-called *Interahamwe* (the name, in Kinyarwanda, means 'those who fight together'), and ceaselessly urged the killers to step up their slaughter. The Rwandan armed forces backed up the *Interahamwe* in those areas where the killers encountered resistance from Tutsi civilians. Pre-positioned transport and fuel permitted the death squads to reach even the most isolated Tutsi communities."[18]

Most of those murdered in Rwanda during that 1994 "season of blood" were hacked to death with machetes. Arms and legs were cut off, so too were male genitals, female breasts, and other body parts. Rwanda's genocide was not a simple matter of mutual hatred between tribes erupting into irrational violence. Neither were the mass killings the result of a huge and sudden outpouring of rage on the part of Hutus following the murder of their president. The killings – and there is ample documentary evidence to prove this – were planned long in advance by a clique close to President Habyarimana himself. This is a legally important fact, because it establishes the clear intent of its architects to commit the crime of *genocide* – "acts committed with the intent to destroy, in whole or in part, a national, ethnical, racial or religious group, as such," in the words of the United Nations Genocide Convention.

According to human rights observers, as well as Rwandan and international medical workers, rape was the rule and its absence the exception. "The number of pregnancies said to have been caused by force suggest that so-called *genocidaires* raped 250,000-500,000 women and girls in less than one hundred days."[19] Although exact figures will never be known, testimonies from survivors confirm that rape was extremely widespread. Some observers believe that almost every woman and adolescent girl who survived the genocide was raped. Thousands of women were sexually violated in the most sadistic and brutal manner imaginable. They were mutilated with sharp objects – sharpened sticks, rifle barrels, and machetes, for example. These were forcibly inserted in their vaginas. Many women were killed immediately after being raped and sodomized. Others, held in sexual slavery (either collectively or through "forced marriages"), were allowed to survive so they would "die of sadness."[20]   Unborn babies were torn from their mothers' bellies, after machete-wielding young men slashed and mutilated the women. *Shattered Lives: Sexual Violence during the Rwandan Genocide and its Aftermath*,[21] published by Human Rights Watch, which investigated and documented the sexual violence in Rwanda, provides grisly reading for anyone who can bear it.

As the twentieth century drew to a close, the world's gaze shifted back to Europe and the Balkans, this time to Kosovo, where on March 24, 1999, NATO began its bombing campaign against the Serb forces of Slobodan Milosevic.   As Serbian police and Yugoslav Army forces continued brutal attacks on civilians, more than 800,000 ethnic Albanians poured out of Kosovo, mostly into Albania and Macedonia. They brought with them eyewitness accounts of atrocities committed by Serb forces against ethnic Albanian civilians. They also brought stories of rapes of ethnic Albanian women. Independent investigators, including Human Rights Watch, found that rape and other forms of sexual violence were used in Kosovo in 1999 as weapons of war and instruments of systematic ethnic cleansing. According to Human Rights Watch, "Rapes were not rare and isolated acts committed by individual Serbian or Yugoslav forces, but rather were used deliberately as an instrument to terrorize the civilian population, extort money from families, and push people to flee their homes. Rape furthered the goal of forcing ethnic Albanians from Kosovo."[22]

In a 1994 report submitted to the United Nations Security Council by a UN Commission of Experts, those who engage in and carry out ethnic cleansing are subject to individual criminal responsibility. Military and political leaders who participate in making and implementing the policy "are also susceptible to charges of genocide and crimes against humanity, in addition to grave breaches of the Geneva Conventions and other violations of international humanitarian law."[23]

Genocide "is distinguished from other international crimes, not by the scope of the acts, but rather by the intent of the perpetrators in committing the acts to destroy a national, ethnic, racial, or religious group."[24] When rape and sexual violence result in killing members of the group, causing serious bodily and mental harm to members of the group, imposing measures intended to prevent births within the group, when they are intended deliberately to inflict on the group conditions of life calculated to bring about its physical destruction, in whole or in part, it is not "simply" ethnic violence or violent conflict between opposing parties, terrible as they may be. Such acts constitute the crime of genocide.

Rape used to be "war's dirty secret," but no longer. Rape is now a conventional weapon in the arsenal of genocide. It is even an act of genocide itself when it is used to destroy a group, as such.[25] Therefore, whenever it rears its ugly head, whenever women are subjected to it in a time of war, rape must be investigated fully, prosecuted vigorously, and punished severely by the international criminal court(s). We owe that to all the women who have suffered the consequences of *genocidal rape*. Otherwise, what does "Never again!" mean?

Notes

1. Susan Brownmiller, "Making Female Bodies the Battlefield," *Newsweek*, 4 January 1993, 17.

2. Israel W. Charny, ed. *Encyclopedia of Genocide*, Vol.II (Santa Barbara, CA: ABC-CLIO, Inc. 1999), "Rape as a Tool of Genocide," Jennifer Balint, 491.

3. Pamela Cooper-White, *The Cry of Tamar: Violence Against Women and the Church's Response* (Minneapolis, MN: Fortress Press, 1995), 81.

4. Jennifer Balint writes, "Although there are instances of men being raped during genocide, the vast majority of rape is perpetrated against women." See further, Balint, "Rape as a Tool of Genocide" in Israel W. Charny, ed., *Encyclopedia of Genocide*, vol. II (Santa Barbara, CA: ABC-CLIO, 1999), 491.

5. Rita Nakashima Brock and Susan Brooks Thistlewaite, *Casting Stones: Prostitution and Liberation in Asia and the United States* (Minneapolis, MN: Fortress Press, 1996), 252.

6. Thom Shanker, "Sexual Violence" in *Crimes of War: What the Public Should Know*, ed. Roy Gutman and David Rieff (New York: W. W. Norton & Co., 1999), 323, 324.

7. Anne Llewellyn Barstow, ed. *War's Dirty Secret: Rape, Prostitution, and Other Crimes Against Women* (Cleveland, Ohio: The Pilgrim Press, 2000).

8. Shanker, "Sexual Violence," 324.

9. Susan Brownmiller, *Against Our Will: Men, Women and Rape* (New York: Ballantine Books, 1975), 58.

10. Roy Gutman, *A Witness to Genocide: The First Inside Account of the Horrors of 'Ethnic Cleansing' in Bosnia* (Rockport, MA: Element, 1993), vii.

11. Cohen quotes the United Nations Commission of Experts' definition for "ethnic cleansing" as found in their January 1993 report to the UN Security Council. See further, Roger Cohen, "Ethnic Cleansing" in Gutman and Rieff, eds., *Crimes of War*, 136.

12. Beverly Allen, *Rape Warfare: The Hidden Genocide in Bosnia-Herzegovina and Croatia* (Minneapolis, MN: University of Minnesota Press, 1996), vii.

13. Gutman, *A Witness to Genocide*, 68.

14. Gutman, *A Witness to Genocide*, 69.

15. Henry R. Huttenbach, "Mass Rape and Gendercide: Gender Victimization as Aspects of Genocide in Bosnia," *The Genocide Forum*, 9 (May 1996): 5.

16. Allen, *Rape Warfare*, vii.

17. Alexandra Stiglmayer, ed. *Mass Rape: The War Against Women in Bosnia-Herzegovina* (Lincoln, NE: University of Nebraska Press, 1994), xi-xii.

18. Mark Huband, "Rwanda – The Genocide" in Gutman and Rieff, eds., *Crimes of War*, 312.

19. Laura Flanders, "Rwanda's Living Casualties" in Barstow, ed., *War's Dirty Secret*, 96.

20. *Shattered Lives: Sexual Violence during the Rwandan Genocide and its Aftermath* (New York: Human Rights Watch, 1996), 1.

21. See further, footnote #22.

22. See further, *Kosovo: Rape as a Weapon of "Ethnic Cleansing,"* (New York: Human Rights Watch, 2000).

23. Quoted in Cohen, "Ethnic Cleansing," 138.

24. *Shattered Lives*, 34.

25. Balint, "Rape as a Tool of Genocide," 492.

13

IDENTIFYING GENOCIDE

Linda Melvern

The first massacre to be discovered by the UN peacekeepers in Rwanda was on Saturday April 9, 1994, three days after the crisis began. The peacekeepers, ignoring warnings about their own safety, had ventured out of headquarters in response to a desperate call for help from two unarmed UN military observers stationed in a parish called Gikondo. When the peacekeepers reached Gikondo, they had gone immediately to the Catholic Church, and it was in the church and all over the terraced gardens that they found the bodies, the members of whole families cut down by machete. Most victims had bled to death. One of the peacekeepers, a major in the Polish army, had noticed a pile of Rwandan identification cards, all with the ethnic designation Tutsi; the cards were charred in an effort to burn them. The peacekeeper filmed the bodies with his camcorder. He thought that the massacre at Gikondo should alert the world. This was genocide.

That afternoon a French journalist called Jean-Philippe Ceppi also visited Gikondo. Ceppi had accompanied a medical team from the International Committee of the Red Cross (ICRC), who had come to search for survivors. In a later newspaper article Ceppi described seeing mutilated bodies in the church compound. All over Gikondo and all over the city of Kigali there were the sounds of screams and gunfire. Ceppi described soldiers from the Presidential Guard touring the streets with lists of victims. A youth militia was battering down doors, chasing Tutsi from house to house, and from room to room. Not even the hospitals were safe for Tutsi, for there were soldiers rampaging through the wards looking for them.

Ceppi's story was published in the French newspaper *Libération* on Monday April 11 and it is of some significance. Ceppi told his readers that this was genocide. He wrote that the genocide of the Tutsi had just begun and given its speed, it would soon be over.

Elsewhere it was a different story with Rwanda described in other Western newspapers as gripped by ancient tribal hatreds. One British journalist reported without question an assertion from a Western diplomat in Kigali that "various clans are murdering others." The basic inference in the news coverage was that the killing represented uncontrollable tribal savagery about which nothing could be done.

The media's failure to adequately describe and report the genocide, and thereby generate public pressure for something to be done to stop it, contributed to international indifference and inaction. With no outcry about genocide in the press, no choices were given and no risks were taken.

We do not yet know who gave the orders for the massacre at Gikondo but I have written several accounts of what happened there and recently I found a survivor who had arrived in Gikondo at dawn on Saturday and had sought the sanctuary of the church. There were hundreds of people already there and some people were so frightened that they hid in cupboards or in the rafters. At 9:00 a.m. the priests had organized a Mass and as it was just about to start there was the sound of shooting and grenades. Two Presidential Guards burst into the church and ordered the people to produce their ID cards and separated them into two groups, Hutu and Tutsi. The Tutsi were ordered to sit down and soon afterwards the militia known as the *Interahamwe* turned up wearing their distinctive clothing, the *Kitenge*, their multi-coloured tunics, and chanting death to Tutsi. They began to kill the Tutsi with machetes. There was total panic.

For three months massacres like this were commonplace in Rwanda and followed a distinct pattern, with the military sealing the exits of places of refuge and the *Interahamwe* called upon to do the killing. It has since been ascertained that the vast majority of victims in Rwanda died in the first six weeks of genocide, in large-scale and organised massacres. There were no sealed trains or secluded camps in Rwanda. The genocide took place in broad daylight. In three months, up to one million people were killed.

Those people who organised and coordinated this crime have yet to see their day in court and so we must turn for an adequate description of them to 1945 and a description of Nazi war criminals:

> We will show them to be living symbols of racial hatreds, of terrorism and violence, and of the arrogance and cruelty of power. They are symbols of fierce nationalism and of militarisation, of intrigue and war-making...[The Nazi defendants] . . . represented sinister influences that would lurk in the world long after their bodies had returned to dust.[1]

These words belong to Justice Robert Jackson, the chief of the prosecution team at the International Military Tribunal at Nuremberg, and in this opening address Jackson described how the Nazi ideology was rooted in racism. So it was with Hutu Power.[2] The Hutu extremists believed that the Tutsi were a different race and that they had come from elsewhere to invade Rwanda. Hutu Power taught that the Tutsi were different, that they were lazy; that they did not want to work the land, that they were outside human existence – vermin and subhuman. The effect of the Hutu Power radio, with its catchy nationalistic theme tunes and its racist jingles must never be underestimated. The broadcasts of *Radio-Télévision Libre des Mille Collines* (RTLM) were an integral part of the genocide plot and it was thanks to the propaganda that spewed over the airways that by April 1994 a large number of people in Rwanda had come to believe that the elimination of the Tutsi, or "cockroaches" as they were called, was a civic duty and that it was necessary work to rid the country of them.

A crime requires motives, means, and opportunity. In Rwanda the motive of those responsible was to continue to monopolise power and to seek a final solution to the political opposition. The primary means was the mobilization of the unemployed into youth militias. Use of the civil administration to encourage ordinary people to participate in killings was a supplementary strategy. Methods of mass killing had been tried successfully during the previous three and a half years and were well documented in a 1993 report of an International Commission of Inquiry into Human Rights violations in Rwanda.

The opportunity for genocide was provided by a conjunction of circumstances allowing the hard-liners to confuse the international community for sufficiently long enough to be able to perpetrate the crime with little international response. No one gave the conspirators reason to pause.

We may never know the moment when the Hutu Power conspirators conceived the genocide, when the oligarchs, threatened with democracy and power-sharing, decided to use genocide as a political weapon. What is known is that by April 1994, when the genocide began, the militia had grown to 30,000 and there were stockpiles of weapons and new agricultural tools hidden all over the country. By now the planning of the genocide had become an open secret, not the least because a series of informers from within Hutu Power ranks had begun to warn of what was in store.

In the weeks beforehand, some Tutsi left the country, while others prepared for emergency evacuation. Still others believed that with the UN peace-keepers in their country they would be safe. In Kigali the ICRC began contingency planning for a huge number of casualties. "Genocide," one of the peacekeepers said just before it started, "hung in the air."

Raphael Lemkin once wrote that genocide followed humanity like a dark shadow, from antiquity to the present time. Lemkin, the remarkable Polish lawyer who coined the word genocide, believed that genocide could be predicted and that with an international early warning system, it was preventable. A key element in genocide was a racist ideology, used to legitimise any act. It is to Lemkin's memory that my book on the genocide in Rwanda, *A People Betrayed: The Role of the West in Rwanda's Genocide*[3] is dedicated. After the Second World War, Lemkin had waged a tireless campaign to establish the Convention on the Prevention and Punishment of the Crime of Genocide and on December 9, 1948, when the Convention was approved by the UN General Assembly, it had marked the introduction of a new world order. The Convention was of unique and symbolic importance for it stood for a fundamental and important principle: that whatever evil may befall any group or nation or people, it was a matter of concern not just for that group, but for the entire human family. The Convention was the world's first human rights treaty, the first truly universal, comprehensive and codified protection of human rights. Lemkin believed that without it, no people on earth could feel safe.

No tragedy was ever heralded to less effect than the genocide in Rwanda. Anyone who knew anything about Rwanda knew what was threatened. The failure to act in accordance with the Genocide Convention before the genocide, and then while one million people were slaughtered, is one of the greatest scandals of the twentieth century. Unless there is widespread understanding of how and why the Genocide Convention was not invoked in 1994, there is little hope that a reformed and accountable international community will be more vigilant in future years.

Copyright: © 2002 Linda Melvern

Notes

1. Justice Jackson's Opening Statement for the Prosecution. Second Day, Wednesday, 21 November 1945. Part 04, in *The Trial of the Major War Criminals before the International Military Tribunal. Volume II, Proceedings: 14 November 1945 - 30 November 1945.* (Official text in the English Language) (Nuremberg: IMT, 1947), 98-102.

2. Editor's note: Hutu power is the name given to an ideology whose adherents were rabidly anti-Tutsi. Racist and nationalistic, they were opposed to democracy. Hutu Power sought the elimination of all Tutsi and pro-democracy Hutu.

3. Linda Melvern, *A People Betrayed: The Role of the West in Rwanda's Genocide* (London: Zed Books, 2000).

14

UNDERSTANDING GENOCIDE

Ervin Staub

A simple but effective definition of genocide was provided by Chalk and Jonassohn: "Genocide is a form of one-sided mass-killing in which the state or other authority intends to destroy the group, as that group and member-ship in it are defined by the perpetrators."[1] This definition includes politi-cal groups which, for political reasons – nations did not want interference in how they treat political opposition – the United Nations Genocide Convention does not. However, this is only one of many definitions.

A great deal of scholarly effort has focused on definitions of genocide and on differentiating violence against groups that is or is not genocide. A benefit of a precise definition and of differentiating between genocide and mass killing – the killing of members of a group without the intention of eliminating the whole group – could be that in the case of genocide, moved by the moral imperative of the Genocide Convention, the international com-munity would act to stop the killings. But instead, the result may be less of a feeling of obligation to act in response to "mere" mass killing. This was dramatically shown when the international community, including the United States, to avoid the moral obligation to act, strongly resisted calling the ongoing extermination of Tutsis in Rwanda in 1994 a genocide.[2]

Another important reason to distinguish between genocide and mass killing is to develop the best theory of the origins and best avenues to the prevention of each. However, the influences leading to mass killing and genocide are similar. In addition, according to Staub,[3] genocide is usually the outcome of an evolution, and mass killing can be a way-station to geno-cide. For example, there were mass killings in the decades preceding the genocides in Turkey against the Armenians and in Rwanda against the Tutsis. While in both countries there were intervening periods with limited violence, the mass killings were part of the evolution that made the genocide more likely.

While good theory can specify how to predict the likelihood of group violence, its exact form is probably impossible to predict. If we want to focus on genocide alone, we can only focus on events that have already taken place. Until, and if ever, further research identifies different origins of genocide and mass killing, it is reasonable to conclude that prevention can only aim at avoiding group violence, not genocide specifically.

Genocide does not have a single cause. There are usually many influences, joining together.[4] The starting points, or "instigators," are usually events in the real world that have great impact on people, both members of a group and their leaders. One instigator is difficult conditions of life – e.g., economic problems, political disorganization, or great social changes, leading to social chaos and disorganization. Worsening social conditions have a greater impact than do bad social conditions to which people have become accustomed.

Conflict between groups is another instigator, especially when it has become intractable – greatly resistant to resolution. For example, the conflict may be over territory needed as living space, or between a powerful group in a society and a subordinate group without power, wealth or privilege. While the conflict is real, it is material. It tends to resist resolution for psychological reasons due to fear, insecurity, mistrust, threat to the group's identity and world-view, pride, and so on. Because conflicts can become intractable and potential starting points for genocide, as in the case of Rwanda, the effective resolution of ethno-political conflict, and other group conflicts, can serve the prevention of genocide.

Both difficult life conditions and persistent conflict frustrate fundamental psychological needs for security, a feeling of effectiveness and control over important events in one's life, a positive identity, positive connections to other people, a meaningful comprehension of reality and of one's own place in the world. These are powerful needs, and when they cannot be fulfilled in constructive ways, people will tend to fulfill them in ways that are potentially destructive. In difficult times groups tend to scapegoat another group, usually a minority, proclaim them as the cause of the societal problems. In the case of group conflict, they come to see the other group as at fault – a form of scapegoating – without seeing their own contribution to the conflict. They tend to justify their actions, including increasingly violent acts, and elevate their own cause, diminishing and blaming the other.[5]

Another contributor to genocide is a destructive ideology, which groups create in response to life problems or group conflict. It provides the vision of a better future, but also identifies enemies standing in the way of its fulfillment. In the case of group conflict, this enemy is the opponent in the conflict. Such ideologies are important danger signals. The Nazi ideology identified superior and inferior races, the latter contaminating the former by their very existence. The Khmer Rouge ideology in Cambodia advocated a society with total social equality, with both members of the old regime and educated people identified as incapable of contributing to or living in such a society. The Young Turk's ideology was nationalistic, with the Armenians seen as standing in the way of creating a greater, more powerful, purer nation.

Cultural characteristics also contribute to the likelihood of genocide. In many societies, some group has been historically devalued. This group then becomes the scapegoat and/or the ideological enemy. In case of conflict, a group may be unwilling to compromise with another group it sees in a negative light, and a devalued group may not trust another that has long treated it badly.

Very strong respect for authority is another contributor. In difficult times, and in case of perceived threat by another group, people who have strongly relied on authorities will yearn for strong leaders. They will question less, obey more whatever they are told to do. A less pluralistic, less democratic society also makes a genocidal process more likely. There will be less opposition when the society increasingly turns against and harms a scapegoat or an identified enemy. These problematic cultural characteristics are less present in democracies.

A common wisdom has become that democracies are unlikely, while authoritarian political/governmental systems are much more likely, to engage in genocide, and other types of violence against their population.[6] This, on the whole, appears to be true, especially in "mature democracies" with a well-developed civic society. While mature democracies may not commit genocide against their own population, they can engage in highly violent acts against others, or support mass killing in other countries, as for example Britain and the US supported the killing of "Communists" in Indonesia in 1965-66.[7]

Another important cultural characteristic is past victimization of a group. Its traumatic effects include a sense of vulnerability and perception of the world as dangerous. Without healing, in response to new threat or conflict, the group may respond by force, thinking that it needs to defend itself, but, in fact, actually becoming a perpetrator. This has been a likely contributor to both Serb violence in Bosnia and Hutu violence in Rwanda.

The joint presence of the starting points and cultural characteristics described is especially likely to give rise to scapegoating and destructive ideologies. These in turn lead to discrimination and limited acts of violence against the scapegoat or ideological enemy. But individuals and groups learn by doing, change as a result of their own actions. Harmful actions are justified by increasing devaluation of the victims. This, combined with the "higher ideals" of the ideology, can lead to a reversal of morality. Killing becomes the necessary and right thing. Along the way, the norms and standards of acceptable behavior, and the institutions of the society, may change. This evolution of increasing violence is a crucial, essential aspect of genocide.

A final important contributor is the passivity of bystanders, both "internal bystanders," members of the genocidal society, and "external bystanders," outside groups and nations. Both usually remain passive. This not only allows perpetrators to proceed, but encourages them, since they take the passivity for approval. More than passive, nations often are complicit. They continue with commerce and diplomatic relations as usual, or, due to historic ties to a country, actively support the perpetrators. This was true to a scandalous extent in the 1994 genocide in Rwanda, with France supporting the genocidal government, and the rest of the world looking on and remaining passive, the UN even withdrawing peacekeepers after the genocide began.

The tremendous changes in the world, which represent difficult life conditions, great poverty in many places combined with awareness of the great wealth of others, often of groups in the same society, and other conditions make genocide a continued threat in this new millennium. What can be done about it?

First, active bystandership by the international community is essential. This means not only actions to stop genocide once it has started, or to stop significant violence that is not yet genocidal, but preventive actions when the conditions for group violence exist. Relevant UN agencies should be reformed and governmental agencies should be established everywhere with this specific responsibility. Their task should not be only early warning, which is of great recent interest, but early action. For this to happen requires the active bystandership of citizens of countries who care enough about the lives of human beings everywhere to demand this of their governments.[8]

I will discuss here a few of the many kinds of important preventive actions that can be taken. First, after violence has already taken place, groups and their individual members need to heal. In small groups, and in large group ceremonies, and in other ways, people need to engage with their past suffering. They need to mourn their losses. The more members of two groups that have harmed each other can do this together, the more this may contribute to reconciliation between them.

When groups that have harmed each other – whether the harm doing was one-sided or mutual – continue to live together, they need to reconcile. This is true both in the case of a history of conflict, in the course of conflict resolution, and after mass killing or genocide have been perpetrated. It is very difficult, but very important, for groups to show empathy for each other and to acknowledge the harm they have done to the other. Recent, important wisdom is that creating a shared, mutually acceptable history, a shared collective memory, is of great importance. Since even when one group was the perpetrator and the other a victim, perpetrators tend to blame the victims, and when harm-doing was mutual, each tends to blame the other. This is a demanding and difficult task. Supportive roles by outsiders, by third parties, can be of great value. In a seminar with the country's leaders in Rwanda, in the summer of 2001, my associate Dr. Laurie Pearlman and I found that the leaders present deeply engaged with the hard task of considering ways to create a history – or collective memory – that would be acceptable to both Hutus and Tutsis in Rwanda.

Reconciliation can be promoted by real engagement of groups with each other. Joint projects that serve both groups' needs offer opportunities for significant human engagement by members of the groups with each other.[9]

The role of leaders is important, when instigating conditions are present. Leaders that create scapegoats or promote destructive ideologies, or blame an opponent in a conflict and elevate their own group, may do so either because they are affected by the combination of instigating conditions and cultural characteristics, as are other members of their group, or because they want to gain followers and strengthen their support, or both. It is important not to neglect the first reason, and to pay attention to the group's history and culture and the group's and the leaders' own woundedness. Diplomats ought to be trained so that they can understand and to be able to respond to the leaders' and the group's needs at psychological, cultural, and even spiritual levels.[10]

Two important avenues to preventing genocide are improving the economic conditions of people, as well as reducing disparity, and democratization. When people are desperate, have little hope in the future and find no purpose for their lives, they are vulnerable to the appeal of destructive ideologies. In many places, desperate and aimless young men became adherents to ideologies that fuel genocide. Democratization is important because it is a significant avenue for culture change. It can contribute to more pluralistic societies in which people will oppose the evolution of increasing violence.

Democratization and pluralism can be furthered if nations help other nations, providing not only financial assistance, but also, more importantly, training that develops knowledge and skills for people to create and improve industry, agriculture, technology, and civic society inside the countries that need them. The more selflessly this is done, the more it will be accepted and reciprocated with positive acts. The more this is done, the more the basis for not only genocide, but also terrorism, will diminish.

Genocide can stop, but it requires changes in our values and actions. If nations consider their own enlightened self-interest, their long-term interests instead of limited, short-term interests, they will engage in actions that prevent violence, with all its negative consequences not only on the victims but on the international community as well. If nations, and their citizens, develop inclusive caring, if they come to see people outside their borders as fellow human beings, they will engage in significant efforts on their behalf. The satisfactions from such values and from engaging in such actions can be great. The transformation required for it is possible. Remember Oskar Schindler, who started out as a high-living opportunist, going to Poland to use Jewish slave labor to enrich himself – and ended up completely devoted to saving human lives, at great cost and danger to himself. Hopefully transforming our governments and national policies is also possible.

It requires, however, citizens who are active bystanders, who exert positive influence within their own countries.

Notes

1. *The History and Sociology of Genocide* (New Haven: Yale University Press, 1990), 23.

2. Alison des Forges, *Leave None to Tell The Story*, (Human Rights Watch, 1999), and Samantha Power, "Bystanders to Genocide," *Atlantic Monthly*, (September 2001), 84–108.

3. Ervin Staub, *The Roots of Evil: The Origins of Genocide and Other Group Violence*, (New York: Cambridge University Press, 1989).

4. See further, Staub, *The Roots of Evil*, as well as E. Staub, "The Origins and Prevention of Genocide, Mass Killing and Other Collective Violence," *Peace and Conflict* 5: 303-336.

5. See further, E. Staub and D. Bar-Tal, "Genocide and Intractable Conflict: Roots, Evolution, Prevention and Reconciliation" in D. Sears, L. Huddy and R. Jarvis, eds., *Handbook of Political Psychology* (New York: Oxford University Press, in preparation).

6. See further, R. J. Rummel, *Death by Government* (New Brunswick, NJ: Transaction Books, 1994).

7. Note by Mark Curtis in the *Encyclopedia of Genocide*, Israel Charny, ed., (Santa Barbara, CA: ABC-CLIO, 1999) Vol. 2: 355.

8. See further, Staub, "The Origins and Prevention of Genocide, Mass Killing and Other Collective Violence."

9. For most of the preceding, see further Ervin Staub and Laurie Ann Pearlman, "Healing, Reconciliation and Forgiving after Genocide and Other Collective Violence," in S. J. Helmick and R. L. Petersen, eds., *Forgiveness and Reconciliation: Religion, Public Policy and Conflict Transformation* (Radnor, PA: Templeton Foundation Press, 2001); see also Staub and Bar-Tal, "Genocide and Intractable Conflict: Roots, Evolution, Prevention and Reconciliation" in D. Sears, L. Huddy and R. Jarvis eds., *Handbook of Political Psychology* (New York: Oxford University Press, in preparation).

10. See further, Staub, "The Origins and Prevention of Genocide, Mass Killing and Other Collective Violence."

Mass graves such as this one, opened by Cambodian civilians and Vietnamese soldiers (circa 1979), contained the remains of some of the estimated 1.5 million people killed by the Khmer Rouge in Cambodia, 1975-1979.

PART III

WHAT CAN BE DONE ABOUT GENOCIDE?

Although opposed by the United States, the International Criminal Court (ICC), the world's first permanent tribunal of its kind, began jurisdiction over genocide and war crimes cases on July 1, 2002. The statute providing for the ICC's creation was part of a 1998 treaty negotiated in Rome and signed by 139 countries, the United States among them, after post-Holocaust era genocides took place in the Balkans and Rwanda. Sixty governments had to ratify the treaty to establish the ICC. With the approval of ten countries – Bosnia, Bulgaria, Cambodia, Congo, Ireland, Jordan, Mongolia, Niger, Romania, and Slovakia – on April 11, 2002, the number of ratifications rose to sixty-six. The ceremony at UN headquarters to celebrate this accomplishment was boycotted by the United States, for the administration of President George W. Bush fears, as have other American administrations, that American forces committed to peacekeeping or other overseas missions could be targeted for inappropriate indictments and unfair trials. China and Russia have left the treaty unratified as well. With these major powers on the sidelines, it remains to be seen whether the ICC can be effective in deterring or prosecuting genocide.

In more ways than one, genocide's perpetrators have the upper hand. Tribunals prosecute the perpetrators after the fact, if at all. If these courts are to be a credible deterrent, they have to act swiftly, thoroughly, and decisively. Such things are easier said than done. Early warning systems and other preventative measures try to anticipate the worst before it happens, but their effectiveness has thus far been in the realm of hope more than fact. Standing between prevention and prosecution there is intervention, but the genocidal debacles in the Balkans and Rwanda are scarcely causes for optimism where intervention is concerned. It is acknowledged that forceful intervention could have prevented the worst offenses in those regions.

Regrets have been expressed about the failure to intervene, but such apologetic hindsight does nothing for the murdered and relatively little to encourage confidence that the world's response to genocidal threats will be better "next time."

Nevertheless, the essays in the third part of this book make a persuasive case that there are steps that can and should be taken to deal with genocidal threats in the present and the future. We understand the roots of genocide better than we used to do. There are ways to identify the precursors of genocide and to issue early warnings. These ways can be made more effective than they have been previously. If there is the political will to act – admittedly a huge *if* – lives can be saved. Prosecution of perpetrators can also play a part, for the UN Secretary General Kofi Annan was right to say that the ICC could deal a "decisive blow" to impunity. Even when justice seems all but impossible, reparations and restitution brought forth by civil litigation – even formal apologies – can be better than nothing. At the very least, the writers in this part say, the term "nothing" must not be the "answer" so long as the question "What can be done about genocide?" remains.

15

WHAT CAN BE DONE?

David Nyheim

Any inquiry into what can be done about genocide inevitably raises a number of questions, including: Do we understand the phenomenon of genocide well enough to do something about it? Can we predict violent conflict and genocide? Are we in any kind of position to act when the threat of genocide emerges? From a practice-based early warning vantage point, the latter two questions can be answered with some certainty.

Prediction. Conflict early warning is now a more firmly grounded discipline and is yielding results. Among established early warning organisations and networks, accurate predictions on the outbreak, escalation, and resurgence of violent conflict have been made. Examples include Macedonia (OSCE/HCNM), Burundi (ICG), Democratic Republic of the Congo (APFO/FEWER), and Chechnya (EAWARN/FEWER).

Action. The simple answer is probably that we are more prone to act than we were prior to the Rwandan genocide in 1994. Since then, action has been taken in Kosovo and East Timor. Nonetheless, advances have been few in galvanising the elusive "political will" to prevent or engage earlier in the management of violent conflicts.

It is clear that a first step towards tackling the lack of political will has to involve understanding its causes and manifestations. Below follows a brief description of the more salient facets of lacking political will among governments, inter-governmental organisations and NGOs.

Challenges

The causes and manifestations of lacking political will are highlighted here as they relate to issues of know-how, politics, and institutional set-ups.

Know-how

Complexity of conflict situations. Conflict situations are highly complex and dynamic. As these situations change, a three-month old fact-finding report will quickly be outdated. Policy makers cannot keep up with developments.

Not knowing what works or what is relevant. Conflict prevention and peace-building is a complex exercise, requiring action at multiple levels (local to international), sectors (security, diplomacy, development) and by a range of actors (state and non-state). Often policy makers will not know what it is they can do that will have an impact.

Not knowing who is doing what. The range of actors and activities involved in conflict-prone/affected areas increases the difficulty of implementing concerted peace-building/making efforts. Actions appear (and often are) disjointed, ad hoc, and unstrategic, sometimes with unfortunate negative consequences and wasted resources.

Politics

Political pressures on decision-making. It is clear that decisions taken with respect to crises are often based on agendas that do not concern themselves with peace and the well-being of people. Conflict and crisis decision-making is rarely evidence-based, i.e., based on a peace-focused situation analysis.

Not wanting to interfere in other states' domestic matters. In conflict situations, the affected state will often be very sensitive about outside interference. Governmental and inter-governmental agencies are therefore hesitant or unable to engage in named "conflict prevention" activities.

Not wanting to invest in unstable situations. A number of donors are highly risk-averse as they manage taxpayers' money. Investing substantial funds in pre-conflict situations (e.g. infrastructure development) is often seen as a bad and risky investment that cannot be justified.

Not wanting to create a self-fulfilling prophecy. Making an explicit and public statement that a region is in a "pre-conflict or genocide phase" may actually precipitate conflict or genocide, for example, either by leading to the withdrawal of investments or by encouraging warmongers to act.

Lack of accountability. Information and analyses on potential conflicts have traditionally remained out of the public domain. There is consequently limited pressure on key players to act or not engage in inappropriate action.

Institutional Set-ups

Restricted mandates. Often key conflict factors (war economies, arms flows, and poor governance) require concerted action from multiple agencies and different departments in the same agency due to institutional/departmental mandates. With prevailing institutional incoherence, this problem reduces the ability of governments and inter-governmental organisations to play an effective role in conflict situations.

Slow response time. The response time to a potential or actual conflict, for example, to deploy United Nations peacekeeping forces, is estimated to be between 6-12 months.[1] A number of organisations are also very slow at disbursing funds for urgent conflict prevention activities. Such slow response time to rapidly changing and escalating situations often undermines efforts to capitalise on "windows of opportunity" for peace.

Short-term versus long-term focus. Given the multitude of priorities faced by decision-makers, and limited human resources, the focus is often on short-term crisis management, rather than long-term conflict prevention. Institutions are chronically "reactive" in nature.

"Early warning noise." Decision-makers are often swamped with information. Furthermore, often it is felt that there is too much early warning and too many false ones. This "noise" reduces the credibility of those groups engaged in effective early warning.

Ways Forward

Tackling these challenges is a tall order and perhaps even a quixotic task. What is needed are practical and commonsensical approaches to tackle the obstacles impeding political will for preventive action. Below follow some strategies/approaches that show value and should be supported.

Division of labor. Based on comparative advantages, like-minded NGOs, IGOs and governments can engage in concerted conflict (and genocide) prevention activities. The development of long-term partnerships between like-minded groups needs to be encouraged (e.g., inter-agency work on the region of Javakheti, in southern Georgia in the south Caucasus).

Public early warning. With several caveats in mind (e.g., self-fulfilling prophecies), public early warning disseminated (or with the threat of dissemination) through the internet or media is an important strategy for reducing the current accountability gap.

Sustained monitoring. Long-term support to peace-focused civil society monitoring networks in conflict-prone regions is a vital tool to ensure that policy makers receive the necessary evidence base for decision-making.

Building on existing activities for peace-building. Donors and other groups often have on-going activities in potentially unstable regions. Rather than seeking to develop a new series of conflict prevention projects, these activities can be re-programmed, co-ordinated and complemented with new activities for improved peace-building impact. Planning forums for integrated/concerted planning and implementation of peace-building strategies are necessary.

Sustained learning. Research on lessons learned and the development of peace and conflict impact assessment methods (PCIA) are important to ensure that the knowledge base for peace-building grows. These experiences should not be used to create blueprints, but serve as "inspiration" and thus strengthen institutional know-how.

Advocacy. A number of NGOs, think-tanks and government departments are engaged in advocacy and research on several important issues, such as: (a) mainstreaming conflict prevention; (b) ensuring donor policy coherence; and (c) institutionalizing a "prevention is better than cure" mentality. Such advocacy and research efforts need to be sustained and supported.

Notes
1.   PIOOM Foundation, 1999.

16

IDENTIFYING PRECURSORS

Jennifer Leaning

The mission of genocide prevention has a paradox at its conceptual core: the more we understand past instances of this most horrible human phenomenon, the more we realize its potential cannot be extinguished from our future.

Scholars from a range of disciplines have sifted through the bloody record of the past several centuries, this last also the bloodiest, to identify precursor conditions for genocide.[1] These enabling conditions are ominously familiar, described as widely observed patterns of malignant group relationships that have in the past led to collective mass violence.

The good news is that although these necessary conditions appear robustly prevalent, they may not in themselves be sufficient. For every instance of documented genocide, as defined by the Genocide Convention of 1948, there are many instances of communal violence or mass killings that do not rise to meet these extreme definitional thresholds.[2] Although much more research is needed on what factors (leadership, economic conditions, or international intervention, as examples) helped to prevent these historical situations from escalating into outright genocidal campaigns, there appears to be historical substance to the notion that the processes leading to genocide can be halted, constrained, or deflected. At any particular historical moment there is space for decision and change, the past does not necessarily determine the future.

The evident contingency of genocide gives reason to talk about ways to identify the escalating steps in these social processes and stop their awful progression. In public health, primary prevention eliminates the root causes of a condition and secondary prevention mitigates or reduces the consequences of a condition once it has occurred.[3] In this context, and based on our current understanding of genocide as the culmination of many prevalent social processes, the task of preventing genocide is really one of secondary prevention. The first important question in this task then becomes how to discern when a society is beginning to accelerate into those collective, deadly activities that signal the embarkation of the genocidal project.

This task of discernment in the midst of complex processes (such as disease and disasters) is called early warning. In public health, early warning is the name given to the process of identifying early indicators of impending epidemic disease. In disaster response, early warning derives from the study of drought and famine, where experts have attempted to define those indicators that point to impending famine catastrophe by following human responses to progressive crop failure and household impoverishment (agricultural practices, market prices, livestock management, and rural-urban migration).[4]

This concept has been adapted by those who investigate governmental abuses of human rights to provide early warning of intensifying patterns of individual oppression, collective punishment, or incitement of group atrocity.[5] The human rights community has built an informal practical checklist, based on historical experience, that allows observers to sound an alarm to the outside world, with all its capacities for denunciation and intervention, and say that in a particular society or region of the world conditions are moving into deeply dangerous zones of communal violence, sufficient even to prompt concerns of potential genocide.[6]

An early warning approach to genocide presupposes a reading of the Genocide Convention that stresses the language regarding the need to intervene before genocide occurs. Attempts to actualize the intent of this language during the war in Kosovo proved controversial. It was politically difficult to talk about impending genocide in a region of Europe, when a scant four years earlier there had been far less civil society and NGO clamor (though still some) regarding the rapidly unfolding genocide in Rwanda. Yet the concern about impending genocide in Kosovo, raised by some human rights and humanitarian groups in the spring of 1999,[7] is best understood in the context of the preceding Balkan wars,[8] rather than Rwanda. In Kosovo, human rights groups saw an evolving pattern of ethnic cleansing, undertaken since the summer of 1998, that looked grimly similar to the pattern of terror and population expulsion that Milosevic had perpetrated from 1991 to 1995 in those former Yugoslav entities to the north.[9] Human rights and humanitarian organizations had time in which to mount advocacy campaigns to impel international action. Further, international outrage over what had occurred at Srebrinica and other "safe areas" in the mid 1990s made it impossible to deny the significance of what was being reported out of Kosovo in 1998-99. The marginal success of early warning in the prevention of genocide during the latter stages of the wars in the Balkans can in large measure be attributed to the same reasons that early warning failed in Rwanda: the pace of events; the baseline level of awareness and interest on the part of the international community; and the imposed sense of urgency. In Rwanda, the obvious early warning signs were not being gathered or interpreted in the months leading up to the ferociously fast onslaught and once the news came out, no one in authority stepped into a place of responsibility to take the necessary action.[10] This fatal lapse derives in part from inadequate use of available information and in part from a collapse in political will at the highest levels.[11] The calamity in Rwanda thus poses a clear challenge for early warning: it is not enough to get the information – advocacy must persuade those in authority to use that information as a basis for policy change.

The check list as provided here contains preconditions and precursors, as well as accelerating ignition points:

Early Issues of Concern

Systematic exclusion of the target group from the benefits of the national project (education, employment);

Formal constriction of rights to movement, practice religion, cultural expression, use of one's own language.

Explicit Signs of State-sponsored or Organized Ethnic Violence

Detention, execution, or assassination of selected leading members of the target group;

Violent methods to force a group to leave a region or territory, including instillation of terror;

Moving members of a target group to designated areas;

Organization of paramilitary forces recruited along ethnic or communal lines;

Denigration or stigmatization of target groups through campaigns in the press, media, public speaking.

Indirect, Population-based Indicators of Social Stress

Increasing arms trade and proliferation of weapons in the aggressive group;

Failure to punish lawlessness or murder directed at the target group;

Growing disparities and economic distress;

Suppression of the press;

Apparently voluntary ethnic separation, people moving from neighborhoods, taking their children out of mixed schools;

An increase in internal migration, passport applications, cross-border movements.

To gather this information, the technical skills required of human rights investigators are wide-ranging:[12] epidemiologic methods for estimating and defining instances of a condition in a large population; survey and interview approaches; forensic techniques; legal and analytic skills in assessing documents and records. Content knowledge is necessary in areas of physical and psychological trauma, torture, public health, arms trade, weapons systems, political organizations, military roles, principles and important details of domestic and international law, including human rights law and the laws of war. The work demands as well a level of physical stamina, experience navigating politically sensitive or even dangerous situations, and good judgment about when to leave the scene.

Cooperation with other groups is essential. In many crisis areas around the world, human rights groups often enter at the request of or in response to quiet concerns raised within the humanitarian community or when press reports suggest a more systematic exploration may be warranted. Relief NGOs are among the first to see that torture, killings, or disappearances are taking place. Although they may not be able to speak out publicly (declamations can lead to expulsion, and for humanitarians, maintaining access to civilian populations is the highest priority), they have learned (especially after experience in Bosnia and Rwanda) that it is necessary to transmit these concerns to some other locus where they can be appropriately dealt with. News reporters have acquired a sophisticated capacity for description and analysis, serving in their own right as credible observers and witnesses of important instances and trends in social and individual oppression, fear, and stigmatization.[13]

Human rights investigators are in the country relatively briefly – two weeks, one month – because their role rapidly becomes too hot. Once they issue a report and engage in advocacy, they cannot remain in the area. In reporting evidence and trends in these categories, the human rights community places high expectations on those who receive the information. It is important to hold these officials accountable for what they knew when, so that later there is little room for denying knowledge and responsibility. Names, dates, titles, and responses received from those who are formally debriefed are an essential part of the reporting and advocacy work.

The focus then shifts to discussions on possible forms of intervention. Although not the focus of this discussion, it is important to note that there are many options available, that many have been used recently, and that those engaged in early warning have a strong interest in encouraging national and international bodies to explore a wide range of possibilities. These include, in ascending order of urgency and aggression:

Official human rights delegations;

Firm denunciations of abuses and outrages;

Diplomatic pressure, involving consultations, veiled threats;

Financial and targeted sanctions against the offending élites or groups;

Insertion of unarmed observers, with agreement of the offending parties;

Arms embargoes;

Humanitarian intervention (military) along just war precepts, abiding by rules of engagement, rule of law, use of proportional force.

All of these actions require focused energy and argument to accomplish. Governments are loathe to engage these issues. Yet it is helpful to those in power who do wish to make a difference on these issues to be subjected to considerable public pressure and to have reports of atrocities widely disseminated.

Genocide does not arise *de novo*, separate from an enabling context and a record of escalating actions and inactions with regard to serious human rights abuses. This escalation leads down an increasingly narrow and terrible path that by now, given how deeply the historical record has been explored, should look familiar the next time we confront it. Early warning is based upon our empirical understanding of the very human ways that a society can turn upon itself. To attempt to prevent genocide is to get continually more precise about what its precursor steps look like and to get increasingly more adept at applying political and public pressure on those who must be moved to act. Near the outset of that familiar path, it is crucial that the word get out, imperative that those with resources and responsibilities be called to act, necessary that the world know – lest once again we lose the fight against our own worst tendencies.

Notes

1. T. S. Szayna, *Identifying Potential Ethnic Conflict: Application of a Process Model* (San Diego, CA: Rand Corporation, 2000); J. G. Heidenrich, *How to Prevent Genocide: A Guide for Policymakers, Scholars, and the Concerned Citizen* (Westport, CT: Praeger, 2001); A. Alvarez, *Governments, Citizens, and Genocide: A Comparative and Interdisciplinary Approach* (Bloomington, IN: Indiana University Press, 2001); Helen Fein, "The three P's of Genocide Prevention: With Application to a Genocide Foretold - Rwanda," in Neil Riemer, ed., *Protection Against Genocide* (Westport, CT: Praeger, 2001), 45-66.

2. D. Chirot and M.E.P. Seligman, eds., *Ethnopolitical Warfare: Causes, Consequences, and Possible Solutions* (Washington, D.C: American Psychological Association, 2001); A. Destexhe, *Rwanda and Genocide in the Twentieth Century* (New York: New York University Press, 1995).

3. J. M. Last and R. B. Wallace eds., *Public Health and Preventive Medicine* (Norwalk, CT: Appleton & Lange, 1992), 4-5.

4. D. S. Mileti, *Disasters by Design: A Reassessment of Natural Hazards in the United States* (Washington, D.C.: National Academy of Sciences, Joseph Henry Press, 1 999), 174-200; R. Yip, "Famine," in E.K. Noji, ed., *The Public Health Consequences of Disasters* (New York: Oxford University Press, 1997), 305-335.

5. Human Rights Watch, *World Report 2001* (New York: Human Rights Watch, 2001); T. B. Jabine and R.P. Claude, "Exploring Human Rights Issues with Statistics," in T. B. Jabine and R.P. Claude eds., *Human Rights and Statistics* (Philadelphia, PA: University of Pennsylvania Press, 1992), 5-34.

6. A. Neier and J. Leaning, "Human Rights Challenges," in J. Leaning, S.M. Briggs, L.C. Chen eds., *Humanitarian Crises: The Medical and Public Health Response* (Cambridge, MA: Harvard University Press, 1999), 195-209.

7. H. Burkhalter, "Facing up to Genocide: The Obligation to Intervene," *Medicine and Global Survival* 6 (1999), 51-53.

8. Human Rights Watch, *Slaughter Among Neighbors: The Political Origins of Communal Violence* (New York: Human Rights Watch, 1995).

9. Physicians for Human Rights, *War Crimes in Kosovo: A Population-Based Assessment of Human Rights Violations against Kosovar Albanians* (Boston: Physicians for Human Rights, August 1999); P. Ball, *Policy or Panic? The Flight of Ethnic Albanians from Kosovo, March-May 1999* (Washington, D.C.: American Academy of Arts and Sciences, April 2000).

10. *Report of the Independent Inquiry in the Actions of the United Nations during the 1994 Genocide in Rwanda* (New York: Office of the Secretary General, United Nations, 15 December 1999). (Report accessed at www.un.org/News/ossg/rwanda_report.htm)

11. S. Power, *A Problem from Hell* (New York: Basic Books, 2002); S. R. Feil, *Preventing Genocide: How the Early Use of Force Might Have Succeeded in Rwanda*, Report to the Carnegie Commission on Preventing Deadly Conflict (New York: Carnegie Corporation, 1998).

12. H. J. Geiger and R. M. Cook-Deegan, "The Role of Physicians in Conflicts and Humanitarian Crises, *JAMA* 270 (1993): 616-620.

13. R. Gutman and D. Rieff, eds., *Crimes of War* (New York: W.W. Norton & Co., 1999).

17

ANTICIPATING GENOCIDE

Henry R. Huttenbach

It goes without saying that the study of genocide (the phenomenon) and of genocides (individual cases) are, in part, devoted to genocide prevention. Finding ways and means of forestalling genocidal crises rests first and foremost on an understanding of both *what* genocide is and *how* it takes place. While predicting genocides is impossible – nothing in the future can be fully known – prudent steps can be taken to lessen the likelihood of an outbreak of genocidal violence.

As we face the uncertainties of the twenty-first century, one thing is certain about the near-term future with regard to genocide, namely, the global dimension and genocidal potential of ethno-conflicts. On all continents, in all cultural regions, and in most countries, ethnic-related tensions have broken out, some assuming genocidal proportions. The brutal break-up of Yugoslavia and the internecine slaughters in Rwanda serve as reminders of what could happen elsewhere: e.g. in multi-national Indonesia, Nigeria, and India; where there are forces of ethno-secessions (Chechnya, the Tamils in Sri Lanka); cross-border ethno-unification irredentism (Albanians); and rival ethnic claims to scarce natural resources. As these gather force, the probability of genocidal violence rises. It is, therefore, a *sine qua non* that monitoring evolving ethnic conflicts lies at the heart of genocide crisis detection, (even though other factors play a role).

What, then are the early warning signals that one can rely on if a global genocide watch system in the context of ethnic strife is to take effect? Impressionistic "evidence" must be avoided. More concrete criteria need to be developed in order to persuade the international community to take preventive actions presently condoned and obligated by international law. In other words, more than mere suspicion is required; instead, reasonably incontestable "hard" evidence has to be mounted in order to pinpoint with reasonable accuracy a trend that a genocide crisis is in the making.

One body of knowledge that can be relatively easily assembled is incidents of violations of collective rights. In its essence, genocide is a violation of the most basic of rights – the right to life, in this case of a group's right to exist. By definition, then, any threat to and endangerment of a group's existence can serve as a signal of potential (possible if not immediately probable) genocide; it can serve as a sign of the deterioration of a group's ability to sustain itself in the face of an aggressively unfriendly foe such as a rival ethnic group. Thus, a careful monitoring of the granting or denying of a group's basic rights can act as a barometer of its existential condition at various times. A record (a timeline) of its actual rights and of those it lacks can serve as a measure of the positive and negative circumstances it enjoys or endures. In turn, a detailed record of a government's rights policies towards a particular group can serve as a measure of the limits of tolerance or intolerance it exercises.

A monitoring of collective rights calls for a categorization and prioritization of collective rights under two rubrics: human rights and civil rights. The former rubric includes a number of universal rights regardless of the political circumstances of a specific group. These include the right to food, shelter and medical services; the right to work and education to facilitate the first three; and the right to cultural identity, e.g. language, religion and (perhaps) territory. The latter rubric includes the standard political rights of citizenship: speech, assembly, press, and democratic representation. Thus, an accurate accounting of the state of collective rights can inform policy advisors on an ongoing basis of the degree of danger, that is, the evolution away or toward a genocidal crisis in the context of ethnic conflict.

A second methodological approach to monitoring the level of security and/or the degree of danger in which a group finds itself is a careful assessment of the rhetoric aimed at it. Rhetoric is a key ingredient in the formulation of the "other." Negative rhetoric is a device to depict a group solely in defamatory terms, ranging from the relatively benign caricature to the extremes of demonization. Hate speeches by government functionaries, inflammatory editorials in state newspapers, violent vocabulary on placards carried by demonstrators, vituperative sermons, and similar negative depictions by the media, popular literature, all belong to the same category of forging a negative image of a group as "the enemy," as "inimicable" to society, as a "fundamental problem" that calls for radical "solutions." Individually, these statements in themselves may not be indicative of a genocidal mind-set in the making. However, cumulatively, these rhetorical attacks can lay the groundwork for a pre-genocidal crisis. Hate words in themselves are not dangerous. However, repeated sufficiently, they do become a call for action. Hence the need for observers to keep a constant eye on the ebb and flow of violent rhetoric as it supports large-scale persecution, mass expulsion, and complete destruction of a targeted group.

Rhetoric is a reasonably accurate reflection of a government's policies especially when seen in conjunction with the denial of collective rights. Thus the nexus of rhetoric and policy can be a useful tool providing the basis for a reliable determination that genocide is or is not in the offing. The monitoring of group rights' violations and of a body of negative rhetoric has to be in the hands of professional observers with special training and qualifications. There is no room here for amateurs and well-meaning persons. The monitoring system will have to be handled by an educated élite, proficient, first of all, in the local language(s), well versed in regional history, and familiar with contemporary conditions of the country in question in which ethnic conflict is feared as a future probability.

To put such a monitoring service into place raises two issues: who will pay for this international endeavor? A UN-supervised fund seems the most practicable in the absence of a better international agency. Secondly, what authority will the monitoring agency have? Will its findings be advisory and subject to review or will they be binding and have the force of law? Obviously these questions cannot be answered here. They are only posed to illustrate the difficulties of prevention even if one has reliable, accurate and ongoing data at one's disposal regarding the possibility and probability of an outbreak of a genocidal crisis brewing on the distant horizon or in the imminent future.

What needs to be understood is that from the perspective of this article, a clear distinction must be made, in the context of genocide prevention, between heading off a suspected genocide and intervention in an ongoing genocide. The latter is *not* the focus of this study: involvement in a genocide in progress is not prevention but genocide termination. Once a genocide is in progress, from the vantage point of the suggestions made above, it is too late. Once genocide is being committed, only violence can stop the crisis. The idea of prevention is to *avoid* genocide by non-violent means by monitoring *pre-genocidal* conditions.

Indexes based on a timeline graphically portraying the rise and fall of the circumstances surrounding a potentially endangered ethnic group are designed to avoid genocide, to stop it before the violence breaks out. This means involvement short of ending violence once in progress. This calls for a great variety of responses: diplomatic (public and secret); economic (boycotts); international condemnation and isolation, etc.

Once the danger of evolution towards genocide is identified, there must be a guarantee of prompt actions: namely, to harness timely response. But that is another topic. Obviously, the means to deploy promptly adequate responses to reverse the trend towards genocide must be in place if monitoring is to be more than an exercise in information-gathering and evaluation. Anticipating genocide is the key to prevention. Without the means to chart in detail events such as the violation of group rights and the use of rhetoric, no meaningful, no pre-genocidal steps can be taken with assurance. Anti-genocide measures cannot be based on false assumptions and sloppy information, but on an unbiased, careful arrangement of information, allowing one to project what will transpire in the near future with reasonable authority. Anticipation must not be idle guesswork. The suspicion of genocide is a matter of suspecting a crime. Preventing a crime must be discriminatory and not a matter of political bias. A strong (if not airtight) case must be made in each instance of anticipated genocide. Towards that end, tabulating the record of violations of group rights and of a group's portrayal as a targeted group is a vital task amongst several others required to rid the world of the scourge of genocide in general, and of genocidal ethno-strife in particular.

In conclusion, while averting a genocide may be a complex assignment, the goal is by no means unprecedented. Skilled diplomacy has prevented wars; occasional international cooperation has fought off famine and diseases. Essentially it boils down more to a matter of political will than of the absence of means, though these definitely need honing and expanding. Sufficient funds are, without doubt, at the heart of a reliable global anti-genocide infrastructure. But that again is in essence a question of political commitment. Failure to ward off future genocides will rest on disinterest and apathy on the part of the rest of the world. It is a question of knowing and acting in response to sufficient information. In the end it is an ethical issue, to do what is right or wrong on the part of states responsible by international law to thwart the plague of genocide that threatens us all in this century. The legacy of the twentieth century is the accountability of everyone in the task to erase genocide from this planet.

18

EARLY WARNING AND GENOCIDE PREVENTION

Barbara Harff

Risk assessment identifies countries and situations with substantial potential for humanitarian crises. I have developed and tested a structural model which identifies, with a high degree of accuracy, the factors that preceded most of the 35 cases of genocides and politicides (political mass murders) that occurred between 1955 and 1998. This provides the basis for identifying countries currently at risk. The approach is currently used by the US government to create a watch list. Tables I and II list 15 high-risk countries identified by this method. (See further, pages 128-129)

Risk assessment does not tell us when an episode is likely to occur, only that the structural conditions for it are present. Geno/politicide may or may not in fact occur in high-risk situations, depending on the occurrence of accelerating events and prevention actions. The aim of the early warning approach I have designed is to narrow the time frame and identify the warning flags that a geno/politicide is in the making six months before its onset. This means identifying the frequency and sequences of political actions – the accelerators and triggers – that either propel or disrupt the escalation of conflict. My accelerator model identifies ten general types of accelerators – examples are aggressive actions by opposition groups, and new discriminatory policies by the regime – each measured using three to seven categories of specific events.[1]

The basic assumption of this approach to early warning is that accelerator events tend to follow similar patterns before the onset of mass killings. The method has been applied to a number of high-risk cases from the last 25 years and the data analyzed using neural net analysis. Initial results show that it is possible to identify with up to 78% accuracy the six months that preceded the onset of a politicide. A team of researchers is now using the approach to analyze and interpret data from high-risk countries.

More accurate risk assessments and early warning should make it easier

EXAMPLES OF COUNTRY RISKS OF GENOCIDE AND POLITICIDE IN THE EARLY 21ST CENTURY

Countries (risk factors)	Risk Factors:						Possible victim groups
	PRIOR GENO/ POLITICIDES	INTERNAL WARS SINCE 1986	MINORITY ELITE	EXCLUSIONARY IDEOLOGY	AUTOCRATIC REGIME	TRADE OPENNESS	
Iraq (6 of 6)	Yes: 1961-75, 1988-91	High	**Yes: Sunni Arabs dominate**	**Yes: Secular nationalist**	Yes	Low	Political opponents of Saddam Hussein, Kurds, Shi'a
Burma (5 of 6)	Yes: 1978	Medium-high	No: Burman majority dominates	**Yes: Nationalist**	Yes	Very low	Democratic opposition; Karen, Shan, Mon; Arakenese Muslims
Burundi (5 of 6)	Yes: 1965-73, 1993, 1998	Medium-High	**Yes: Tutsis dominate**	No	Yes	Low	Supporters of militant Hutus; Tutsis
Rwanda (5 of 6)	Yes: 1963-64, 1994	Medium-High	**Yes: Tutsis dominate**	No	Yes	Low	Supporters of exiled Hutu militants
Pakistan (4 of 6)	Yes: 1971, 1973-77	Medium-low	No: Punjabi majority dominates	**Yes: Islamist/ Nationalist**	Yes	Low	Sindhis, Hindus, Shi'a, Christians
Ethiopia (4 of 6)	Yes: 1976-79	High	**Yes: Tigreans dominate**	No	No: Transitional	Low	Supporters of Oromo, Somali secessionists; Islamists
Somalia (4 of 6)	Yes: 1988-91	Very high	No: clan rivalries but no dominance	No	Yes	Very low	Isaaq in Somaliland, clan rivals in south

Country	Past geno/politicides	Magnitude	Ethnic/political elite	Ideology	Regime type	Risk	Possible victim groups
China (4 of 6)	Yes: 1950-51, 1959, 1966-75	Low	No	Yes: Marxist	Yes	Low but growing	Uigher and Tibetan nationalists, Islamists, Christians
Congo DRC (3 of 6)	Yes: 1964-65, 1977	Very high	? No ?	No	Yes	Medium	Hutus, Tutsis, political and ethnic opponents of Kabila regime
Liberia (3 of 6)	No	High	Yes: Americo-Liberians, Gio, Mano dominate	No	Yes	Medium	Krahn, Mandingo; political opponents of Taylor regime
Uganda (3 of 6)	Yes: 1972-79, 1980-86	Medium-low	Yes: Ankole dominate	No	No: Transitional	Low	Supporters of Lords Resistance Army
Algeria (3 of 6)	Yes: 1962	High	No	Yes: Secular nationalist	No: Transitional	High	Islamists, government supporters, Berbers
Indonesia (2 of 6)	Yes: 1965-66, 1975	Medium-high	No	No	No: Transitional	Medium	Acehnese, *transmigrasi*; Chinese, Christians
Sri Lanka (2 of 6)	Yes: 1989-90	Medium-high	No: Sinhalese majority dominates	No	No: Democratic	Medium	Supporters of Tamil separatists
Turkey (2 of 6)	No	Medium-low	No	Yes: Secular nationalist	No: Transitional	Low but growing	Kurds, Islamists

Note: This is a revision of a table prepared for Barbara Harff in "Genocide and Politicide in Global Perspective: The Historical Record and Future Risks," in Stan Windass, ed., *Just War and Genocide* (London: Palgrave, for the Foundation for International Security), 2002. Countries are listed according to their number of risk factors, as identified in Barbara Harff's structural model, using recent information. Shaded cells signify high-risk conditions. The table includes most countries with four and five risk factors plus a sampling of those with two and three. Afghanistan, which was high on all six factors in 2001, is not included because of its rapidly changing status. Sudan and Angola, which have ongoing geno/politicides, are not included. Possible victim groups are identified based on country-specific information from the authors' case files on countries, minority groups, and political opposition movements.

for governments to plan preventive actions. The same information, if publicly available, should also help NGOs anticipate humanitarian crises. And it also may be useful in promoting citizen action campaigns that can deflect genocidal action in high-risk countries. Citizen groups in Western countries may take the lead in such action, and so could citizen self-help groups in high-risk countries themselves.

What kinds of preventive action are most likely to be effective in specific situations? It is necessary to develop a toolbox of preventive actions and to identify the circumstances in which they are most likely to be effective. Preventive action by governments includes diplomatic efforts, sanctions, and military action – both threatened and overt. The range of preventive action by NGOs and citizen groups is potentially much wider. It includes campaigns aimed at publicizing abuses, using informal political means to encourage preventive action, and organizing rescue and humanitarian work. The larger issue is this: researchers and policy makers need to learn much more about what tools have been tried in what situations, and whether or not they have had positive effects.

Notes

1.   See Barbara Harff, "Could Humanitarian Crises Have Been Anticipated in Burundi, Rwanda, and Zaire? A Comparative Study of Anticipatory Indicators," in Hayward R. Alker, T. R. Gurr, and Kumar Rupesinghe, eds., *Journeys Through Conflict: Narratives and Lessons* (Lanham, MD: Rowman & Littlefield, 2001), pp. 81-102.

19

CONTROLLING GENOCIDE IN THE TWENTY-FIRST CENTURY

Herbert Hirsch

If one allows one's mind to wander through the events of the last century, it is difficult to avoid the pessimistic conclusion that we have failed to control the seemingly endless spiral of genocide, war, and ethnic conflict that raced through that century and continues to plague humanity in this century. In this brief essay I am going to argue that the failure of the international community to stop the massacres in places such as Bosnia and Rwanda is not only immoral but impractical as well. Policy toward genocide must be dominated by what I call the "practicality of morality." By this I mean that action to halt and prevent genocide and political massacres is practical because without it all the basic building blocks of international life, commerce, travel, and the international and intra-national interchange of goods and information, are subject to severe disruption. It is, therefore, in the interest of all to end that disruption and create an environment of peaceful interchange. In short, moral imperatives are the most practical way to pursue a nation's interest.

Specifically, I argue that if we are to proceed in the direction of controlling genocide, it will be necessary to take both long and short-term actions. In this essay I am going to discuss the immediate problem, that of saving life and preventing genocide in the short-term. It must never, however, be forgotten that in the long run it is also necessary to replace the present ethic of life destruction with one dedicated to life preservation. That, however, is for another essay, and to prevent genocide in the short-term, three broad steps to develop a coherent strategy to achieve that goal must be taken.

First, devise a multilateral strategy to curtail and prevent genocide and political massacres. This will be facilitated by assembling a coalition of support to halt the violence by developing a policy to bring together the international laws of war and the United Nations Convention on the Prevention and Punishment of the Crime of Genocide.

Second, development of an "Early Warning System" and instruments of humanitarian intervention to recognize and curtail future genocides and political massacres.

Third, these actions should result in the punishment of instigators of genocide and political massacres, demonstrating to the world that violence is not an acceptable means to achieve political ends.

International Law and the Prevention of Genocide

If prevention is ever to become a reality, it is essential to create, within the United Nations, a set of institutions which have the power to act to prevent mass killing. These should be based on international law, and full implementation of the International Criminal Court, along with a reformulated and strengthened UN Convention on the Prevention and Punishment of the Crime of Genocide.

Remedies in international law must be created which will guarantee that perpetrators of genocide will be brought to justice and that international violence will not be seen as a legitimate mechanism to achieve territorial or other aspirations. International law has been virtually powerless to stop the large-scale destruction of human life and the primary reason is that international politics is dominated by the nation state and the idea of sovereignty. In fact, international law is often defined as "the body of rules that nations recognize as binding upon one another in their mutual relations"[1] and is the result of consensus among nations. That is, international law is what the nations of the world agree it is. Any program to stop the violence will have to confront the nation state's claim to sovereignty within its borders.

This cannot be accomplished unilaterally. It will require the kind of coalition building and support inducement manifested in the Persian Gulf War and in the new coalition against terrorism formed after the horrible events of September 11, 2001 when aircraft were piloted into the World Trade Center and the Pentagon. This coalition should concentrate on building support for the policy of bringing together the UN Convention on the Prevention and Punishment of the Crime of Genocide and invoking international laws defining crimes of war as procedures to punish perpetrators and demonstrate to the world that international violence is not to be tolerated by the world community. The precedents for such action are, of course, found in the Nuremberg Trials, the numerous war crimes trials throughout Europe, and the war crimes trials held in the Far East at the conclusion of the Second World War.

Unfortunately, the role of international law has been underestimated by many observers. The basic idea is that, since it appears unrealistic to believe war will be abolished, the next best thing is to attempt to control the worst effects of warfare by trying to maintain the idea that there are standards of civilization by which conduct is to be judged. While participants in war do not always adhere to the laws regulating warfare, certain basic ideas have gained widespread acceptance. For example, prisoners of war are not to be killed and must be treated humanely; hospitals are not to be targets; non-combatants, persons not taking an active part in the conflict, for example, children, are not to be harmed; and torture is not to be allowed.

States and armed participants comply with the laws for a variety of reasons. These include the role of world public opinion which might condemn gross violations, the fear that if the laws are violated there will be military or other reprisals – including political consequences, such as the loss of friends and allies, and possible judicial consequences such as war crimes trials which, while they may not have enforcement sanctions, could very well brand the perpetrators as pariahs in the world of international politics. Even when international law does not appear to be effective, it provides standards of behavior to be considered in the policy-making process.

This basic idea that war is governed by rules appears to have existed in almost all societies, but it was only in the second half of the nineteenth century that laws to regulate war were codified. Since that time, the international agreements regulating war have taken the form of declarations, conventions, and protocols.

These precedents established the concept that international law applied to individuals as well as nations. Using them as a foundation, it is possible to create institutions to prevent future genocides and to punish perpetrators. This, in turn, may contribute to creating the environment within which the life-preserving ethic may flourish and begin to create a new form of memory – memory of the common struggles to implement international law to protect the rights of all individuals.

Some progress in this direction has, of course, been made. The creation of the International Criminal Court and the creation by the United Nations of the International Criminal Tribunals for the former Yugoslavia, meeting in The Hague, and for Rwanda, meeting in Arusha, Tanzania, are the most important examples. While there are many objections and problems standing in the way of further implementation of such actions, it is crucial to point out that, if the violence is to be stopped, permanent, international institutions have to be developed and empowered to act.

Genocide and Justice: Prevention and Punishment

If future massacres and genocides are to be prevented, individuals who wage aggressive war, or plan and execute genocide, must be apprehended and held accountable. While this is the first step, it is usually after the fact. Prevention is the key.

There have been many proposals to create variations of what have been called "Genocide Early Warning Systems." The United States government has participated in studies to determine how such a system might operate and at least two recent books and several new organizations are devoted to this task. Basically, there are two major tasks to be performed during the early warning stage.

The first is to alert international public opinion. This involves gathering, processing, and disseminating information, and then mobilizing coalitions to bring this information to world attention.

Second, exert pressure on the offending party to attempt to convince them that it is in their interest not to continue on the path toward genocide.

Pressure is exerted through a variety of techniques including petitions and representative missions to government officials. Since these are unlikely to have much impact, the next step is to move to campaigns such as those undertaken by groups like Amnesty International, Human Rights Watch, Prevent Genocide, or other non-governmental organizations. Even these are unlikely to deter a group or government determined to use genocide as a policy. If they fail, an "international alert" is declared. This would be followed by activating UN or other international organizations. This stage is crucial because it is much more difficult to dislodge perpetrators from territory already taken than to prevent the invasions at the outset. It is of the utmost importance, therefore, to be able to identify the genocidal possibility in a society.

Observers such as Franklin Littell, have identified five general indicators that might serve as portents of the potential for genocide.

First, instruments and mechanisms of recruitment. When a group or movement prints, uses or distributes antisemitic or racist or other dehumanizing material for recruitment of members, this is a possible demonstration of genocidal possibility.

Second, the use of the media or other means to distribute antisemitic, racist, or other dehumanizing appeals.

Third, the mechanisms used to achieve political power involve the techniques identified above which are attached to the use of violence and intimidation. The violent tactics encouraged or used against opponents include the creation of paramilitary training camps to teach the use of weapons, bombing, beating, assassination, etc.

Fourth, the construction of an environment of unquestioning obedience to authority. The movement or state uses religion to repress the population to establish a situation in which individuals lose any semblance of identity and believe that they owe their allegiance to the leader.

Fifth, the use of secrecy and other methods to create an exclusionary organization which separates insiders from outsiders. These include secret binding rituals established to cement the followers' relationship to the organization. Among these are rituals of induction and separation, as well as the use of deception or disinformation to confuse the public and maintain extreme secrecy. Tactics may include the use of infiltration and subversion of public and other institutions such as the police, schools, and perhaps others.

When these are present, the institutions created to deter atrocity and genocide must be prepared to act to prevent the assertion of power of terrorist groups or to intervene to save lives.

This means that the creation of some common rules, along with mechanisms to enforce adherence, have to be placed on the agenda. It would appear that, in an interdependent and fragile world all too prone to the abuse of human rights, nations and groups can no longer be afforded the right to unlimited self-determination if that determination does harm to the greater, international good.

In spite of the problems, if there is ever going to be a convincing demonstration of the world's desire to create institutions to stop the violence, the inaction must be replaced by action. Action to stop genocide usually is called "humanitarian intervention."

Humanitarian Intervention

The basic idea of a right of states to intervene in the affairs of another state to save lives is controversial. Humanitarian intervention was first discussed by the Dutch writer Hugo Grotius who argued that a state could use force to prevent another state from mistreating its own citizens. Grotius insisted that the state's oppression of its own citizens had to be "so ruthless and widespread that it would shock the sensibility of the international community." While it seems perfectly logical to assume that nation states should have the right to intervene in cases of massive abuse of human rights, humanitarian intervention is suspect among the nations of the world because in the past some states used humanitarian intervention as an excuse to pursue their own political and economic ends.

Most scholars suggest that intervention is justified if several overlapping criteria are met:

1. The existence of large-scale atrocities or gross violations of basic human rights in the offending society;
2. Humanitarian motives must take precedence over other motives such as territorial acquisition;

3. Other possible remedies are exhausted and intervention will not
cause significant harm elsewhere.

Even if these were accepted by the nations of the world as triggers to cue
action, humanitarian intervention might remain a rare and endangered species
of international activity. Nation states are generally unconcerned about the
plight of peoples unless there is some threat to their interest. Thus, one must not
forget that the most common occurrence in the face of violations of human
rights and human dignity is for nothing to happen. Generally, states have been
given the right to kill their populations because outside intervention would
violate their sovereignty and no state wants to set the precedent of intervention
because it might find itself being accused of human rights violations.

Conclusions

At one time, prior to the rise of the nation state, individual rights were
not generally imagined, as people existed in small communities often at the
whim of a ruler or local authority figure. Today we are face to face with the
state and, as we have seen, the state has repeatedly killed large numbers while
it continues to repress even larger numbers. The difficulty presented by the
recent examples of genocide demonstrates how intractable the modern nation
state remains when faced with horrible crimes of war and genocide. Most
nation states, it would seem, are unwilling to stand forthrightly behind "real"
attempts to implement my policy of the "practicality of morality." Yet, even
though we continue to witness examples of violence and genocide, there are
optimistic signs that some lessons may have been learned from the crimes of
the past. Optimistic portents include:

The creation of the International Criminal Court;

Discussion about creating a United Nations rapid-reaction force to
engage in humanitarian intervention;

Discussion about a similar force for the European Union;

The creation of the International Criminal Tribunal for the Former
Yugoslavia;

The creation of the International Criminal Tribunal for Rwanda;

The indictment of General Augusto Pinochet;

Discussion of trials for the Khmer Rouge;

The extradition of Slobodan Milosevic to the International Criminal
Tribunal for the former Yugoslavia in The Hague;

Discussion of universal jurisdiction under which a perpetrator of
genocide might be tried by any jurisdiction which apprehends the
criminal; and

The appearance of a number of organizations devoted to ending the scourge of genocide.

In short, these and many other trends point out that in many parts of the world, the sad history of genocide has led to new awareness that something modern must be done to prevent this ancient crime.

Notes

1. William R. Slomanson, *Fundamental Perspectives on International Law* (St Paul, MN: West Publishing Company, 1990), 1.

THE MEDIA AND GENOCIDE PREVENTION

It seems logical to begin any discussion of the media and its relationship to genocide with Rwanda in 1994. But here, the media which became infamous for its part in mass murder, was not CNN or any other international broadcaster. It was Radio Milles Collines, *a local station with huge audiences. It was easy to access, and it continued its transmissions day after day, combining popular music and witty presentation with murderous undertones to which many of the Rwandan population could relate. The main issues that arise from this notorious example are: Why was the nature of this program not picked up by the international community? (The UN had a mandate in Rwanda at the time.) Why was preventive action not taken?*

Preventing genocide, mass violence, or endemic conflict is something that the media has attempted to undertake, but they are local rather than international initiatives and content focuses on solutions rather than reciting problems. One simple example is Radio Dwenza *near Timbuctu, Mali, which successfully tackled the worsening seasonal conflict between farmers and herders in the area of Mali where it broadcasts. It encouraged farmers to post notices on the radio when they had finished their harvests, alerting the herders that they could now drive their sheep and cattle across the farmed land without damaging the crops.*

Another is Studio Ijambo, *a project of Search for Common Ground, based in Burundi, which has set a high standard for reporting ethnic conflict.* Studio Ijambo *regularly challenges government bans on rebel activities and personalities, and it produces and broadcasts a soap opera called* Our Neighbors, Ourselves, *a vehicle for getting people to put themselves in the perceived enemy's shoes, in an effort to humanize them. The impact is not enormous, but it is noticeable.*

Robert Manoff of the Center of War, Peace and News Reporting at New York University (USA) notes that the media has the ability to help build peace in a context of conflict because it can:

 - *Counter misconceptions, reduce rumor and "humanize the enemy";*
 - *Build confidence and consensus among warring parties, and allow "face saving";*
 - *Facilitate communication and promote dialogue across front lines;*
 - *Analyze the conflict's origins and educate people about conflict resolution;*
 - *Propose solutions;*

- *Influence the balance of power; and*
- *Demonstrate shared concerns and suffering on both sides of the divide.*

For media responses to smaller-scale conflict, the evidence points to local media as the way forward, but this requires a lot more training, and a great emphasis on collaboration with community groups and professional conflict resolvers. International media could help by providing resources and forging closer links with local media to disseminate good practice worldwide. Sustained action of this kind could consign Rwanda's Radio Milles Collines to the dustbin of history, and elevate Burundi's Studio Ijambo as the example for broadcasters to emulate.

Gordon Adam (UK)
Managing Director,
Media Support.

20

STUDYING THE ROOTS OF GENOCIDE

Ben Kiernan

Legally, genocide is the most serious criminal act, an "aggravated" crime against humanity. This is for a specific reason. International law on genocide requires proof of the intent of a perpetrator to destroy a human group. Other crimes against humanity do not require such intent to be proven, merely the criminal action itself. This state of mind of the genocide perpetrator is widely accepted. There is more disagreement on which human groups are legally protected.

The varying definitions of genocide often depend on how differently the victim groups are defined – by perpetrators, judges, or scholars – and to what extent such definitions describe groups of the kind that allow individual members to escape persecution and death by concealing or abandoning their group identity and taking up another. Again from the legal perspective, the 1948 United Nations Convention on the Prevention and Punishment of the Crime of Genocide defines victims of this crime as members of a targeted "national, ethnical, racial or religious group, as such." To the extent that it is most difficult, if not impossible, for a member of a racial group to "escape" that racial identity and assume another, it is an absolute injustice, indeed the most criminal of acts, to exterminate people on the basis of their membership of a race. This is largely true also of religious, ethnic and national groups. Additionally, some scholars believe, social and political groups, or even imaginary "groups" invented by the perpetrator and falsely accused of communal or conspiratorial activity, can also become victims of genocide and should be protected by the Convention. Such groups are, however, already protected by most interpretations of international law on crimes against humanity. In practice, genocidal regimes also tend to be both domestically repressive, even of their own "favored" ethnic community, and expansionist. They usually commit both crimes against humanity and war crimes, and often ethnic cleansing as well, along with genocide. But these common features of genocidal regimes are not the most useful for predicting their activities early enough to allow timely intervention to prevent them. For that purpose, we need to explore their thinking, detectable in public statements, internal documents, and secret activities, well before they come to power.

Analysis for Detection and Prevention of Genocide

During 25 years of research on the history of the Khmer Rouge and the Cambodian genocide,[1] I found many common features shared by this and other outbreaks of mass murder. Sometimes, these were ideological, such as the warped lessons Pol Pot learned from Mao's disastrous "Great Leap Forward" in China. Sometimes the links between genocides are more pragmatic, such as in 1965, when Pol Pot watched from Beijing as the Suharto military regime in Indonesia massacred half a million Communists in Java and Bali. Pol Pot later wrote that, "If our analysis had failed, we would have been in greater danger than the Communists in Indonesia."[2] Resolving to prevent such a disaster from happening to his own party, Pol Pot in turn massacred his opponents and suspected rivals in Cambodia ten years later.

From such historical examples, we may conclude that if essential common features and antecedents of genocides can be identified and studied, perhaps they can also be detected in advance of future cases, notably by studying the philosophical and pragmatic preoccupations of potential perpetrators. Such early recognition would give opponents of genocide the time and opportunity to prevent these vast human tragedies from recurring.

Genocides do not merely spring from similar perpetrator predilections. Often they are related events. The twentieth century opened with the genocide of the Hereros in the German colony of Southwest Africa. Participants in this brutalizing colonial experience included the father of Hermann Göring (a main thoroughfare in Windhoek is Göring Street). Immediately afterwards, Eugen Fischer carried out his racialist research on miscegenation among the mixed Dutch/Hottentot "Rehoboth Bastards" of Southwest Africa. In his 1913 study, as Henry Friedlander has pointed out, Fischer advocated protecting "an inferior race... only for so long as they are of use to us – otherwise free competition, that is, in my opinion, destruction." Fischer, who later became head of the Kaiser Wilhelm Institute for Anthropology, Human Heredity, and Eugenics, also denounced "coloured, Jewish, and Gypsy hybrids." His publisher delivered a copy of one of Fischer's works to Hitler in jail before he in turn wrote *Mein Kampf*. In 1933, Hitler appointed Fischer Rector of the University of Berlin, where Fischer took up the task of removing its Jewish professors.[3]

Further illustration of the historical linkage between genocidal events is provided in Vahakn Dadrian's study, *German Responsibility in the Armenian Genocide*.[4] In turn, in launching World War II, Hitler remarked, "Who ever heard of the Armenians?", suggesting his awareness that genocide could conceivably be perpetrated with impunity.[5] Regarding more recent events, there is evidence that the perpetrators of the Rwandan genocide in 1994 took the slow pace of the world's reaction to genocidal crimes in the former Yugoslavia as a sign that even worse ethnic "cleansing" in central Africa would not provoke rapid international intervention. While perpetrators of genocide seem to have benefited from their own comparative analysis of the potential and possibilities for genocide in the modern era, the rest of humanity has so far failed to learn all the lessons from the past that could lead to meaningful intervention in such catastrophes.

Genocide Studies

The interdisciplinary field of comparative genocide studies has long been dominated by sociologists: Irving Louis Horowitz, Leo Kuper, Helen Fein, Kurt Jonassohn, Vahakn Dadrian. Rarer work by historians such as Frank Chalk (*History and Sociology of Genocide*, 1990, co-edited with Kurt Jonassohn), and by political scientists such as Robert Melson (*Revolution and Genocide*, 1990), and Roger Smith on genocide denial, has been of great value to researchers. It is important to build on this work in an interdisciplinary fashion. More research on the history, anthropology, economics, demography, and psychology of genocide is much needed.

The Genocide Studies Program (GSP) at Yale University is a comparative, interdisciplinary research program pursuing state-of-the-art approaches to the study of genocide and trauma, and policy-oriented solutions to detecting and preventing genocide, as well as alleviation of its far-reaching sequelae. The GSP has built on the experience of its component project, the Cambodian Genocide Program (CGP) at Yale, which established and funded from 1994-2001 the Documentation Center of Cambodia in Phnom Penh (see further, www.yale.edu/cgp). In 2000, the CGP and GSP trained two Rwandan scholars to establish internationally accessible multi-lingual electronic databases on the perpetrators and victims of the Rwandan genocide of 1994 (www.yale.edu/gsp/rwanda_rgp.html). And in 2001, the GSP provided similar documentation training to 28 survivors of the genocide in East Timor (www.yale.edu/gsp/easttimor/index.html), and developed training manuals in Bahasa Indonesia for future trainees.

Documentation and Deterrence

"You are stupid," Pol Pot's deputy Nuon Chea told Deuch, former commandant of the Khmer Rouge's Tuol Sleng prison, after learning that Deuch had failed to destroy the prison's archives before his flight from Phnom Penh in 1979.[6] Deuch had stayed behind for several hours after Vietnamese forces entered the city, but instead of burning the archives, he had preferred to ensure that his last prisoners were murdered.[7] Over 100,000 pages fell into the hands of the Vietnamese and were soon made available to scholars. A "Tuol Sleng Museum of Genocide" was set up, with an archive of the Khmer Rouge "bureaucracy of death." British journalist Anthony Barnett visited Cambodia in early 1980 and brought back an extensive set of photocopies, which formed the basis for a cover story in the *New Statesman* magazine.[8] When a journalist presented copies of the documents to Pol Pot's brother-in-law Ieng Sary, he admitted that they were genuine.[9] His wife, Ieng Thirith, added: "We left all our records there... nobody thought we would leave Phnom Penh for good. We left all our things there, even our clothing."[10]

The couple's acknowledgement of the extensive documentation of their regime's torture and murder was quickly denied by an anonymous Khmer Rouge aide, in an unsigned letter to the *Far Eastern Economic Review*.[11] A decade later, another leading Khmer Rouge official, Son Sen, read through the Genocide Convention and underlined passages that might be used to prosecute him, including the definition of the crime, the "intent" requirement, and the sections asserting that "whether committed in time of peace or in time of war, [genocide] is a crime under international law."[12] Publication of their incriminating internal records had made the Khmer Rouge very uncomfortable. They had absolutely no idea that one day these records would be made available on the world wide web. Perhaps this possibility will serve as a small deterrent to future *genocidaires*.

Notes

1. "Bringing the Khmer Rouge to Justice," *Human Rights Review*, 1, 3, (April-June 2000): 92-108.

2. "Abbreviated Lesson on the History of the Kampuchean Revolutionary Movement Led by the Communist Party of Kampuchea," Document VII in *Pol Pot Plans the Future: Confidential Leadership Documents from Democratic Kampuchea, 1976-77*, D. P. Chandler, B. Kiernan, and C. Boua, eds., (New Haven: Yale Southeast Asia Studies Monograph no. 33, 1988), 218. See also Kiernan, *How Pol Pot Came to Power: A History of Communism in Kampuchea, 1930-1975* (London: Verso, 1985) 222.

3. Henry Friedlander, *The Origins of Nazi Genocide: From Euthanasia to the Final Solution* (Chapel Hill: University of North Carolina Press, 1995), 11-13, 19.

4. Vahakn N. Dadrian, *German Responsibility in the Armenian Genocide* (Cambridge: Blue Crane, 1995).

5. William Schabas, *Genocide in International Law* (Cambridge: Cambridge University Press, 2000), 1.

6. Jean-Claude Pomonti, "Le 'repentir' d'un tortionnaire khmer rouge," *Le Monde*, 3 septembre 1999; see also Nick Dunlop and Nate Thayer, "The Confession," *Far Eastern Economic Review*, 2 May 1999.

7. Ben Kiernan, *The Pol Pot Regime: Race, Power and Genocide in Cambodia under the Khmer Rouge, 1975-1979* (New Haven: Yale University Press, 1996), 452.

8. Anthony Barnett, Chanthou Boua, and Ben Kiernan, "Bureaucracy of Death: Documents from Inside Pol Pot's Torture Machine," *New Statesman*, London, 2 May 1980, cover and pp. 669-676.

9. Elizabeth Becker, "An Innocent Abroad," *Far Eastern Economic Review*, 7 August 1981; Anthony Barnett, "NS evidence forces Ieng Sary to confess," *New Statesman*, 7 August 1981, p. 3, and "Don't blame me, it was my brother-in-law," in John Pilger and Anthony Barnett, *Aftermath: The Struggle of Cambodia and Vietnam* (London: New Statesman, 1982), 130-31.

10. Elizabeth Becker, "The Death Chambers of the Khmer Rouge: the No. 2 Man Verifies the Horror," *Washington Post*, 2 August 1981. (Ieng Sary was in fact No. 3 in the Khmer Rouge hierarchy. Nuon Chea was No. 2 after Pol Pot.)

11. Unsigned, "Democratic Denial," *Far Eastern Economic Review*, 11 September 1981, p. 3.

12. "Salvaged Khmer Rouge Documents Show Direct Reports to Pol Pot," Sheri Prasso, *Agence France-Presse*, Phnom Penh, 2 December 1991. Prasso kindly provided copies of Son Sen's underlined documents.

21

PROSECUTING THE PERPETRATORS

Kurt Jonassohn

When the editors asked me to write a chapter on the topic, "What Can Be Done about Genocide?", I accepted with trepidation. After all, it seems safe to assume that all authors who write about genocide share the motivation to answer this question – either explicitly or implicitly. I finally accepted the editors' invitation because I suspect that some of my answers to their question will not duplicate those of most other genocide scholars.

The first thing to be done about genocide is to limit or to abolish the impunity of perpetrators. This will be difficult because throughout history the perpetrators of genocide have celebrated their deeds as victories. Notions about the rights of man, although of ancient vintage, gained political prominence in the Western world only with the advent of the French Revolution. Its message of liberty, equality, and fraternity did not prevent it from performing its own genocide in the Vendée; it even coined a word for it: populicide.

Only after World War II did it become important to prosecute the perpetrators. Several countries set up tribunals to deal with the perpetrators of war crimes. These trials exposed a wide public to the violations of human rights that were committed under the cover of war. The evidence that they produced made it obvious that such tragedies must be stopped. Much has already been accomplished in that direction since the horrors of two world wars, including the genocides associated with them, finally convinced the international community that it was high time to stop these slaughters. This conviction has, in fact, until now succeeded in preventing a Third World War. The realization that the majority of the casualties had not been the result of combat led to the passing of a number of conventions to affirm and protect the rights of man. The most important of these are the United Nations Convention on the Prevention and Punishment of the Crime of Genocide on December 9, 1948, the Universal Declaration of Human Rights on December 10, 1948, and the

Helsinki Accord on August 1, 1975. These and similar documents greatly increased the respect for human rights in at least some parts of the world. But since they did not lead to the establishment and acceptance of an enforcement mechanism, they neither prevented violations nor punished violators.

Many authors advocate reliance on the United Nations to enforce international law, to set up an international military unit, and to intervene in potential and actual genocidal situations. Other authors have grave doubts about the United Nations' ability to reach the consensus necessary for concerted action. They have advocated a variety of interventions based on other international bodies and non-governmental organizations (NGOs). These range from early warning systems to so-called humanitarian interventions by which they mean the mobilizing of armed intervention. Ideally, that would be the role of a United Nations force. But until such a force comes into existence, regional groups of countries can agree to act to mount such an effort. The few cases in which this has so far been tried have not produced very encouraging results. It seems that such military intervention is most successful when it is applied very early. This has led to demands for the establishment of early warning systems. So far, they have not been implemented.

Other proposals for action have ranged from unfavorable propaganda to economic boycotts to disbarment from meetings of sports and cultural groups. When these measures have been applied, they too have so far produced rather mixed results. Their major weakness is that they apply to a country as a whole where their effect on the governing classes is minimal, while the brunt of their burden is felt by the poor. While the various international agreements in favor of the rights of man have been observed mainly in the breach, they are having a significant effect. The enormous number of victims that this century produced not only led to the widespread acceptance of these documents in the community of nations, but also assured them of increasing popular support. The developments in modern means of communication exposed the masses to information on massacres and genocides around the world. The increasing number of NGOs devoted to assisting the victims is just one indication of the extent to which people are affected by these tragedies. Other NGOs provide information on human rights violations and organize protests to alert individuals and governments against their perpetrators. Thus, one thing to do is to further raise the popular consciousness against genocides by supporting grass roots movements and pressure groups.

Now, at the start of the twenty-first century, an International Criminal Court has finally come into existence although its legitimacy is being challenged and many of its legal aspects remain to be worked out. However, it embodies the widespread hope that the prosecution and punishment of perpetrators will discourage future genocides. So, one of the things that we can do is to support these efforts to destroy the impunity of the perpetrators. Thus, modern perpetrators are reviled rather than celebrated. An increasing consensus has been developing against their impunity. Perpetrators have fewer options in finding safe havens after they are deposed. They are defined as criminals who should be judged in an appropriate court of justice. An international court that could issue international arrest warrants was established for that purpose; but its jurisdiction was undermined by countries that felt that it interfered with their sovereignty. While that argument was used by some countries to maintain the impunity of their perpetrators, other countries avoided that interpretation by setting up their own so-called tribunals. These developments make the life of a perpetrator much less attractive. Far from being admired, he is now branded a criminal. Finding a safe refuge is becoming more difficult and travel exposes him to the risk of being arrested. One can only wonder how many candidates will find this an attractive career in the future.

A number of authors have dealt with the question of what to do about genocide from a psychological or social-psychological perspective. They address such issues as educating people to lower the level of discrimination, to reduce ethnic tensions, and to lower tendencies to intolerance. Such efforts need to start with the young during their schooling. This requires new teaching materials and new teachers. Similar efforts will be required to improve relations between ethnic, political, religious, etc., groups in order to reduce potential or real conflicts. This will also require thorough revisions of the materials that are distributed by the mass media and related propaganda methods. While such recommendations for reducing aggression are certainly desirable, it is not at all clear that their implementation would reduce future genocides in situations where a genocide is planned by a totalitarian central authority. To the extent that these recommendations focus on improving individuals or small groups, it remains to be established whether they will also solve the problems of society unless greater attention is focused on the perpetrators.

In the second half of the twentieth century, ideas of civil liberties, human rights, and the rule of law have reached many parts of the world. Where they facilitated the spread of wealth beyond the élites, they have raised the standard of living of much of the population in addition to improving public health, education, and social services. This has meant that people could aspire to improvements in their own life-chances and make plans for their children. Countries where such increases in wealth and well-being are occurring are most unlikely to engage in massacres and genocides. Thus, significant increases in the wealth of peoples in the poorer parts of the world are most likely to result in dramatic decreases in gross human rights violations, massacres, and genocides. This is likely to be true no matter what other causative factors are at work.

This is not the place to explore the ways in which the wealth of the poor can be increased. That clearly involves enormous difficulties and will continue to be the subject of protracted controversies. Because the ruling élites seem more interested in increasing their power and their wealth than in alleviating poverty, it will be important to enlist the growing involvement of an informed and committed public. Thus, the future lies in the raising of the consciousness and growing awareness of the public in the free part of the world. The great surprise is that these processes are in fact already taking place in spite of the efforts of those in power to suppress their spreading manifestations. Recent history has shown that it is possible to mobilize public opinion in support of the environment, wildlife, aid to the sick and the poor. Organizations in support of the Bill of Human Rights and of an international criminal court system are already active. The enormous support that the public already accords the many non-governmental organizations that are active in alleviating poverty promises that they will have increasing influence and effects. It does not seem utopian to anticipate that when a wealthier public's outrage and support for such organizations reaches critical levels, gross human rights violations and genocides will dramatically decline. Thus, the most important thing that can be done about genocide is to support the movements that want to increase the wealth of the poor.

Unfortunately such wide-ranging social changes occur only very slowly, which confirms the pessimists and tries the patience of the optimists. Finally, I must add that I make the above suggestions for reducing future genocides in full awareness of the dismal record of futurology.

22

USING CIVIL LITIGATION TO ACHIEVE SOME JUSTICE

Michael J. Bazyler

This essay discusses one aspect of the role of law in dealing with genocide. The specific focus is on the use of civil litigation as an instrument for achieving some measure of justice, separately and apart from bringing criminal proceedings against the perpetrators.

The only courts that have been ready so far to use civil litigation as an instrument for remedial action in response to genocide have been courts of the United States. And the most dramatic use of civil litigation for this purpose has been with regard to the Holocaust.

This essay initially examines the legal doctrine of monetary restitution and discusses the role that such restitution plays in the aftermath of genocide. It then discusses the Holocaust restitution movement in the United States, launched in the late 1990s which, to date, has yielded over $8 billion in payments. Finally, the essay touches upon the emerging debate about the propriety of seeking monetary damages for historical wrongs, especially as it has now emerged in the sphere of Holocaust-era litigation in the United States.

Monetary Restitution as a Response to Genocide

In the aftermath of a genocide – the so-called crime of crimes – what legal remedies are available? Part of the healing process involves a call for justice: that the perpetrators of the genocide be punished. Criminal punishment, of course, does not bring back the dead victims. It does, however, play an important role in bringing closure both to the surviving relatives and to the entire surviving victim group. Punishment also plays a critical role in the prevention of future genocides. Without punishment, the victim group, through its collective memory, lives with an open wound that may only begin to heal when the victims themselves become the victimizers.

Civil justice can also play a critical role in the aftermath of a genocide.

Just as criminal proceedings provide some measure of closure, civil remedies likewise play an important role in making the survivors feel that the wrongs committed against them have been recognized. As explained by Elazar Barkan, in *The Guilt of Nations*, for victims of historical wrongs (and their heirs), "the desire for recognition is insatiable."[1]

Civil courts accomplish this recognition by awarding monetary damages to be paid by the perpetrators or their cohorts to the survivors. In the transfer of funds between the perpetrator group and the survivor group, both sides benefit. According to Barkan: "The process of restitution leads to a reconfiguration of both sides. While the perpetrators hope to purge their own history of guilt, and legitimize their current position, the victims hope to benefit from a new recognition of their suffering and to enjoy certain material gains."[2]

Monetary restitution, of course, is not the only proper non-criminal response to genocide. As Roy Brooks, in *When Sorry Isn't Enough*, explains: "The list of responses is dizzying. Some governments have issued sincere apologies; others have not. Some have followed up their apologies with payments to victims or their families; others have not. And still others have invested money, services, or both in the victims' community in lieu of compensating victims individually."[3]

Of course, monetary compensation in the aftermath of a genocide can never fully compensate the surviving victims. Nevertheless, no matter how remorseful an apology, monetary restitution of even an insignificant amount, still must follow. Without monetary payments, the apology does not seem real.

Civil remedies, however, play an additional critical role. Genocide involves not only the killing of the target group. Concomitant with the killing almost always there is theft – often massive – of property from the victim group. Justice requires that such property be returned to the victims or their surviving heirs or compensation paid for the theft. When no heirs are alive, such restitution or compensation is made to representatives of the victim community.

The Holocaust provides the best-known example in the modern era of massive theft being part and parcel of a genocide. It also presents, to date, the best example of a model form of restitution. Not only has Germany undertaken to atone for the sins of the Nazis by repeatedly expressing profound remorse, but, as Brooks points out, "[i]n total, [Germany] has paid more reparations [– over $70 billion –] ...than perhaps any other government in world history."[4]

The Holocaust Restitution Movement in US Courts

One of the most dramatic – and wholly unexpected – events in the aftermath of the Holocaust has been the recent restitution payments made by European and American corporations for their nefarious financial dealings during World War II. The impetus by these corporate entities to make such payments did not come as a voluntary act, as was done by post-war West Germany in the 1950s, but rather through pressure exerted from civil suits being filed against them in American courts beginning in 1996.

Brooks, though an American law professor, argues that civil courts are not the proper forum to address claims of redress. "[T]he demands or claims for redress must be placed in the hands of legislators rather than judges. Legislators, quite simply, can do more than judges. In every nation of the world, the judiciary has the least lawmaking authority of any branch of government."[5]

This makes the fact that American courts are being used today to deal with wrongs committed during World War II – over one-half century after the events took place – even more remarkable. In an astoundingly short period of time since the Holocaust restitution movement began in the United States – six years – pledges to settle Holocaust-era claims now total over $8 billion. The pledges have come from Swiss banks (stemming from their nefarious financial dealings with the Nazis during World War II), German and Austrian companies (for their use of slave labor and involvement with other genocidal policies of the Nazis), European insurance companies (for failing to pay on insurance policies purchased by Holocaust victims) and French, British and American banks (for their role in the Aryanization of accounts of their Jewish account holders in their branches of Nazi-occupied Europe). Various European governments, and even the United States government, have also made financial contributions. And, finally, museums worldwide, including those in the United States and even Israel, are only now returning art in their possession which they discovered to have been looted by the Nazis.

These financial claims from the Second World War have captured the public imagination. The American media has featured more stories about the Holocaust in the last six years than in the past thirty. Most of these involve Holocaust restitution.

The Holocaust did not occur in the United States, but in Europe. Most Holocaust survivors also reside outside of the United States. It is the United States legal system, however, that has taken the lead in delivering the latest dose of justice to aging Holocaust survivors.

Why the United States? As with all transnational litigation today, the highly-developed and expansive system of American justice makes the United States the best – and, in most instances, the only – legal forum for the disposition of such claims. American courts have a long history of recognizing jurisdiction over defendants where courts of other countries would find jurisdiction lacking. American-style discovery, mostly unknown in Europe, allows the plaintiffs' lawyer to develop the case during the pre-trial process, rather than having all the evidence available at the outset of the litigation. Guarantee of jury trials in civil cases – and a culture where juries are accustomed to granting awards in the millions (or even billions) of dollars, both as compensation and punitive damages – makes the filing of a Holocaust-era lawsuit in the United States more likely of financial success. The existence of the concept of a class action, where representative plaintiffs can file suit not only on their behalf, but also on behalf of all others similarly situated, creates a more efficient system of filing suits and raises the prospect of large awards against the wrongdoers.

Moreover, American attorneys are greater risk-takers than their European counterparts and, unlike in most other countries, can take a case on a contingency basis, so that the client does not need to pay if the case is unsuccessful, but must share a percentage of the award if the case succeeds. Moreover, in the United States, a losing party, except in unusual cases, does not pay the attorneys' fees of the successful litigant. As a result, an American lawyer has less to lose if the case fails and, therefore, is more likely to file suit.

The recognition of American courts as the most desirable forum for transnational litigation was recognized by the great British jurist Lord Denning, when he wryly observed in a 1983 English court opinion, "As a moth is drawn to light, so is a litigant drawn to the United States. If he can only get his case into their courts, he stands to win a fortune."[6]

The Beneficial Consequences of Holocaust Restitution

Does the taking of moneys by the survivors demean the memory of the deceased victims? Does it allow the perpetrators or their heirs now to claim that their debt has been paid, and any moral guilt extinguished? Such questions are raised whenever monetary damages are sought from, or freely offered by, those responsible for a genocide.

Misgivings over the Holocaust restitution litigation appeared not long after the onset of the litigation. Abraham Foxman, head of the US-based Anti-Defamation League and himself a Holocaust survivor, in a December 1998 commentary decried that this struggle for restitution from the private defendants makes money the "last sound bite" of the Holocaust.[7] According to Foxman, this is a "desecration of the victims, a perversion of why the Nazis had a Final Solution, and too high a price to pay for justice we can never achieve." Nationally syndicated columnist Charles Krauthammer, that same month, published a similar critique,[8] suggesting that "[i]t should be beneath the dignity of the Jewish people to accept [money], let alone to seek it."

In 2001, as the litigation was now being settled, Efraim Zuroff, director of the Israeli office of the Simon Wiesenthal Center, again echoed these concerns. "I think this is a dangerous thing, that people are getting hung up on the financial aspects. This is not what the *Shoah* [Hebrew word for the Holocaust] is about. People are going to think: Why are Jews so obsessed with the Holocaust? Because they want to give a bill at the end of the day."[9]

That same message was a theme in an angry diatribe published in 2000, with the sensational title, *The Holocaust Industry*. In the book, American professor Norman Finkelstein, in an over-the-top style, accused Jewish organizations in the United States of using the Holocaust to perpetuate their existence. Finkelstein claims that these organizations are extorting money from European concerns who are vulnerable to blackmail because they dealt with the Nazis during the war.

A more serious critique appeared the same year in the Jewish monthly *Commentary*, written by its senior editor Gabriel Schoenfeld.[10] Schoenfeld, while not denying the legitimacy of seeking Holocaust restitution payments from the European wrongdoers, expressed concern about how the movement was being conducted. He accused the Jewish community leaders involved in the restitution efforts of ignoring concerns of the individual survivors, frequent lack of adherence to historical truth in making their accusations against the wrongdoers, and failing to see the impact that the movement is having on other Jewish vital interests, primarily the security of the state of Israel and the impact on antisemitism.

Schoenfeld and other critics, of course, are partially correct. The movement is not without its faults. Moreover, actual payments which the Holocaust claimants will receive are minuscule (whether $7,500 or $50,000) compared to the personal and financial losses they suffered.

Nevertheless, not seeking financial restitution in the face of documented proof that financial giants worldwide are sitting on billions of funds made on the backs of World War II victims, which they then invested and reinvested many times over during the last half-century, amounts to an injustice that cannot be ignored. Allowing these corporate concerns to escape financial liability amounts to unjust enrichment.

Equally significant, as explained above, forcing a wrongdoer to pay up is an important element of retributive justice. As Stuart Eizenstat, the top US official involved in the Holocaust restitution effort, noted, "[T]here is a certain symbolic quality that only money can convey to repair the injustices."[11] Israel Singer, rabbi and a leader of the World Jewish Congress who was intimately involved in crafting many of the settlements, explains as follows:

> I don't want to enter the next millennium as the victim of history... Himmler said you have to kill all the Jews because if you don't kill them, their grandchildren will ask for their property back. The Nazis wanted to strip Jews of their human rights, their financial rights and their rights to life. It was an orderly progression. I want to return to them all their rights.[12]

Richard Cohen, another nationally syndicated columnist, also answers criticism that seeking compensation and making the wrongdoers pay demeans the memory of the Holocaust: "An immense calamity was committed in Europe, a moral calamity that left a black hole in the middle of the 20th century. Money is the least of it. But money is part of it. Holocaust victims paid once for being Jewish. Now, in a way, they or their heirs are being asked to pay again – a virtual Jewish tax which obliges them not to act as others would in the same situation. But in avoiding one stereotype, they adopt a worse one – perpetual victim."[13]

Conclusion

The new trend by governments and corporations to pay monetary restitution and finally "come clean" about the wrongs committed by them in the past would not be occurring without the spotlight being shined on their activities through the lawsuits in the United States.

The ultimate goal is that the Holocaust restitution cases can serve as a template for a new era of financial relief and recognition to victims of genocide and other crimes against humanity – but, this time, without the fifty year wait for justice. As a result of the victories achieved by victims of the Nazi genocide in the courts of the United States, individuals and corporations presently engaged in human rights abuses are being put on notice: eventually you also will be held responsible for your misdeeds.

Notes

1. Elazar Barkan, *The Guilt of Nations: Restitution and Negotiating Historical Injustices* (New York & London: W.W. Norton, 2000), 320.
2. Barkan, 321.
3. Roy L. Brooks, ed., *When Sorry Isn't Enough: The Controversy Over Apologies and Reparations for Human Injustice* (New York & London: New York University Press, 1999), 8.
4. Ibid., 9.
5. Ibid., 6.
6. *Smith Kline & French Labs v. Bloch*, 2 All E.R. 72.
7. "The Dangers of Holocaust Restitution," *Wall Street Journal*, 4 December 1998, p. A18.
8. "Reducing the Holocaust to Mere Dollars and Cents," *Los Angeles Times*, 11 December 1998, p. A26.
9. Elli Wohlgelernter, "Compensation Issue Clouds Holocaust Message," *Jerusalem Post*, 19 January 2001, p. 6A.
10. "Holocaust Reparations – A Growing Scandal," *Commentary*, September 2000, p.1.
11. Richard Wolffe, "Putting A Price On the Holocaust," *Irish Times*, 16 March 1999, p. 15.
12. Ibid.
13. "The Money Matters," *The Washington Post*, 8 December 1998, p. A21.

Exhumed in 1997 from a mass grave in Srebrenica, the corpses of these Bosnian Muslims, victims of the Serbian militia who killed 7,000 members of that group in July 1995 after UN forces withdrew, were temporarily kept in this tunnel in Tuzla.

PART IV

WILL GENOCIDE EVER END?

"I have nothing to feel ashamed of and my conscience is clean," Dragoljub Ojdanic was quoted as saying in a Reuters news report on April 25, 2002. At that time, Ojdanic, a 61-year-old Serbian general who has been accused of forcing some 800,000 ethnic Albanians from Kosovo in 1999, had traveled from Belgrade to The Hague, where he gave himself up for trial on war crimes charges. Ojdanic claimed innocence. He also denied that he had anything to tell that would incriminate his previous superior, Slobodan Milosevic, who, at the time of this writing, was standing trial for war crimes and genocide in the Balkans. The United States has put pressure on Belgrade, indicating that it will block economic aid and loans to Yugoslavia unless Serbs indicted by the United Nations appear before the tribunal in The Hague. Ojdanic is an exception to prove the rule that very few of those fugitives – including Radovan Karadzic and Ratko Mladic, who are accused of genocide – have bowed to that pressure.

When perpetrators of genocide remain at large, that fact is significant enough in its own right, for it is emblematic of the world's inability thus far to try the accused and to bring the guilty to justice. But the fact that perpetrators of genocide remain at large signifies something that may be even more ominous. It suggests that the attitudes and ambitions, the hostilities and hatreds, that breed genocidal tendencies also remain at large in the world. Time will tell, but it seems unlikely that Ojdanic's innocence is as great as he has claimed, and his insistence that he feels no shame and has a clean conscience compounds the problem. For the problem is not restricted to particular perpetrators such as Milosevic, Karadzic, Mladic, and probably Ojdanic, too. The problem extends to the conditions that fuel genocidal mentalities and the circumstances that provoke the acts that have made ours an age of genocide. Genocidal leaders such as Milosevic, the Khmer Rouge's Pol Pot, or

Léon Mugesera, the Rwandan ideologue who incited Hutus to "wipe out this [Tutsi] scum," do not appear in vacuums. Without followers, without bystanders who might intervene but do not, they could do very little. Leaders may "think genocide," but it takes large numbers of people and many institutions, as well as perpetrator-leaders, to commit it. Will genocide ever end? That question haunts every essay in this book, as its title suggests, but in this fourth part the authors turn explicitly to that topic. As John Heidenrich puts the key point, genocide is everyone's problem. To make that claim is not to disperse responsibility in banal ways. To the contrary, the intent is to show that genocide-producing conditions, as well as the individuals and groups that commit this crime-of-crimes, must have the determined attention of the United Nations, of governments, non-governmental organizations, and individual persons if there is to be realistic hope that the answer to this book's governing question can be *yes*.

Humankind has abolished some of its ills. Diseases such as smallpox and polio no longer plague us as they once did. Abolition did not eliminate slavery entirely, but concern about human rights is greater than it used to be. As James Smith suggests, perhaps we can claim cautious optimism that genocide may yet become a thing of the past. Uncertain though that judgment may be, of this much we can be sure: Genocide will not go away unless and until we – our governments and ourselves – really want that outcome and want it sooner rather than later.

23

GENOCIDE: EVERYONE'S PROBLEM

John G. Heidenrich

Genocide is the intended destruction of a group identity, typically a religious, racial or ethnic group, chosen to be a scapegoat by a more powerful group identity, which is almost always a regime or quasi-government that is either extremely tyrannical or aspires to be. Genocide is the ultimate form of intolerance. Elsewhere, in societies where constitutional democracy is part of the culture, we are taught that tolerance is a virtue, indeed an essential virtue when the alternative is violence or, worse, a cycle of violence. In return for this tolerance we enjoy a remarkable amount of political freedom, certainly more freedom than most populations have enjoyed historically or even possess today in countries where tyranny reigns. We have so much political freedom that we have even the freedom to *not be political* – an enviable freedom indeed when its absence is filled with boringly frequent political indoctrination sessions (or worse). Our elected officials urge us to be individually responsible for our collective political affairs: to vote, to speak out, to volunteer in civic ways. Yet we can evade these responsibilities if we want to, even not think to do them. We can busy ourselves, daily, with personal routines blissfully ignorant of politics and of the wider world around us. Quite a lot of us do.

Consequently tolerance is, to far too many of us, not something active but only passive: not the act of learning about other peoples and cultures to discover more about life, not actively defending the rights of others, not personally trying to overcome our own misconceptions, prejudices and ignorance – but, rather passively, not doing very much at all. This passivity allows us to keep our misconceptions, prejudices and ignorance, and use them to rationalize yet more passivity. *Whatever happens elsewhere is none of my business. It's not something I know much about. It's not something that interests me. I'm too busy to care. Those other people have their own ways of doing things. Let them sort it out. It's their problem.*

The truth is that genocide is everyone's problem, a truth universally

161

enshrined in the Convention on the Prevention and Punishment of the Crime of Genocide – more legally binding than the Universal Declaration of Human Rights. Unfortunately, a remarkable number of people, perhaps even a majority, do not know what the word "genocide" even means. The man who first coined the word, Raphael Lemkin, warned us as long ago as the mid-twentieth century of "how impoverished our culture would be if the peoples doomed by [Nazi] Germany, such as the Jews, had not been permitted to create the Bible, or give birth to an Einstein, a Spinoza; if the Poles had not had the opportunity to give the world a Copernicus, a Chopin, a Curie; the Czechs, a Huss, a Dvorak; the Greeks, a Plato and a Socrates; the Russians, a Tolstoy and Shostakovich."[1]

Lemkin's warning is a powerful argument against genocide, resonating for each of us as individuals as much as for humanity as a whole. It defines why genocide is a crime against humanity, literally, because all humankind suffers the loss. Yet when people today ask why we should care, we rarely hear this powerful reason offered. The Dalai Lama has raised it in reference to the Tibetan genocide, warning for a very long time that the Chinese Communist government is destroying Tibet's Buddhist monasteries, including their priceless religious treasures and insightful spiritual writings. He calls it a "cultural" genocide. That description is redundant, because all genocides are cultural genocides. The crime harms all of us, even if most of us do not realize the loss.

When tolerance means accepting mass murder and cultural annihilation, if "only" by foreigners against foreigners, then tolerance is no longer a virtue but a vice. For the opposite of love is not hate, but indifference. What can be done about genocide? Most of us can start by not being indifferent to genocide. We may claim that we care, even believe that we care, but care without action is hypocrisy. Each of us alone may not be able to do very much, but each of us can do more than nothing at all.

But that's the government's responsibility, a common reply counters, or *All governments do sinister things* – ergo, we "powerless" voters are wasting our time trying to change things.

If only such people knew what a report by the United Nations determined back in 1985, commissioned to find ways to improve the Genocide Convention. It concluded: "Without a strong basis of international public support, even the most perfectly drafted Convention will be of little value. Conventions and good governments can give a lead, but the mobilization of public awareness and vigilance is essential to guard against any recurrence of genocide and other crimes against humanity and human rights."[2]

"I think you could start by convincing a friend," suggests Aung San Suu Kyi, a recipient of the Nobel Peace Prize for her leadership of the embattled democracy movement in Burma, or *Myanmar* as that country's military dictatorship calls it. "You have to start with a first step, and there are many ways of starting," she explained in *Shambhala Sun* magazine in January 1996. "I take heart that some big international movements have started with a letter to a newspaper, and people who read that take it up. Every movement, ultimately, was started by one person."

Sending a personal letter, preferably several, to newspapers, news magazines, radio shows and television programs also informs those news organizations of what interests you. They have a product to sell – news – and you are the consumer. When the most desired news is Hollywood gossip, pop culture, and domestic news reports that are more shallowly sensationalist than substantive, that is the product they largely deliver. Substantive foreign news coverage is available, such as from newswire services on the Internet, but it is the domestic and entertainment news that most people consume. Sometimes our political leaders get asked tough, newsworthy foreign policy questions, but to a remarkable extent they do not, even during election campaigns, because most news editors do not perceive that most people care much about foreign policy issues. Many journalists do want to ask those tough questions and keep asking until they get some satisfactory answers – but they need your own demonstrated interest, i.e., your letters, to justify their effort. They are less likely to ask if they doubt that many of us even care.

Some people like to stage public protests using rallies and marches. These noisy forms of expression can be newsworthy, but there are more effective ways to change public opinion. Most protests are tiny, staged for a few hours, typically on a university campus or in front of an embassy or a government building, more successfully amusing passers-by than changing any minds. A protest may focus public attention upon an issue today and perhaps even tomorrow, but eventually the public loses interest, no matter how committed the protest's organizers or how important the issue. The most persuasive protests are massive and, ironically, occur in dictatorships – where political expression is very limited, necessitating courage among the protesters. Convincing a democratic government to pursue genocide prevention as a permanent foreign policy objective, keeping it regardless of which political party is in power, requires a permanently interested general public – the right, center, and left – and not just a few scattered protests.

Novels and television programs, such as the mini-series *Holocaust* in the 1970s, as well as motion pictures such as *The Killing Fields* and *Schindler's List*, have raised our common awareness of genocide. In 1997, Hollywood released two major motion pictures about the Tibetan genocide, *Kundun* and *Seven Years in Tibet*. Even science fiction sometimes contributes: for example, the film *Star Trek: Insurrection* considered the issue of genocidal "ethnic cleansing." In 2000, the American television series *Touched By An Angel* ran an episode that dramatized contemporary slavery and genocide in Sudan – and probably did more to encourage public activism in response, both in the United States and Canada, than all the relevant editorials, press releases, academic papers and Sudanese human rights campaigns had before. Storytellers have known for a long time that genocide makes for a powerful story, either as the theme itself or a backdrop. Their accuracy is sometimes questionable, but at least the public is made more aware. A much more serious problem is that the various genocides these artistic pieces depict have already occurred. More helpful would be a motion picture that shows how future genocides can be foreseen and probably prevented by international involvement – if the international community was not so unprepared and unwilling to act decisively. A dramatization of the 1994 Rwandan genocide could show this.

Perhaps more of us would care if a popular myth was dispelled that genocide's cause is only common bigotry, not political expedience and propaganda. Contrary to how it is too often portrayed, genocide is not spontaneous; rather, it is a premeditated crime – planned, prepared for, and orchestrated. It can therefore be predicted, months or even years in advance, by monitoring the likely perpetrator-group's ideology, hate speech, and other manifestations of its "identity" politics, as well as by tracking trends in human rights abuses. Caring individuals can do this monitoring themselves – surprisingly feasible with Internet-based resources – but Western governments can do it better, drawing upon their embassies, intelligence agencies, and consultants. By noticing and acting upon the ominous signs, democratic governments can lead the international community toward helping to calm a troubled country's situation by encouraging more respect for human rights, sending material aid, envoys, negotiators, and, where applicable, peacekeepers. The details are complicated and may not work everywhere, but a strategy of genocide prevention is basically this simple.

What has retarded this strategy has been a lack of political will among Western and other governments, unconvinced that institutionalizing genocide prevention is cost-effective and worth their sustained commitment, afraid that their voting publics are too fickle to care consistently. Few if any of these governments have institutionalized systems of genocide forecasting and early warning. Proposals to reform UN peacekeeping – such as establishing a standing rapid-reaction force of UN peacekeepers or, short of that, privatizing peacekeeping, so that, either way, governments would not have to risk their own troops – have proven too controversial to implement without any energetic push by the Great Powers, particularly by the United States. Meanwhile, worldwide, a small number of genocidal potentialities continue to brew toward otherwise avoidable eruptions, most likely to be followed by Western claims of surprise and excuses. This longstanding, unconscionable *status quo* is unlikely to change until enough ordinary people – motivated by humanity, faith, and civic responsibility – actively demand that their governments change it, that we stop tolerating what ought to be intolerable.

What impresses an elected official almost as much as getting a campaign contribution is receiving an old-fashioned "snail mail" letter from an ordinary constituent. Form letters do not excite as much attention. Email messages might, but, being so easy to write and zip away, are not always taken very seriously by politicians who receive queues full of them everyday. Telephone calls tend to be even less impressive. To most politicians, the most convincing form of constituent communication is the old-fashioned postal letter because it demonstrates that that constituent is interested enough in the issue to spend the time to write something formal and pay some money to mail it. It almost certainly reveals how that constituent will vote in the next election – as well as how other constituents, those who did not bother to write letters but who feel the same, will vote. Mail does matter. Even if a particular elected official does not represent your views, that official should still be mailed a letter, if not several, expressing how you feel about an issue, such as genocide prevention, and what you want done. Your letters may not change anything, but they might.

Politicians and political parties are in the business of getting your vote. Tell them what they should do to deserve it.

Notes

1. Raphael Lemkin, "Genocide," *The American Scholar Magazine* (April 1946), 227-230.
2. Benjamin C. G. Whitaker (Special Rapporteur), *Report on the Question of the Prevention and Punishment of the Crime of Genocide* (United Nations document E/CN.4/Sub.2/1985/6), 2 July 1985, with corollary 29 August 1985. Quoted in the entry "Genocide" in Edward Lawson ed., *Encyclopedia of Human Rights* (New York: Taylor & Francis, 1991), 668.

24

A TASK WHOSE TIME HAS COME

Samuel Totten

Humanity has split the atom, probed the far reaches of the universe, and explored the ocean's depths. Man has landed and walked on the moon. Heart and other organ transplants are regular occurrences. The Internet allows individuals instantaneously to share information and communicate across the greatest divides of the earth. And yet, we still have not devised an efficacious way to prevent the genocide of our own species. Granted, solving problems that deal with people's beliefs, feelings, and actions is vastly more complex than solving technical problems, but that does not preclude finding a solution.

The three purposes of this essay are to succinctly (a) delineate some of the many issues/actions that have been and are being considered and/or implemented *vis-à-vis* the issues of the intervention and prevention of genocide; (b) highlight some of the past failures to intervene and/or prevent genocide; and (c) present recommendations for the United Nations, NGOs, and scholars of genocide to consider.

Issues and Efforts Under Consideration

Over the past twenty-five years or so, genocide scholars (as opposed to those in fields such as peace studies, conflict resolution, international law, and criminal law) have basically focused on nine major concerns *vis-à-vis* the intervention and prevention of genocide: 1. Defining what genocide is and is not; 2. Examining and delineating the processes of genocide; 3. Analyzing specific genocidal events, including their causes, the individuals and groups involved (e.g., perpetrators, collaborators, victims, bystanders, rescuers), the ways in which the genocides are perpetrated, the horrific results, and the aftermath; 4. Analyzing data from genocidal incidents in order to ascertain early warning signals; 5. Developing risk databases; 6. Undertaking incipient work on the development of genocide early warning systems; 7. Delineating and analyzing the adverse impact of the denial of past genocides by perpetrators and others; 8. Arguing the need to try and punish perpetrators of genocide, and analyzing the adverse impact of impunity; and 9. Developing and implementing educational efforts at different levels of schooling (secondary, college and university) and/or within governmental agencies (including legislative, judicial and executive bodies, as well as the military). All of these efforts are of major importance and constitute a significant contribution to the effort to develop efficacious means to intervene and prevent future genocides. However, as significant as these developments are, they only begin to touch the proverbial tip of the iceberg in regard to what needs to be done in order to develop the most effective methods possible to intervene and/or prevent genocides from being perpetrated.

The fact is, an eclectic group of organizations and individuals outside the field of genocide studies is also interested in, writing about, and working on the problems of the intervention and prevention of genocide (many of which, it should be noted, most genocide scholars have dedicated little to no time to studying/examining). Among the varied issues they are working on are the following: international law (accords, covenants, conventions, treaties); information-gathering and analysis; intelligence-sharing; the development and/or analysis of various types of early warning systems; analyzing data from genocidal incidents in order to ascertain early warning signals; the development of data risk bases; attempting to ascertain effective confidence-building measures; developing and implementing preventive diplomacy, Track I diplomacy, and/or Track II diplomacy; examining, developing and/or implementing such varied measures as conflict prevention, conflict management, conflict resolution, peacekeeping, diplomatic peacekeeping, peacemaking, peace enforcement, sanctions, partitioning, temporary protection measures for refugees fleeing internal and other types of conflict, humanitarian intervention, various types of policing efforts (such as regional police forces, constabulary forces, private security forces), military intervention, institution building, and the list goes on and on.

In an essay this brief, it is impossible to discuss much more than a couple of these issues, and thus the primary focus of this essay is humanitarian intervention. *It must be stated if there is to be even a hope of developing effective means of intervening and preventing genocide, genocide scholars and others must undertake an effort that brings the aforementioned strands together in a synergistic manner.*

Past Genocides

Over the course of the past century, many perpetrators of genocide have gone unfettered in their efforts to eliminate certain groups of people, while only feeble to somewhat robust attempts have been made to staunch genocide. When all is said and done, the record of staunching genocide in the twentieth century is nothing short of a record of infamy. Tens of millions have died horrible deaths at the hands of perpetrators: the Armenians at the hands of the Ottoman Turks, the so-called Kulaks by Stalin and his lackeys, the Jews and other victims by the Nazis and their collaborators, the Cambodians by the fanatical Khmer Rouge, the Tutsis and moderate Hutus by the extremist Hutus in Rwanda, and on and on.[1] *The terrible fact is that in more cases than not, when the world community did act it was after a particular genocide had already begun; and as a result, the murdered and the maimed already numbered in the tens of thousands, if not higher.*

Indeed, far too little has been done to intervene in ethnic strife and other types of conflict *prior* to the outbreak of a genocidal act. Of course, and this is the most obvious of points, in some, if not many, cases it is often excruciatingly difficult to ascertain whether, for example, a civil war is going to eventuate and explode into a genocidal situation. At one and the same time, during the course of many past genocides there have been warning signs that a potential genocide may be on the horizon and yet the world community has not taken the time, effort, and means to attempt to prevent the genocide from becoming a reality. For example, as Alan J. Kuperman notes in *The Limits of Humanitarian Intervention: Genocide in Rwanda,* prior to the 1994 genocide in Rwanda,

Numerous reports of ethnic violence in Rwanda surfaced in the months and years preceding the genocide. Death squads were exposed in 1992, and death lists containing hundreds of names came to light in the succeeding two years. In spring 1992 the Belgian embassy in Kigali reported an anonymous allegation of a "secret headquarters charged with exterminating the Tutsi of Rwanda to resolve definitively... the ethnic problem in Rwanda and to crush the domestic Hutu opposition." In March 1993 an international human rights panel reported that most victims of sporadic massacres in Rwanda were killed because they were Tutsi. During the first week of December 1993 several ominous indications arose: a Belgian cable reported the Presidential Guard conducting paramilitary training of youths; a Rwandan journal reported weapons being distributed to militias; and UNAMIR received an anonymous but credible letter, purportedly from leading moderate Rwandan army officers, warning of a

"Machiavellian plan" to conduct massacres throughout the country starting in areas of high Tutsi concentration and also targeting leading opposition politicians. On December 17 the Rwandan press exposed details of a planned "final solution," including militia coordination, transportation arrangements, French military aid, and "identification committees" to compile death lists. These danger signs were usually conveyed to Brussels within days via cable – the anonymous letter of December 14 and the press report of a final solution on December 23, 1993.[2]

A complicating factor in some, if not many, situations, is that certain warnings may come from unknown parties, and thus it is difficult to ascertain the validity of the warnings. This was exactly what happened during the Holocaust period. More specifically, as Pauline Jelinek writes in her article "File: Allies Tipped Off to Genocide in Early '42,"[3] it is now believed that "The West may have been informed about Nazi Germany's plans for the Holocaust months earlier than previously thought. 'It has been decided to eradicate all the Jews,' says a newly declassified document believed to have been obtained by British and American intelligence by March 1942. Previously, historians have judged that the West didn't learn until August 1942 that the Holocaust was happening."[4] As to why the British and US governments did nothing in response to such news, Holocaust historian Richard Breitman answered with a question: "Why would any British or American official pay particular attention to the views of an unknown Chilean diplomat in Prague?"[5]

It is also true that repeated warnings of a pending genocide over a period of years tend to be dismissed by those receiving them. The 1994 Rwandan genocide offers a classic example along this line. A US government official, Colonel Tony Marley, the US State Department's political-military advisor in the region, has asserted that, "'We had heard them cry wolf so many times' that the new warnings fell on deaf ears."[6]

It is also a fact that intelligence-gathering is not as strong as it could or should be when racial, religious, national, political and ethnic strife is taking place, and thus early warning signals are either missed altogether, not pieced together to indicate that there is a pattern of an ever-increasing likelihood that genocide may result, and/or situations where one intelligence body (a specific nation or a specific organization within a nation) neglects, for whatever reason, to share its intelligence with other parties (including leaders of various key organizations, including the United States and the United

Nations) that actually indicates a pattern or process possibly moving towards the genocidal.

Hesitant to send their own armed forces into dangerous situations, and especially desirous of avoiding fatal attacks on its troops, many nations, including the United States, have been lukewarm at best in regard to undertaking or even supporting humanitarian intervention efforts to prevent genocide. (It must be acknowledged that the danger to their troops was not the only aspect that tempered various nations' support for such interventions. Indeed, there were other major concerns, including the issues of sovereignty, internal affairs, *realpolitik*. All three of the latter are instrumental concerns that need to be taken into serious consideration when discussing humanitarian intervention, but space constraints preclude doing so herein.)

In regard to the United States' position, such hesitancy, today, is a direct result of the so-called "Somalia factor." More specifically, the United States government and citizens were outraged in October 1993 when eighteen US soldiers were killed in Somalia – some of whom were shot and then dragged through the streets – while attempting to apprehend faction leader Muhammad Farah Aideed. Not only was the US government outraged, but from that point on governmental leaders became extremely reluctant to risk troops overseas for anything but threats to primary national interests.

As of late, even when intervention is agreed upon, all efforts are made to avoid sending in ground troops. Such an intervention can and has had tragic consequences. For example, in March 1999, a decision was made by NATO to use air power – versus ground troops – across Yugoslavia and against Serb troops accused of violence, repression and "ethnic cleansing" against the ethnic Albanian majority in Kosovo. The controversial NATO air attack lasted for 78 days. As Alex Alvarez notes in *Governments, Citizens, and Genocide: A Comparative and Interdisciplinary Approach*, ironically and tragically, "the attacks incited the Serb leadership to speed up the policies of ethnic cleaning of Kosovar Albanians, resulting in widespread massacres and the uprooting and dislocation of the majority of the population."[7]

Another key issue *vis-à-vis* intervention is the factor of time – the time it takes either the United Nations, a coalition of nations such as the North Atlantic Treaty Organization (NATO), or individual nations to mobilize and respond to a genocide once a decision has been made to intervene. Such preparation involves, for example, transporting and shipping the troops to the area of conflict as well as the *matériel* (vehicles, weapons, medical supplies, food, et al.) needed to implement the intervention. Obviously, the greater the distance between the location of the conflict and the location of the initial staging area of the intervenors, the greater amount of time it is going to take to implement the intervention. In his provocative book *The Limits of Humanitarian Intervention: Genocide in Rwanda*, Alan J. Kuperman, who contests the opinions of various UN personnel who were in Rwanda during the genocide (as well as various human rights organizations such as Human Rights Watch) in regard to the number and type of troops that would have been needed to staunch the 1994 genocide, argues as follows:

> [T]he time required to deploy the intervention force would have been a function of its weight. Estimates of the weight and other characteristics of a division-size task force built around one brigade each from the 101st, the 82nd, and a light division can be taken as the average of those divisions – 26,550 tons, including 200 helicopters and 13,373 personnel.... At the maximum credible rate of 800 tons daily, such a force would have required thirty-three days of airlift...Thus, U.S. troops would not have begun stopping genocide in the countryside [versus in Kigali] until about three weeks after the president's order, or May 11, 1994.[8]

What has been addressed above is only a fraction of the many problems that come into play *vis-à-vis* the issues of intervention and prevention of genocide, but they are significant ones nonetheless. The question that remains, of course, is what can be done to address or ameliorate the aforementioned concerns. Next, I present some radical yet, I believe, doable solutions. Ultimately, what is needed to implement all of them is a deep and abiding world-wide concern about genocide, along with a burning desire to prevent genocide wherever and whenever it is about to erupt.

Recommendations Regarding Potential Solutions

1. Under the auspices of the United Nations, a sizable, well-financed, highly qualified and dedicated, and thoroughly independent genocide investigative team should be established. The investigative team's express purpose would be to (a) maintain an eye on any "hotspots" across the globe where either serious and/or ongoing human rights infractions and/or civil unrest/war are taking place, and (b) deploy to those areas for the express purpose of conducting the most *comprehensive and objective investigation* into whether the situation is slouching towards genocide or not. Upon completion of the investigation and documentation of the situation (or, in the most dire of circumstances when the situation demands it), the investigative group should dis-

seminate its report to the major governments of the world, the United Nations, and other inter-governmental and non-governmental organizations (NGOs), give interviews to the media (e.g., newspapers, radio and television), and issue calls to act to prevent the genocide from being perpetrated.

Rationale: More often than not, in the past, outside governments, the media, and even peacekeeping forces have been incorrect in assessing whether a genocide is about to take place or not. In some cases, even as massive killing is taking place, there have been debates over whether a situation is genocidal or not. An investigative team whose express task is to document and ascertain whether a situation is moving toward genocide could prove to be extremely valuable in providing the type of objective, detailed information needed to make a definitive assessment.

2. The establishment of a cable channel – with the ability to transmit to the far reaches of the earth – whose sole purpose would be to focus on the issue of genocide in the most accurate, unbiased/objective, and comprehensive fashion possible. Among the issues that such a station could address are: (a) the perpetration of contemporary, outright genocides; (b) situations where the deprivation of human rights and/or civil war are possibly moving towards the perpetration of genocide; (c) regular updates in regard to how major governments, the United Nations, NGOs, and other inter-governmental organizations are addressing situations that are slouching towards genocide or that have exploded into genocide; (d) regular updates regarding the trials of perpetrators (in national courts, special tribunals, and, eventually, the International Criminal Court (ICC); (e) the efforts to track down perpetrators of genocide; (f) the ways in which individual citizens could become involved in anti-genocide work, etc.

Rationale: Such a station would provide up-to-date information for both governmental officials, inter-governmental and non-governmental organizations, other activists, and ordinary citizens. It would be a means for everyone concerned to keep apprised of the latest situations and issues germane to genocide. It would also serve as a means to expunge the excuse that government officials and others were not fully informed about a genocide or genocidal situation and thus could not act due to incomplete information or a lack of access to adequate and accurate information.

3. Under the auspices of the United Nations, a volunteer rapid-action anti-genocide force should be established. The force must be well-manned, well-equipped, well-financed, and well-trained and highly qualified for various types of intervention assignments. Volunteers would come from virtually any area of the globe, and they would be trained by highly qualified officers with ample military and intervention experience.

Rationale: As previously mentioned, many, if not most, nations (including the United States and the United Nations) are hesitant, leery, and sometimes outright against providing troops for deployment in dangerous situations where genocidal activity is taking place (and this includes civil wars). As a result, United Nations missions are either not deployed at all, or when they are, they are sorely under-staffed. In regard to the latter, the troops deployed are unable to carry out the mission adequately. More specifically, they are incapable of protecting potential victims and/or halting a genocide that is, literally, taking place in front of their eyes. The 1994 genocide in Rwanda was a classic example of the latter.

Again, as previously noted, averse to sending in ground troops to halt the "ethnic-cleansing" campaign in Kosovo, NATO carried out an air attack that, ironically and tragically, allowed Slobodan Milosevic's forces to hunt, harm, and chase ethnic Albanians from their homes and communities. Hundreds of thousands of Kosovars were forced to flee their homes, which were often burned to the ground along with the rest of their villages. Many people were also summarily executed.

If the United Nations and its members are averse to providing troops for extremely dangerous missions, and in many ways that is understandable, then another means to halt genocide must be put in place – either that, or the international community must honestly and forthrightly state that genocidal victims are, more often than not, going to be on their own and at the mercy of the perpetrators. An all-volunteer rapid-action force would alleviate the need for individual nations to supply troops, and it would allow the United Nations the means to act swiftly in deploying troops for it (the UN) would no longer have to beg nations to provide troops for such missions. If such a force were substantial in number, it would also eliminate the excuse that the United Nations does not have the personnel for the purpose of quelling the violence and mass killing by perpetrators.

4. Under the auspices of the United Nations, anti-genocide forces should be established across the globe, on virtually every continent with the exception of Antarctica. The express purpose of such forces – which must be well-manned, well-equipped, well-trained, and well-financed – is to be on alert and available for quick mobilization and intervention whenever a situation was slouching towards genocide in its particular region of the world.

Rationale: Too often intervention forces are deployed to a genocidal situation after tens of thousands, if not more, innocent individuals have already been murdered. Part of the problem is the inordinate amount of time it takes to mobilize and deploy troops and transport *matériel* to far-flung areas across the globe. The permanent deployment of large, well-trained and well-equipped rapid-action forces across the globe could possibly ameliorate such deadly situations.

Conclusion

Almost every time a genocide is perpetrated, politicians, Holocaust and genocide scholars, activists, and various members of the public decry the horrific situation, and assert that it must not happen again. But it does, somewhere else, time and again.

Up to this point in time, it seems as if the international community has either not cared enough to put in the time, effort and money to devise effective ways to prevent genocide or it has perceived the task as next to impossible. My sense is that while it would be extremely complex, difficult, time-consuming, and costly, it is not impossible. However, if humanity truly cares about its fellow humans, then the means must be devised, and soon, to staunch genocide. It is a given that the longer it takes to accomplish this task, the greater number of victims there will be who will have fallen victim to the hands of *genocidaires*.

Notes

1. For critical analyses and first-person accounts of these and other genocides, see further, Samuel Totten, William S. Parsons and Israel W. Charny, eds., *The Century of Genocide: Eyewitness Accounts and Critical Views* (New York: Garland Publishers, 1997).

2. Alan J. Kuperman, *The Limits of Humanitarian Intervention: Genocide in Rwanda* (Washington, D.C.: Brookings Institution, 2001), 102.

3. *Arkansas Democrat Gazette*, 3 July 2001, p. 4.

4. Ibid.

5. Ibid.

6. Kuperman, 105.

7. Alex Alvarez, *Governments, Citizens, and Genocide: A Comparative and Interdisciplinary Approach* (Bloomington: Indiana University Press, 2001), 139-140.

8. Kuperman, 66, 67.

25

GENOCIDE IS HISTORY

Ahmedou Ould-Abdallah

To my generation, genocide is history. An exception in an exceptionally murderous, inhuman century. Until very recently, genocide was understood as a proper noun, a name with a big capital "G," similar to Gabriel or Gabon. Indeed, genocide is history. However, with the passing of time and witnesses, its reality was fading away, questioned and even under siege by revisionists. With the end of the Cold War and subsequent unleashing of hatred, new wars erupted in many countries. The cruelties of these civil conflicts, broadcast throughout the world by global networks, was a chilling reminder of earlier genocide.

One of the outcomes of these developments is that the reality of genocide is now less challenged. State-sponsored mass killings intended to destroy whole religious or ethnic groups have become almost routine in the former Yugoslavia and in Central Africa. In 1994, government-organized killing took the lives of about 800,000 people. In one hundred days, one Rwandese ethnic group was almost wiped out. It took time for observers to realize the magnitude of the tragedy and even more time to recognize that it was genocide, not "ritual murders" as advanced by a few "African specialists." Since 1994 genocides intended not to wipe out whole groups but to destroy parts of them, have multiplied, and were witnessed or reported in different regions of the globe.[1] Whereas once it signified a horror so extreme that it was used as a proper noun, genocide, a crime combining many crimes, has now become sufficiently familiar that it is a common noun with a small "g" like gap or gown. This recurrence of genocide – an unacceptable aberration – should be a major concern to all. Today, the priority is to ask what can be done to keep genocide as an exceptional criminal deviation of the past and not a fact of normal life. Effective respect for democracy and human rights could help prevent policies that lead to genocide and isolate, very early, those who would think, plan, or perpetrate genocide. Furthermore, recent progress in international law to address impunity should help to create a climate conducive to national reconciliation and peace, and to eliminate the fear, exclusion, and other factors that could lead to genocide.

Deterrence of Genocides

Violence, mass or selective killings do not appear overnight in a peaceful country. Storms or hurricanes are never spontaneous although for centuries they took populations and authorities by surprise, sowing death and devastating large territories. There are seasons for storms and hurricanes, and seasons for blue skies and nice weather. Today, deadly climate turbulences are detected early enough, and are identified and monitored long before they hit the ground, thus limiting their destructive impact. But this has not always been the case. Similarly, genocides, *de facto* social and human hurricanes, occur only when a number of pre-conditions are assembled. It is therefore possible to detect, identify, and monitor these crimes long before they bring chaos, take or shatter the lives of the weakest innocents, and spill over into neighboring countries with vast exodus of refugees.

Today, in an era of globalization and mass communication, one haunting question is how to detect mounting violations of human rights or early government-sponsored massive abuses of power, all of which announce the potential for genocide. The international legal order – the Geneva Conventions and Protocols – and the fight for the respect of human rights, if well supported and implemented, could help to prevent violence and in particular to stop the cruel treatment of innocent populations. There are seasons of peace and tolerance, but there are also seasons favorable to genocides, similar to the seasons of hurricanes.

Genocide develops in specific conditions. Failing development, leading to poverty, inequality, corruption and exclusion are all fertile grounds for social conflicts, and hence preconditions for abuse of power and violence. These often lead to manipulation of conflicts by unscrupulous leaders inflaming cultural, religious or ethnic diversity. Corrupt dictators exploit their countrymen's failed expectations, and thwarted ambitions, resulting in a rise in ethnicism and the polarization of people along religious or ethnic lines. Excessive unchecked power is a factor in genocide. When in a country or a sub-region a group sees itself as superior, or where failed ambitions are manipulated, the season of violence and potentiality of genocide is not far away. Repeated small or "retail" violence could be signs announcing that "wholesale" killing could be expected.

Genocide, the most horrendous of all crimes, is the culmination of many successive and diverse violations of human rights, often sponsored and encouraged by state authorities, and left unpunished. Impunity favors a climate that often leads to suspicion and fear, both a cause of civil war when they become pervasive. Impunity prevents healing and reconciliation. Appeasement or international indifference to arbitrary government action and to the cruel treatment of people by their own government also makes fertile soil for genocide.

Ending Genocide

Progress in the elaboration and codification of international criminal law is one of the best means to combat genocide. But it is neither enough nor sufficient. The Convention for the Prevention of Genocide – a crime under international law – is still not effectively implemented. The use of state power to murder and suppress a distinct group "as a matter of policy" was overlooked, and possibly tacitly encouraged during the Cold War. Each political camp in the East and even in the West was either silent or condoned the barbarian activities of its protégés. Peaceful citizens were declared guilty, not by their action or even by their association, but because they possessed the same descriptive characteristics.

A favorable national and international environment, where scrutiny but also tolerance prevail, should help end genocide. Strong determination of the international community should result in uncompromising condemnation of any violence, especially when targeted toward a designated group. In this era of tolerance, openness and mass communication, there is no room for genocide. It should be more and more difficult to hide behind national sovereignty to perpetrate crimes against humanity and other gross violations of fundamental human rights. As globalization links different states' interests, the international community should not turn a blind eye on abuse of power, a frequent practice during the Cold War. A *de facto* limitation of sovereignty is necessary, given that state-sponsored violence threatens not only the state's own ability, but also that of its neighbors, through the flow of refugees, and other countries through immigration, terrorism, and all kinds of illegal trafficking.

In a situation of genocide, there is not only a right to intervene but a duty and an obligation to end the violence. The UN Charter in Article 2.7 makes a reservation about external interference in a country's domestic affairs. There is no dispute regarding this in normal conditions when a government respects a minimum of democratic principles, and refrains from international crime, cruelty and genocide. But the UN reservation should not be an excuse to kill behind closed borders, or not to intervene when a regime oppresses its citizens.

An agreement between international actors should help to confront humanitarian crises. This confrontation could be at two levels: political, primarily through dialogue, but also with determination in the field when deemed necessary. To its credit, the international community has intervened with particular resolve in Kosovo, saving lives but also sending a clear and strong message to all dictators and their accomplices that they will be held accountable. Dictators are now aware that there is no more tolerance for those who conceive, plan or carry out genocide. However, we should ensure that there are no double standards. In terms of moral principles, policies promoting genocide are wrong. Furthermore, they constitute additional penalties on most vulnerable populations, precisely those in countries either prone to or more exposed to abuses of power, civil wars and potentially, to genocides. Hence, the international community should not accept compromise or appeasement with oppressors. There should be no reasons for strategic interests to outweigh the plight of the victims. Excessive and continued abuse of power and violation of human rights cannot lead to peace or stability and often constitute security risks in far-away states.

Joint responses by the international community are feasible. A number of modest and not costly but effective actions could be designed and implemented, including: follow-up of situations and monitoring to prevent escalation. But when these peaceful means have failed, cooperation between states is needed to ensure decisive and concrete action. Assistance to internally displaced persons and refugees could help to lessen tensions as well as provide shelter, food and medicine. But these soft interventions should not replace or prevent robust and effective action when there is risk of mass killing.[2]

Preventing Genocide

Preventing genocide is an obligation under international law. It is also necessary to protect the security of all states, especially the major powers in an era of vast movements of populations with all the connected health and terrorism risks. Morally it is essential to think and take care of the victims, those without hope and who live in fear. Coherent and effective action by the international community could help avert genocide just as forecasters help concerned areas protect themselves against hurricanes. But it must always be remembered that hurricanes are acts of nature, forces beyond the control of man. Genocide is not. It is neither inevitable nor uncontrollable. We all have a moral responsibility to ensure that it is prevented, and that those who would encourage it are condemned.

Notes

1. Gregory H. Stanton, "The Burundi Genocides" (Unclassified Briefing Paper: US State Department, 1995).

2. Barbara Harff, "Rescuing Endangered Peoples: Missed Opportunities," in Albert J. Jongman, ed., *Contemporary Genocides: Causes, Cases, Consequences* (Leiden: PIOOM, 1996), 117-130.

26

WAR CRIMES TRIALS

Richard J. Goldstone
Nicole Fritz

Genocides have punctured human history. Yet this type of activity has for centuries had no name. It was the Holocaust – the tragedy that became emblematic of the term "genocide" – for which the term was coined. Indictments issued by the Nuremberg Tribunal charged German war criminals with conducting "deliberate and systematic genocide, viz. extermination of racial and national groups, against the civilian populations of certain occupied territories in order to destroy particular races and classes of people and national, racial or religious groups."[1] Yet the Charter of The International Military Tribunal did not provide specifically for jurisdiction over the crime of genocide. Instead, genocide was understood as a particularly egregious manifestation of crimes against humanity.

The 1948 United Nations Genocide Convention provides for trial of individuals accused of genocide before courts of the state in which the genocide was committed or before an "international penal tribunal." It was not until half a century after the drafting of the Convention that it could be said that international tribunals were up and running. Failure to establish these tribunals in the Cold War years may account for the lack of clear understanding of the crime of genocide. Despite this ambiguity, some of the most significant Conventions of the period, notably the 1973 United Nations Convention on the Suppression and Punishment of the Crime of Apartheid, deliberately followed the language of the Genocide Convention.

The end of the Cold War and the horrible specters of Bosnia and Rwanda provoked new initiative on the part of the United Nations – the establishment of the International Tribunals for the former Yugoslavia and for Rwanda in 1993 and 1994, respectively. The statutes of both tribunals afforded jurisdiction for the crime of genocide. Unsurprisingly, while some state officials cautioned against using the term "genocide" to describe the carnage lest they inflame calls for action, media coverage of the conflicts showed the public scenes as much like genocide as they could imagine.

The first judgment to interpret the Genocide Convention was handed down by the Rwandan tribunal in 1998. The decision was a monumental one – holding that the sexual assault of women of the Taba commune in Rwanda constituted genocidal acts. The decision made clear that genocide included acts other than the actual killing of the members of the group. The deliberate infliction of "serious bodily or mental harm to members of the group" (in this instance, rape), intended to violate the very foundation of that group, would also amount to genocide. The decision was significant too in that the court's reasoning suggested a possible dilution of the stringent interpretation of the intent requirement – a particularly onerous hurdle which required proof of intent, which excluded foresight or knowledge, "to destroy in whole or in part a national, ethnical, racial or religious group." This type of reasoning will go some way to ensuring that the charge of genocide is less exclusively symbolic and more fully enforceable. Other decisions of the Rwandan Tribunal, such as that of The Prosecutor v Clement Kayishema and Obed Ruzidana,[2] which found the accused guilty of genocide, but not of crimes against humanity in that the latter charge had been subsumed by the former, have highlighted the intersection of genocide and crimes against humanity. This pronouncement, that genocide was a species and particular manifestation of crimes against humanity, has contributed to a more sharply defined understanding of the crime of genocide.

Although the jurisprudence of the tribunals has given content to the legal elements of genocide, both tribunals have also importantly provided a better understanding of the process of genocide. The judgments have been laudable in setting out not only the immediate context of the individual accused's acts but also the larger context in which the conflicts of the former Yugoslavia and Rwanda took place.

Hannah Arendt famously wrote of the banality of evil, when observing the trial of Adolf Eichmann. The description has seemed fitting when applied to those who have appeared before the Rwanda Tribunal. There has been no characteristic, nothing immediately identifiable which marks those convicted as capable of evil. Prime minister, *bourgmestre*, radio announcer: the disparate, seemingly innocuous appearance of these individuals has belied the carefully orchestrated nature of the Rwandan genocide. Each judgment, however, has been careful testimony to the character of genocide: the extent to which, in climates of economic and political instability, the most negligible differences can be marshaled to create fear and distrust, to scupper civil society, and unravel communities. Many of the judgments have eloquently chronicled the frightening potential of modern media to be put at the service of individuals bent on genocide, and many have sadly pointed to the very many warning bells which should have alerted and activated the regional and international community to the impending inferno.

Yet it would be hard to say that prosecution and punishment of systematic human rights abuses have had a deterrent effect. The International Tribunal for the former Yugoslavia, convened at the time of the war in Bosnia, seems to have had little impact on the scale of the atrocities committed within Kosovo, despite the fact that these crimes fell within the jurisdiction of the Tribunal. At Nuremberg, US Chief Prosecutor, Justice Robert Jackson, observed that judicial action on its own could have little deterrent effect: "Judicial action always comes after the event. Wars are started only on the theory and in confidence that they can be won. Personal punishment, to be suffered only in the event the war is lost, will probably not be a sufficient deterrent to prevent a war where warmakers feel the chances of defeat are negligible."[3]

The paradigm of international justice may have shifted; punishment is no longer meted out only to those defeated. The two ad-hoc tribunals and the International Criminal Court are supported for their premise that all individuals, irrespective of their positions within conflict, are to be prosecuted should they be accused of committing genocide, crimes against humanity or war crimes. But in light of ongoing, widespread atrocities the world over, it may be too early and too difficult to maintain that international tribunals serve a preventative purpose.

While we may hope that international tribunals come to act as deterrents to would-be *genocidaires*, they serve another immediate purpose – justice. They allow the victims of the worst type of atrocities some sense of redress, of equanimity. International prosecution and punishment can and does provide a sense of justice being done – that justice being an acknowledgment, in a public space, of the crime committed and of punishment meted out in accordance with responsibility for the crime.

Notes
1. *Trials of the Major War Criminals Before the International Military Tribunal*, Nuremberg 14 November 1945 – 1 October 1946, 43-44.
2. ICTR–95–1; 1: ICTR–95—1; 2:ICTR–96—10.
3. *Trials of the Major War Criminals Before the International Military Tribunals*, Nuremberg, 14 November 1945 – 1 October 1946, 153-54.

27

WILL GENOCIDE EVER END?

Hubert Locke

"Nearly 50 years after the defeat of Nazi Germany,
the world, to all our shame, has not yet found
a morally and militarily adequate response
to this recurring crime against humanity."
D. C. Unger,
"UN Troops Cannot Stop Genocide,"
New York Times, 31 July 1994

Asking whether genocides will ever end is akin to asking whether wars will ever cease – with one significant difference. For well over two thousand years, humans have cherished the hope that warfare might be abolished – that nations, in the words of the prophet Micah, "would beat their swords into plowshares and their spears into pruning hooks ... [nor] learn war any more."[1]

No such optimism surrounds the phenomenon that is the attempt to physically annihilate an entire group of people because of its race or ethnicity. Students of genocide will recognize that I have drawn a decidedly narrow definition around a phenomenon that, in some quarters, is broadened to include the bombing of Hiroshima and the conditions of life in America's inner cities.[2] Such breadth, though it encompasses events and circumstances many find abhorrent, detracts not only from the utility of the term, it leaves us with a concept that has been stripped of its potency to pinpoint and specify one of the principal brutal behaviors of our time.[3]

Admittedly, genocide is a far more recent phenomenon, but it is almost as if, having observed and labeled this modern evil, we have become resigned to its perpetual existence. For having witnessed, in the middle of the last century, one of, if not the worst, experience of genocide on record – an experience that gave rise to the term itself – it would appear that contemporary societies have determined to repeat this peculiar horror rather than put an end to it. That which earned the twentieth century the designation of "the century of genocide" shows no sign of abating in the twenty-first.

Two scholars in the field of genocide studies point to the "coarseness and brutality of human existence throughout much of history" as factors which have contributed to the prevalence of genocide.[4] What is ironic, however, is its prevalence in the modern era. There may be, in fact, considerable dispute over whether the Roman destruction of Carthage in the second century B.C.E. or the disappearance of the indigenous population of Tasmania in the nineteenth century properly constitute, as some scholars suggest, incidents of genocide.[5] No one whose opinions are taken seriously doubts that the slaughter of Jews and Gypsies by the Nazis, or Bosnians by Serbs in the former Yugoslavia, or Tutsis by Hutus in Rwanda was genocidal, no matter how broadly or narrowly it is defined.

Perhaps the most disturbing feature of genocide is its prevalence in an era in which it is assumed there has been an increasing valuation of human life among civilized peoples. It is not modern arrogance but a matter of record to note, beginning with the Enlightenment, the genesis and growth of ideas about human freedom, dignity and worth that have brought radical change to societies and the conditions of life in the western world. From the ideals espoused in the American and French revolutions to the abolition of slavery and the emancipation of women, there has been not only an assertion of human values, but also their extension to groups previously beyond their orbit.

This valuation of human life reached new heights in the post-World War II period. For the first time in history, in the aftermath of a war, military and civilian leaders of the defeated nation were brought before an international tribunal on charges of having committed crimes against humanity. A few years later, member-states in the newly-formed United Nations adopted a Declaration of Human Rights, as well as a Convention on the Prevention and Punishment of Genocide. More recently, the UN has established a Permanent International Criminal Tribunal where military, political and civilian leaders of nation-states can be charged with and tried for crimes of genocide and crimes against humanity.

It is possible to see this sequence of events as an indication of the unrelenting progress that the world continues to make toward higher forms and ideals of the human spirit. But it is impossible to ignore the fact that these developments – clustered in or near the second half of the twentieth century – owe their impetus to the persistent outbreaks of genocide during the same period: in Burundi and Rwanda, Cambodia, East Timor, Bosnia, Serbia, and the Sudan. The prospects for eliminating genocide, therefore, do not seem great. They are further dimmed by Leo Kuper's observation that genocides occur frequently within nation-states that have the characteristics of pluralistic societies. Thus, it would seem that those features and virtues of the modern world in which we have come to place the greatest reliance for stemming the tide of barbarism and brutality offer no real assurance that this tide will not continue to wash over humanity.

While the prospects for bringing an end to genocide are bleak, they are not hopeless. An important clue to their curtailment is found in the passage from the prophet Micah, cited earlier. Speaking of war, he anticipates a period in which nations will not rise up against one another and in which they will not learn or study the art and rules of military combat. We may debate the reality of Micah's vision but the clue is invaluable. It is that war is learned behavior. Even more so is genocide.

Scholars may dispute whether aggression is a biological instinct, of which war is one of its massive and unavoidable expressions, but there is nothing instinctive in humans that makes genocide inevitable. Humans engage in acts of genocide only because they first succumb to the powerfully mistaken idea that there is a biological reality called race and a culturally significant phenomenon termed ethnicity in the world. Once these are accepted as givens or "facts," all else becomes the potential for genocidal commentary. One "race" or "ethnic group" decides to dominate or oppress some other "race" or "ethnic group"; physical annihilation of the oppressed group is the surest and most effective means of domination. Thus have the worst chapters of modern history been written.

The so-called facts of race and ethnicity are matters that have to be taught and learned. Infants and toddlers in every culture do not have an innate sense that differences in physical characteristics have some significance; they have to be taught whatever meaning – positive or negative – that becomes attached to this reality. Likewise, to imagine that the linguistic, religious, cultural group with which one identifies has some unique importance or significance is to be taught a set of myths and legends that are ostensibly harmless, but that can become lethal if they are taken seriously.

Throughout the modern world, nationalism is the cloak in which race and ethnicity often become wrapped. In each genocidal occurrence of the past century, other features or elements may be seen: class, caste, religion, et al. But it is the deadly combination of assumptions about racial or ethnic superiority in tandem with an excessive nationalism that has produced the mass slaughters that mar the modern era.

We know that genocides are always performed by a state or other political authority, that they require a high degree of centralized organization, that they are difficult for ordinary people to carry out, and that they require the dehumanization of the intended victims before they can be implemented. Dehumanizing intended victims of a prospective genocide requires a massive educational effort; only the state – and a totalitarian state at that – has command of the resources (e.g., the media, schools, political propaganda) that are needed to persuade ordinary people to commit unspeakable deeds.

The resources that can be mobilized against the genocidal mind and process may not be as powerful as the state, but they are all we have, and we must make the best use of them that we can. One of the principal and, at the same time, most problematic of resources is religion in its various forms and settings. Because genocides often take the form of religious crusades or invoke religious traditions or teachings in their support, religious institutions and their leaders have an especial obligation to place the wisdom of the world's great religions clearly, unmistakably, and unequivocally on the side of human dignity and equality. They must be in the forefront of those who denounce and condemn genocidal efforts. Just as Christians, because of the culpability of Christian antisemitism in the genocide of European Jewry, had a direct and specific obligation to reexamine and renounce centuries of Christian dogma that contributed to contempt of the Jewish people, so every major faith in the world must open itself – its teachings and traditions – to self-scrutiny. Every faith must do so in recognition of the fundamental principle that any religious belief or practice that does not honor and value the life of everyone respects no one and thereby desecrates whatever religious claims it makes. One of the encouraging signs, in the dawning of the twenty-first century, is the growth of non-governmental organizations (NGOs) whose efforts are specifically focused on and directed toward genocide prevention. The work of organizations such as the Aegis Trust, under whose auspices this volume appears, is of critical importance and merits the widest possible support.

Notes

1. Micah 4:3.
2. See Charles B. Strozier and Michael Flynn, *Genocide, War and Human Survival* (New York: Rowan and Littlefield, 1996), Chapters. 3 & 10.
3. See the immensely helpful discussion of this point in Frank Chalk and Kurt Jonassohn, *The History and Sociology of Genocide: Analyses and Case Studies* (New Haven: Yale University Press, 1990), 3-4.
4. Ibid., 7.
5. Ibid., 75, 204.

28

CAUTIOUS OPTIMISM

James M. Smith

In the spring of 1994, the Rwandan government joined the United Nations Security Council. Unashamed that they were systematically planning to kill their entire Tutsi population, Rwandan *genocidaires* had become part of the UN's most powerful decision-making body. More alarming still, the other permanent and non-permanent members of the Security Council continued with business as usual, apparently unaware or unaffected by the situation in Rwanda.[1] Once the murder started in April 1994, arguments began about whether the term *genocide* could be applied to what was happening there. If it could be applied, would the UN Convention on the Prevention and Punishment of the Crime of Genocide oblige international intervention or merely provide the right for it to take place? As the scale of human suffering mounted, decision-makers procrastinated.

Recent history contains many instances where people of goodwill have allowed the fate of others to go unchecked, either because of ignorance, inability to predict, or political expediency. The central question raised by these failures is, "How can we avoid their repetition?" If a more secure future is to be created, the international community must remain attentive to the salutary lessons of the past.

To prevent genocide, the international community needs to act with pertinent tools. While largely in place, these tools need refinement. Their effective use, moreover, depends on political will. British Prime Minister Tony Blair has insisted that prevention of humanitarian disaster is within the interest of the West.[2] Signals from other political and UN leaders in the past decade indicate a shift in foreign policy from reactive crisis management to proactive prevention. This development is welcome, particularly for potential victims of genocide.

However, we must not underestimate the influence of *realpolitik* on the West's response to future crises. Prevention is always colored by regional politics and economics and also by the level of risk perceived by the electorate at home. The world's apathy to Rwanda can never be justified, but the horrific images from Somalia in October 1993 left the American public reeling, with little appetite to be further involved in African conflict. Ultimately, the deaths of eighteen US rangers played a large role in the abandonment of a million Rwandans.[3] That said, preventive action should not be undertaken by Western-led coalitions alone, especially if the action is required in a developing country, for mistrust of Western agendas understandably runs deep in developing countries. On the other hand, fear or resentment about possible neo-imperialism will not save life either. Ending genocide remains dependent on numerous factors, but the potential for developing the tools of intervention and the political will to use them gives cause for cautious optimism.

Speaking the Same Language

Political leaders need to be more aware about genocide and its human, social, moral, political, and economic implications. Genocide emerges out of complex political and social scenarios, and there needs to be a fuller and wider under-standing of how it evolves, what can be done about it, and when. Even if there is political will to respond, observers face a challenge to recognize genocide in a climate of crisis and probable state failure. There may be many urgent prior-ities for relief agencies: displaced persons, starvation, and economic collapse. Politically there may be a focus on the democratic process or a threatened *coup d'état*. How then, in such circumstances, should one recognize specifically the threat of genocide, and how should that recognition alter the management of the situation or policies on the ground?

There is a difference between prevention and intervention. Genocidal ide-ologies creep incrementally toward a crisis point,[4] although they may often undergo sudden transformation when precipitated by certain triggering events. Imagine a continuum in which a stable society moves, sometimes almost imper-ceptibly, into an increasingly genocidal environment. The period prior to mass murder is characterized by a prolonged "gray zone" containing many destabi-lizing factors, each of which is insufficient to cause genocide, but many of which may be necessary for its occurrence.

stable society	the grey zone	genocide

Responses within this period need to be measured according to how far the situation has progressed, but with awareness of where it could ultimately lead. Once genocide is imminent or underway – toward the right of this model

– response must be rapid and firm; at this stage, it will probably require military intervention. Late-stage response, however, is *not* prevention. Henry Huttenbach calls this late-stage intervention "genocide termination,"[5] while Jim Fussell refers to "suppression of genocide."[6] True prevention must occur at an earlier point – toward the left of this model – if lives are to be saved.

Legal or Moral Obligations?

The UN Genocide Convention relies for its definition on demonstration of intent. Without intent to murder a group in whole or in part, there is no genocide, according to this definition. An unfortunate consequence of the emphasis on intention is that it can support the view – since intention is exceedingly difficult to prove – that there is no need to respond, no matter how many people are being killed. If we wait until an event can safely be defined as genocide before there is a response, the only thing that will be safe is the definition. Once genocide is happening, one might assume that proving intentionality becomes easier to demonstrate. The trials of élite Rwandan *genocidaires* in the International Criminal Tribunals for Rwanda (ICTR) in Arusha, and of Slobodan Milosevic in the International Tribunal for the Former Yugoslavia (ICTY) at The Hague, emphasize that this is not so. While the events in Rwanda – and arguably those in Bosnia and Herzegovina – constituted clear-cut genocide, the cases against these *genocidaires* rest on demonstrating intent to commit genocide. This exercise is costly, lengthy, and complex. Even after genocide has taken place and been witnessed by the world, these tribunals take months or years to establish a case for successful prosecution.

From a legal perspective, if preventive action depends on demonstrating intent, prevention becomes more difficult still. The need arises to describe or define what is happening when mass death is not yet occurring. For instance, how can hate-media be countered in a situation where few, if any, people are being killed, but the media is clearly dehumanizing a group and inciting violence? Where to draw the line is a difficult political decision, a decision upon which people's lives may depend. Preventive policies, then, may need to operate in the legality's gray zone. They must be based upon the *threat* of genocide, when events are referred to as *genocidal*, rather than being based upon genocide itself.

Avoiding Legal Loopholes

To end genocide, legal loopholes used to impede political action must either be filled, circumvented, or explained. The legal conflict between state sovereignty versus intervention is a central dilemma of international law faced by the UN and intergovernmental bodies. This conflict requires clarification.[7]

At what point along the pathway toward genocide does international law provide the international community with sufficient justification to prevent *possible* genocide? Does the term "prevention" in the UN Genocide Convention refer to true prevention or to termination of genocide? Chapter VII of the UN Charter provides for intervention at a late stage once genocide "erupts" – on the right of this model. Article 39 states:

> The Security Council shall determine the existence of any threat to the peace, breach of the peace, or act of aggression and shall make recommendations, or decide what measures shall be taken... to maintain or restore international peace and security.[8]

The remaining articles, especially 42 and 43 of Chapter VII, lay out explicitly the measures that may be taken.[9] While these provisions may save some lives, they only allow for crisis management. Some will argue too that if the genocide does not impact on neighboring states, it is not a threat to international peace and security, and therefore remains an internal issue of the accused state.

If the Genocide Convention does refer to true preventive policy, another dilemma arises. When lives or international security are not in imminent danger, it may be concluded that Chapter VII does not provide a sufficient mandate for early intervention. Article 2.4 of the UN Charter, which was designed to protect state sovereignty from outside interference, restricts intervention if, for instance, the conflict is considered to be a civil war. It states:

> All Members shall refrain in their international relations from the threat or use of force against the territorial integrity or political independence of any state.[10]

This UN language creates a significant problem because conflict and genocide are increasingly intra-state affairs. Indeed, Article II has been used to restrict the mandate of UN peacekeeping forces. As a result, life may be lost because UN member states do not want to interfere. As with defense of freedom of speech, protection of state sovereignty is a right that can be used and abused.[11]

Pivoting response around purely "legal determinants" is largely unhelpful in prevention, as it may be used to avoid the moral duty to save lives. US State Department spokeswoman Christine Shelly, and other western officials, avoided using the term "genocide" in 1994 because it was believed that the UN Genocide Convention would oblige its signatories to intervene in Rwanda.[12] The US State department and British officials were misinformed on four counts and, as a result, misled others. First, they denied that genocide was happening even when the evidence indicated that it clearly was. Second, they erred about being legally obliged to respond under the UN Genocide Convention. The Convention does not create a duty, but a legal right to respond. Third, even if it was arguable that genocide was under way, available information made clear that people were being killed in huge numbers and the head of operations on the ground concluded it was logistically feasible to stop the slaughter. A moral duty existed to do so. Last, and perhaps most importantly, Chapters VI and VII of the UN Charter give clear authority to the UN Security Council to provide a mandate for intervention should it determine that matters "endanger the maintenance of international peace and security."[13]

This last point provides a strong argument against pivoting response to genocide on legal determinants. The key to effective response in the future lies not in changing international laws, even if they are insufficient or contradictory, but in the UN member states having the will to intervene, and in strengthening UN bodies to enable them to respond effectively. The UN Security Council has the right, but not sufficient support from the member states. All the articles in Chapter VII rely on the UN member states being *invited* to provide the means once a Security Council decision has been made.

> When the Security Council has decided to use force it shall... invite that Member, if the Member so desires, to participate in the decisions of the Security Council...[14]

The compulsion to respond is therefore a political rather than a legal one.

Clearing Confusion: "Calling a Spade a Spade"

Looking back to 1994, once the genocide erupted in Rwanda, there was little doubt among many of those on the ground about what was happening. Three weeks after the mass killing began, the UK-based aid agency Oxfam declared in a press release that it feared genocide was under way in Rwanda.[15] But a review of international newspaper articles and photograph archives from Spring 1994 indicates that not all those responsible for transmitting information understood what they were witnessing. Until mid-May 1994, the bloody situation in Rwanda was largely described as "civil war" or "tribal violence." The militias who were systematically slaughtering men, women and children were described as "fighting alongside Rwandan Government soldiers defending against RPF rebel advances."[16] Most people in the West accepted the confusing but horrific analysis, albeit with growing unease.

If confusion exists during a genocide, it begs the question about how clear the picture is to those in a position to inform and influence international response in the months or years prior to genocide. Do diplomats, journalists and NGO workers always understand what they are looking at? Major Brent Beardsley, General Romeo Dallaire's executive assistant, remarked on their assignment with the UN peacekeeping force in Rwanda in the fall of 1993,

> We were under the impression that the situation was quite straightforward: there was one cohesive government side and one cohesive rebel side, and they had come together to sign the peace agreement and had then requested that we come in to help them implement it.[17]

Philippe Gaillard of the International Committee of the Red Cross had been in Kigali for nine months prior to the outbreak of systematic killings. He acknowledges that the day before it broke, he knew terrible things were going to happen but did not know how severe they would be; even now, he explains that when he refers to the "genocidal atmosphere" of early 1994, it is described *ex post facto*.[18]

The relationship between conflict and genocide warrants emphasis here. The potential for confusion remains a danger that could lead to misdiagnoses and mismanagement of the problem in the future. While much conflict exists without genocide, we are hard-pressed to find examples of genocide that have not been associated with a war. The Armenian genocide, the Holocaust, Cambodia,[19] Bosnia, and Rwanda all took place in an environment of inter-state or intra-state conflict. To avoid similar tragedies, we need to be better at recognizing the latent genocidal ideologies that often emerge during a state of conflict. This lesson has been made clear in numerous inquiries following the genocide in Rwanda.[20] Actors in the field need to be trained to see the wood of genocide through the trees of conflict.

Peacemakers involved in diplomacy must be certain that a ceasefire in a civil or ethnic conflict does not create an illusion of peace that places a target group in a vulnerable position. Samantha Power made it clear: "Genocide differed from ordinary conflict because, while surrender in war normally stopped the killing, surrender in the face of genocide only expedited it."[21]

The Need for Independent Advice

A danger exists that the terms *genocidal* or *threat of genocide* may become devalued by overuse or politicized by groups who stand to gain from "genocide publicity." To avoid this outcome, it is crucial to have independent authoritative advice around which to build a consensus of opinion. A future body serving the UN secretariat and member states should act as the diagnostic and advice center, focusing on the danger of genocidal ideology. It should be easily accessible so that diplomats and NGOs know where to turn when they are concerned about a situation. The prime purpose of such a recognized body would be to link genocide early warning with regional knowledge in order to present pragmatic solutions. Its work clearly needs to dovetail with broader conflict prevention initiatives. While acting as an observation portal, such a body would also be able to advise on the priority areas with regard to responses from the international community. The UN needs to use its limited resources in prevention in the areas where populations are most at risk, in those scenarios that are moving rapidly, and those which are most feasible to stop. An attempt to save lives should not make matters worse; as with all advice and intelligence, it should be placed in context with a sound understanding of the possible repercussions of action or inaction. Such a body should have a wide range of military and intelligence expertise, and must also understand the complex regional circumstances. The independence of an observation and advice body must also be extended to any preventive policy or interventional force that results. General Romeo Dallaire is right to insist that single state-led coalitions run the risk that real or perceived interests lie beyond the humanitarian.[22]

Looking ahead then, there will not be a quick fix to genocide. As with cancer, however, treatment does not stop just because we lack the full pathogenesis. Instead, treatment continues concurrently with research for better cures. It is essential to foster a political culture in which people matter more than "interests." If persistent, concerted effort from numerous disciplines and actors continues, anti-genocide understanding can gradually evolve and policies improve. It may take generations, but genocide can be prevented.

Notes

1. "In the first four weeks of the genocide, the fact that a systematic and continuing slaughter was taking place in Rwanda was not once discussed at length in [Security] Council meetings. Everyone in the Secretariat in New York was preoccupied with the civil war." Linda R. Melvern, *A People Betrayed: The Role of the West in Rwanda's Genocide*, (London: Zed Books, 2000), 166.

2. "We are realizing how fragile are our frontiers in the face of the world's new challenges.... the yearning is for order and stability and if it doesn't exist elsewhere, it is unlikely to exist here. I have long believed this interdependence defines the new world we live in.... The critics will say: but how can the world be a community? Nations act in their own self-interest. Of course they do. But what is the lesson of the financial markets, climate change, international terrorism, nuclear proliferation or world trade? It is that our self-interest and our mutual interests are today inextricably woven together," Tony Blair, speaking on 3 October 2001 at the Labour Party conference. See further, www.labour.org.uk/lp/new/labour/docs/LONGSPEECHES/TBCONFSPEECH2001.TXT

3. "The US intervention in Somalia is now widely considered to have been a fiasco.... It was the major factor in the tragic US refusal to intervene – either unilaterally or through the UN – to prevent the genocide in Rwanda during the spring of 1994," Stephen Zunes, Associate Professor of Politics and Chair of the Peace & Justice Studies Program at the University of San Francisco. See further, www.foreignpolicyinfocus.org/commentary/2002/0201somalia_body.html

4. This model corresponds to the pathogenesis of some diseases such as cancer. As with pre-cancerous cells, the severity of progression can be conveniently divided into three grades according to the presence of warning indicators at a micro level. This helps clinicians judge the urgency of treatment or how closely to observe the patient. The United States Holocaust Memorial Museum's Committee on Conscience refers to three levels leading to genocide. Greg Stanton, Director of Genocide Watch, has identified eight stages of genocide.See further, www.genocidewatch.org/8stages.htm

5. See further, Henry Huttenbach's essay in this volume, "Anticipating Genocide, " pp. 123-126.

6. Jim Fussell; personal communication with the author.

7. For further reading, I recommend the report *The International Commission on State Sovereignty and Intervention,* created by the Canadian Department for Foreign Affairs, December 2002.

8. See further, www.un.org/Overview/Charter/chapter7.html

9. Ibid.

10. United Nations Charter, see www.un.org/Overview/Charter/chapter1.html. Note also that Article 2.7 both emphasizes and qualifies this issue.

11. One reason for the zeal with which nation states protect the principle of Article II corresponds to the fear they have that others may one day interpret their own actions as a transgression of human rights and thus justify an intervention.

12. PBS/BBC broadcast, "The Triumph of Evil," 26 January 1999.

13. See further, Articles 33, 34, www.un.org/Overview/Charter/chapter6.html

14. Article 44, www.un.org/Overview/Charter/chapter7.html

15. Melvern, *A People Betrayed,* 178.

16. To give a typical example, the original press caption of one Reuters' photograph read: "28 May 1994 – A Rwandese man wounded by machete is helped by an unidentified journalist and a United Nations representative. UN officers reported rebel gains in Rwanda's civil war but said they still hoped to evacuate hundreds of civilians trapped in the capital." (Reuters/Popperfoto NAI04.) The caption fails to make any mention of the genocide in which its central subject is caught up.

17. Samantha Power, "Bystanders to Genocide," *The Atlantic Monthly*, September 2001. See further, www.bard.edu/hrp/events/fall2001/bystanders.to.genocide.htm.

18. In dialogue with Gerald Caplan at the Aegis-UK Foreign and Commonwealth Office Genocide Prevention Conference, Beth Shalom, Newark, UK, 22-25 January 2002.

19. Most of the victims of the Khmer Rouge were Cambodian peasants, leading some scholars to exclude Cambodia as a genocide as they were not identified by the perpetrators on "ethnic, religious or racial grounds" and therefore do not fall within the UN definition of genocide. Barbara Harff coined the term "politicide" to describe the mass killing of people identified as political enemies of the state. Others describe it as "autogenocide" since the Khmer killed people of the same ethno-religious identity as themselves. Genocidal regimes are characteristically totalitarian and see extermination as a means to an end. Political opponents therefore usually form part of the victim groups: Socialists and Communists in Nazi Germany, Hutu moderates in Rwanda. In Cambodia it could be argued that the Vietnamese and other ethnic groups were victims of genocide and the million or so Khmer peasants were victims of politicide. With regard to the ideological motives and outcome, it was the same, and I therefore include Cambodia in this short list of genocides.

20. As for instance in Gerald Caplan's report for the Organization of Africa Unity in statements by the United Nations and by Kofi Annan, the Secretary General of the United Nations, who was the head of the Department of Peace Keeping Operations (DPKO) during the genocide in 1994. (The Organization of African Unity's *Special Report of the International Panel of Eminent Personalities to Investigate the 1994 Genocide in Rwanda and the Surrounding Events*, also known as the OAU IPEP Report. See further, www.oau-oua.org/document/ipep/ipep.htm)

21. See further, Power, "Bystanders to Genocide."

22. "I believe that all these new initiatives of single nation-led coalitions [are] marginalizing the UN ... But there is no transparent, impartial entity in the world still existing that is better than the UN. One must be very wary of single nation-led coalitions because it's not altruism that conducts the operations and the decisions to be involved," General Romeo Dallaire, Interview, BBC News Online's *Talking Point/Forum*, 24 January 2002.

Claire Kabahizi is sitting at Nyanza, Rwanda thinking about her parents and other family members who were among several thousand Tutsis slaughtered there by Hutu militia in 1994, only hours after the UN withdrew its protection from the ETO school where they and other Tutsis had sought refuge.

Photo © James M. Smith

29

EPILOGUE

BEYOND THE DARKNESS?

Carol Rittner, John K. Roth, and James M. Smith

As this book went to press, the former Yugoslav president Slobodan Milosevic became the first head of state ever to be taken to court on allegations of geno- cide. Proceedings against Milosevic began in The Hague on February 12, 2002, long after the alleged genocidal atrocities took place in the 1992-95 Bosnian war. The Milosevic trial will last for months. It remains to be seen whether this trial, or any genocide-related court action, will have results that deter genocide in the future. Prudence dictates against too much confidence in that regard, a judgment that holds good as well for the future of the International Criminal Court (ICC), which was proposed in Rome in 1998. Although the minimum of sixty national ratifications needed to bring the ICC into existence has been achieved, it is unlikely that the world's superpowers will sign on. If they do not, the ICC's power to act meaningfully in response to genocide will be crippled. As these developments suggest, the future of credible international action to prevent, check, or redress genocide remains full of problems and predicaments.

"The beast of genocide," says Gregory H. Stanton, director of the International Campaign to End Genocide, "lurks in the dark." Romeo Dallaire, the Canadian general who headed the United Nations Assistance Mission in Rwanda, makes a counterpoint when he urges that "the need is to stop the dis- connect between the experiential and the intellectual."[1] Heeding Stanton's warning, the essays in this book also seek to advance Dallaire's imperative. To the extent that they succeed, the answer to the fundamental question, "Will genocide ever end?" can at least be *perhaps*. That realistic conclusion is ever- so-tentative. Yet it is not without hope and substance because international awareness about what it will take to move beyond genocide is becoming clearer. As this book draws to a close, here is a summary of those directions.

Overarching Themes

At least five overarching themes have found expression – implicitly if not explicitly – in these pages. First, the essays show that genocide prevention is a goal that exceeds any single person's expertise, any discipline's methodology, or any government's reach. Genocide prevention requires working together at every point.

Second, no automatic link exists between intellectual analysis of genocide and the action that is needed to prevent it. That connection can be made only through political will. How to muster and sustain that political will is among the most important questions raised by the continuing threat of genocide in our world.

Third, governments, even if they are alert and activated, will not – indeed, cannot – do everything that is necessary to prevent, stop, or heal the wounds that genocide inflicts. That fact requires the mobilization of other agencies that may be able to lend a hand in this crucial work.

Fourth, at times there is no substitute for international military intervention, which is essential to maintain stability and security. Military intervention, however, is not enough to meet the needs that genocidal threats present. Crucial needs include political, economic, and educational aid – somewhat along the lines of a post-World War II Marshall Plan – to defuse potentially genocidal situations.

Fifth, prevention of and intervention in genocide are long-term commitments, otherwise genocide prevention will remain ineffective. The long-term commitments must involve all sorts of institutions, and not least of all the media, which have the power to alert, inform, and urge the need for action.

Good News/Bad News

This book's contents focus on philosophy and religion, the responsibilities of governments and non-governmental agencies, to name only a few of its perspectives. Individually and collectively, the authors offer good news about genocide prevention, but at the same time they point to areas that must command greater attention and resources if genocide is to end. Here, very compactly, are some of the good news/bad news implications that flow from the research and reflection.

1. We have the concept of genocide. It is defined, for example, by the United Nations Convention on the Prevention and Punishment of Genocide. The concept helps us to identify genocide when it happens and, importantly, when it may be coming. But the bad news is that education about genocide is lacking, and, in addition, the scope and meaning of the concept remain debat-

able. As a result, there are loopholes in the legal frameworks about genocide. The concept's definition, moreover, is not likely to be universally agreed upon. Even if it were agreed upon, the sense of obligation to prevent genocide may remain ambiguous. Deeper study and better education about genocide are needed if genocide is to end.

2. Prevention and proof of genocide depend on determining perpetrator intent, which is not easily done, especially in pre-genocidal situations. Nevertheless, there is good news about demonstrating intent, because we know that ideologies can show it. Some ideologies are genocidal; their presence can be a factor in early warnings. Yet, even if we can sense genocide's coming by study of ideologies, the control of hate-inflaming communication, education, and media – crucial though it is – remains both problematic and lacking. If genocide is to end, there must be media usage and control in that direction.

3. The good news includes the fact that we have worthwhile analyses of risk assessment and credible approaches to early warning where genocide is concerned. Nevertheless, too often no one gives the perpetrators – potential or actual – reason to pause. Early warning is an important piece, but still a small one, in a very large and complicated genocide puzzle. If genocide is to end, early warning systems must produce policies and actions that give its agents reason to pause.

4. Military intervention can be effective in preventing and stopping genocide. Such intervention is crucial for establishing security in which genocide cannot erupt or prevail. Yet, military power is state-focused; what it can do depends on state authority, and states jealously guard their sovereignty. Where genocidal situations are involved, how states will allow their military power to be used, if at all, for prevention and intervention remains at issue. Genocide's threats are unlikely to disappear until more effective international military cooperation against genocide becomes operational.

5. We know too much for it to be a surprise when genocide happens. Nevertheless, genocide indicators are difficult to operationalize for genocide prevention. Accountability is among the most crucial aspects of this problem. Who, for example, does one call to get preventative action going when genocide is threatened or under way? If genocide is to end, calls of that kind must be placed and answered. Accountability for genocide prevention must be put in place.

6. The good news is that we know a great deal about what to do to check genocide or to keep it from re-erupting after it has happened. Those steps include: establishing security, neutralizing genocidal leaders, engaging in regional planning, ensuring that political moderates have a voice, avoiding

ethnically-based governments. In spite of such knowledge, however, geno-cides continue. They reveal either the failure or the inadequacy of basic institutions – political, religious, humanitarian. Genocide's threat will not end until those institutions perform better than they have thus far done.

7. National interest is not always a barrier to genocide intervention. The case can be made that prevention and intervention are parts of a nation's values and thus of its interest. On the other hand, decisions are often made on the basis of political considerations that override appeals to "higher values." When that happens, value-based appeals for prevention and intervention are muted and unheeded. Genocide is unlikely to end unless the tendency to override ethical considerations is reversed.

8. It is good news to know that religion can be a powerful and persuasive force in genocide prevention. The negative example of Rwanda bears witness to this claim, for virtually all analysts of that genocide are convinced that it could have been prevented or stopped if strong religious protests against the genocide had been raised. But that same negative example also shows that religion is a key part of the problem where genocide is concerned. Religion can separate people; it can legitimate violence that is genocidal. If the quality of religious life improves by becoming less exclusive and more inclusive, so will the odds in favor of genocide prevention.

9. Reports, testimonies, acts of memory and memorialization – these responses keep attention focused on what happens in genocide. They make it more difficult to ignore the brutality, the killing, and its aftermath. Unfortunately, reports can be buried. The past recedes. Life goes on. Justice does not take place. Long-term rebuilding falters. Denial gets a hearing. Perpetrators go back to business as usual. The antidotes for genocide include resistance against the disappearance of what has been seen and felt in genocide's killing fields.

10. Not only are there many non-governmental organizations (NGOs) that do have deep commitments to humanitarian causes, but those organizations, along with many governmental ones, are staffed by individuals who often display immense courage, persistence, and resilience in battling against genocidal threats. Yet the bad news includes the fact that NGOs may unwittingly aid and abet potentially genocidal regimes by creating or intensifying one set of problems as they respond to another. When to disengage as well as when to engage remain issues that can often be riddled with ambiguity and unintended negative consequences. Such difficulties are among those that never make it possible for us to say with complete assurance that genocide will end.

11. The media possess immense power and sophistication to report accu-

rately, to keep us informed of events in real time, and to cover the globe. Where genocide is concerned, the excuse that "I did not know" or "we were unaware" can no longer have much credibility. But the bad news is that too often the media spin, simplify, and scoop. The spins are multiple, contested, incomplete, more-or-less true, and they reflect "interests" – political, economic, philosophical – that contribute to the ideologies and mistrust in which genocidal dispositions thrive. In no small part, then, the prevention of genocide depends on media committed to that goal.

The Key Word: Accountability

Genocide prevention depends first and foremost on establishing institutional accountability – governmental and non-governmental – aimed in that direction. As a result, the questions that most need answering include the following: How do we best establish, support, and encourage institutions to take responsibility to prevent or check genocide and to keep that goal among the highest priorities?

Giving testimony about his experiences in Bosnia, Kemal Pervanic, a survivor of genocidal ethnic cleansing in the Balkans, said that his story, unfortunately, "is nothing new." Then he added: "I heard the concept of genocide first *after* it happened."[2]

The beast of genocide does lurk in the dark, as Gregory Stanton said, but the dark is not only the darkness of murderous ignorance, lethal discrimination, and bloodthirsty arrogance. Instead, genocide lurks largely in the darkness of irresponsibility and non-accountability, which prevents too little and intervenes too late. General Dallaire got it right: the disconnection between the experiential and the intellectual must be stopped. If it is stopped, then *perhaps* genocide will end. We have no right to regard striving for that objective as hopeless.

Notes

1. Stanton and Dallaire made these comments at the Aegis Trust–British Foreign and Commonwealth Office (FCO) Genocide Prevention Conference, a significant international inquiry, which took place at the Beth Shalom Holocaust Centre in England, January 22-25, 2002. This conference included participants from government, the military, non-governmental organizations, the media and universities, as well as genocide survivors.

2. Pervanic was one of the genocide survivors who participated in the Aegis–FCO Genocide Prevention Conference, January 22-25, 2002.

APPENDICES

CONVENTION ON THE PREVENTION AND PUNISHMENT OF THE CRIME OF GENOCIDE

Approved and proposed for signature and ratification or accession by General Assembly Resolution 260 A (III) of 9 December 1948 Entry into Force 12 January 1951, in Accordance with Article XIII

The Contracting Parties,

Having considered the declaration made by the General Assembly of the United Nations in its resolution 96 (I) dated 11 December 1946 that genocide is a crime under international law, contrary to the spirit and aims of the United Nations and condemned by the civilized world,

Recognizing that at all periods of history genocide has inflicted great losses on humanity, and

Being convinced that, in order to liberate mankind from such an odious scourge, international co-operation is required,

Hereby agree as hereinafter provided:

Article I

The Contracting Parties confirm that genocide, whether committed in time of peace or in time of war, is a crime under international law which they undertake to prevent and to punish.

Article II

In the present Convention, genocide means any of the following acts committed with intent to destroy, in whole or in part, a national, ethnical, racial or religious group, as such:

(a) Killing members of the group;

(b) Causing serious bodily or mental harm to members of the group;

(c) Deliberately inflicting on the group conditions of life calculated to bring about its physical destruction in whole or in part;

(d) Imposing measures intended to prevent births within the group;

(e) Forcibly transferring children of the group to another group.

Article III

The following acts shall be punishable:

(a) Genocide;

(b) Conspiracy to commit genocide;

(c) Direct and public incitement to commit genocide;

(d) Attempt to commit genocide;

(e) Complicity in genocide.

Article IV

Persons committing genocide or any of the other acts enumerated in article III shall be punished, whether they are constitutionally responsible rulers, public officials or private individuals.

Article V

The Contracting Parties undertake to enact, in accordance with their respective Constitutions, the necessary legislation to give effect to the provisions of the present Convention, and, in particular, to provide effective penalties for persons guilty of genocide or any of the other acts enumerated in article III.

Article VI

Persons charged with genocide or any of the other acts enumerated in article III shall be tried by a competent tribunal of the State in the territory of which the act was committed, or by such international penal tribunal as may have jurisdiction with respect to those Contracting Parties which shall have accepted its jurisdiction.

Article VII

Genocide and the other acts enumerated in article III shall not be considered as political crimes for the purpose of extradition.

The Contracting Parties pledge themselves in such cases to grant extradition in accordance with their laws and treaties in force.

Article VIII

Any Contracting Party may call upon the competent organs of the United

Nations to take such action under the Charter of the United Nations as they consider appropriate for the prevention and suppression of acts of genocide or any of the other acts enumerated in article III.

Article IX

Disputes between the Contracting Parties relating to the interpretation, application or fulfillment of the present Convention, including those relating to the responsibility of a State for genocide or for any of the other acts enumerated in article III, shall be submitted to the International Court of Justice at the request of any of the parties to the dispute.

STATUTE OF THE INTERNATIONAL TRIBUNAL FOR YUGOSLAVIA

Adopted 25 May 1993 by Resolution 827
As Amended 13 May 1988 by Resolution 1166
As Amended 30 November 2000 by Resolution 1329

Article 1
Competence of the International Tribunal
The International Tribunal shall have the power to prosecute persons responsible for serious violations of international humanitarian law committed in the territory of the former Yugoslavia since 1991 in accordance with the provisions of the present Statute.

Article 2
Grave breaches of the Geneva Conventions of 1949
The International Tribunal shall have the power to prosecute persons committing or ordering to be committed grave breaches of the Geneva Conventions of 12 August 1949, namely the following acts against persons or property protected under the provisions of the relevant Geneva Convention:
- (a) Wilful killing;
- (b) Torture or inhuman treatment, including biological experiments;
- (c) Wilfully causing great suffering or serious injury to body or health;
- (d) Extensive destruction and appropriation of property, not justified by military necessity and carried out unlawfully and wantonly;
- (e) Compelling a prisoner of war or a civilian to serve in the forces of a hostile power;
- (f) Wilfully depriving a prisoner of war or a civilian of the rights of fair and regular trial;

(g) Unlawful deportation or transfer or unlawful confinement of a civilian;

(h) Taking civilians as hostages.

Article 3
Violations of the laws or customs of war

The International Tribunal shall have the power to prosecute persons violating the laws or customs of war. Such violations shall include, but not be limited to:

(a) Employment of poisonous weapons or other weapons calculated to cause unnecessary suffering;

(b) Wanton destruction of cities, towns or villages, or devastation not justified by military necessity;

(c) Attack, or bombardment, by whatever means, of undefended towns, villages, dwellings, or buildings;

(d) Seizure of, destruction or wilful damage done to institutions dedicated to religion, charity and education, the arts and sciences, historic monuments and works of art and science;

(e) Plunder of public or private property.

Article 4
Genocide

1. The International Tribunal shall have the power to prosecute persons committing genocide as defined in paragraph 2 of this article or of committing any of the other acts enumerated in paragraph 3 of this article.

2. Genocide means any of the following acts committed with intent to destroy, in whole or in part, a national, ethnical, racial or religious group, as such:

(a) Killing members of the group;

(b) Causing serious bodily or mental harm to members of the group;

(c) Deliberately inflicting on the group conditions of life calculated to bring about its physical destruction in whole or in part;

(d) Imposing measures intended to prevent births within the group;

(e) Forcibly transferring children of the group to another group.

3. The following acts shall be punishable:

(a) Genocide;

(b) Conspiracy to commit genocide;

(c) Direct and public incitement to commit genocide;

(d) Attempt to commit genocide;

(e) Complicity in genocide.

Article 5
Crimes against humanity

The International Tribunal shall have the power to prosecute persons responsible for the following crimes when committed in armed conflict, whether international or internal in character, and directed against any civilian population:

   (a) Murder;

   (b) Extermination;

   (c) Enslavement;

   (d) Deportation;

   (e) Imprisonment;

   (f) Torture;

   (g) Rape;

   (h) Persecutions on political, racial and religious grounds;

   (i) Other inhumane acts.

Article 6
Personal jurisdiction

The International Tribunal shall have jurisdiction over natural persons pursuant to the provisions of the present Statute.

Article 7
Individual criminal responsibility

1. A person who planned, instigated, ordered, committed or otherwise aided and abetted in the planning, preparation or execution of a crime referred to in articles 2 to 5 of the present Statute, shall be individually responsible for the crime.

2. The official position of any accused person, whether as Head of State or Government or as a responsible Government official, shall not relieve such person of criminal responsibility nor mitigate punishment.

3. The fact that any of the acts referred to in articles 2 to 5 of the present Statute was committed by a subordinate does not relieve his superior of criminal responsibility if he knew or had reason to know that the subordinate was about to commit such acts or had done so and the superior failed to take the necessary and reasonable measures to prevent such acts or to punish the perpetrators thereof.

4. The fact that an accused person acted pursuant to an order of a Government or of a superior shall not relieve him of criminal responsibility, but may be considered in mitigation of punishment if the International Tribunal determines that justice so requires.

STATUTE OF THE INTERNATIONAL TRIBUNAL FOR RWANDA

Established by Security Council Resolution 955
Acting under Chapter VII of the UN Charter
8 November 1994

Article 1: Competence of the International Tribunal for Rwanda
The International Tribunal for Rwanda shall have the power to prosecute persons responsible for serious violations of international humanitarian law committed in the territory of Rwanda and Rwandan citizens responsible for such violations committed in the territory of neighboring States between 1 January 1994 and 31 December 1994, in accordance with the provisions of the present Statute.

Article 2: Genocide
1. The International Tribunal for Rwanda shall have the power to prosecute persons committing genocide as defined in paragraph 2 of this article or of committing any of the other acts enumerated in paragraph 3 of this article

2. Genocide means any of the following acts committed with intent to destroy, in whole or in part, a national, ethnical, racial or religious group, as such:
   a) Killing members of the group;
   b) Causing serious bodily or mental harm to members of the group;
   c) Deliberately inflicting on the group conditions of life calculated to bring about its physical destruction in whole or in part;
   d) Imposing measures intended to prevent births within the group;
   e) Forcibly transferring children of the group to another group.

3. The following acts shall be punishable:
a) Genocide;
b) Conspiracy to commit genocide;
c) Direct and public incitement to commit genocide;
d) Attempt to commit genocide;
e) Complicity in genocide.

Article 3: Crimes against Humanity

The International Tribunal for Rwanda shall have the power to prosecute persons responsible for the following crimes when committed as part of a widespread or systematic attack against any civilian population on national, political, ethnic, racial or religious grounds:
a) Murder;
b) Extermination;
c) Enslavement;
d) Deportation;
e) Imprisonment;
f) Torture;
g) Rape;
h) Persecutions on political, racial and religious grounds;
i) Other inhumane acts.

Article 4: Violations of Article 3

... These violations shall include, but shall not be limited to:
a) Violence to life, health and physical or mental well-being of persons, in particular murder as well as cruel treatment such as torture, mutilation or any form of corporal punishment;
b) Collective punishments;
c) Taking of hostages;
d) Acts of terrorism;
e) Outrages upon personal dignity, in particular humiliating and degrading treatment, rape, enforced prostitution and any form of indecent assault;
f) Pillage;
g) The passing of sentences and the carrying out of executions without previous judgment pronounced by a regularly constituted court, affording all the judicial guarantees which are recognized as indispensable by civilized peoples;
h) Threats to commit any of the foregoing acts....

Article 6: Individual Criminal Responsibility

1. A person who planned, instigated, ordered, committed or otherwise aided and abetted in the planning, preparation or execution of a crime referred to in articles 2 to 4 of the present Statute, shall be individually responsible for the crime.

2. The official position of any accused person, whether as Head of State or Government or as a responsible Government official, shall not relieve such person of criminal responsibility nor mitigate punishment.

3. The fact that any of the acts referred to in articles 2 to 4 of the present Statute was committed by a subordinate does not relieve his or her superior of criminal responsibility if he or she knew or had reason to know that the subordinate was about to commit such acts or had done so and the superior failed to take the necessary and reasonable measures to prevent such acts or to punish the perpetrators thereof.

4. The fact that an accused person acted pursuant to an order of Government or of a superior shall not relieve him or her of criminal responsibility, but may be considered in mitigation of punishment if the International Tribunal for Rwanda determines that justice so requires.

ROME STATUTE OF THE INTERNATIONAL CRIMINAL COURT JULY 17, 1998

*[as corrected by the procès-verbaux of
10 November 1998 and 12 July 1999]*

Article 1
The Court
   An International Criminal Court ("the Court") is hereby established. It shall be a permanent institution and shall have the power to exercise its jurisdiction over persons for the most serious crimes of international concern, as referred to in this Statute, and shall be complementary to national criminal jurisdictions. . . .

Article 5
Crimes within the jurisdiction of the Court
1.   The jurisdiction of the Court shall be limited to the most serious crimes of concern to the international community as a whole. The Court has jurisdiction in accordance with this Statute with respect to the following crimes:
   (a)   The crime of genocide;
   (b)   Crimes against humanity;
   (c)   War crimes;
   (d)   The crime of aggression.
2.   The Court shall exercise jurisdiction over the crime of aggression once a provision is adopted in accordance with articles 121 and 123 defining the crime and setting out the conditions under which the Court shall exercise jurisdiction with respect to this crime. . . .

Article 6
Genocide

For the purpose of this Statute, "genocide" means any of the following acts committed with intent to destroy, in whole or in part, a national, ethnical, racial or religious group, as such:

(a) Killing members of the group;

(b) Causing serious bodily or mental harm to members of the group;

(c) Deliberately inflicting on the group conditions of life calculated to bring about its physical destruction in whole or in part;

(d) Imposing measures intended to prevent births within the group;

(e) Forcibly transferring children of the group to another group.

Article 7
Crimes against humanity

1. For the purpose of this Statute, "crime against humanity" means any of the following acts when committed as part of a widespread or systematic attack directed against any civilian population, with knowledge of the attack:

(a) Murder;

(b) Extermination;

(c) Enslavement;

(d) Deportation or forcible transfer of population;

(e) Imprisonment or other severe deprivation of physical liberty in violation of fundamental rules of international law;

(f) Torture;

(g) Rape, sexual slavery, enforced prostitution, forced pregnancy, enforced sterilization, or any other form of sexual violence of comparable gravity;

(h) Persecution against any identifiable group or collectivity on political, racial, national, ethnic, cultural, religious, gender as defined in paragraph 3, or other grounds that are universally recognized as impermissible under international law, in connection with any act referred to in this paragraph or any crime within the jurisdiction of the Court;

(i) Enforced disappearance of persons;

(j) The crime of apartheid;

(k) Other inhumane acts of a similar character intentionally causing great suffering, or serious injury to body or to mental or physical health.

2. For the purpose of paragraph 1:
   (a) "Attack directed against any civilian population" means a course of conduct involving the multiple commission of acts referred to in paragraph 1 against any civilian population, pursuant to or in furtherance of a State or organizational policy to commit such attack;
   (b) "Extermination" includes the intentional infliction of conditions of life, inter alia the deprivation of access to food and medicine, calculated to bring about the destruction of part of a population;
   (c) "Enslavement" means the exercise of any or all of the powers attaching to the right of ownership over a person and includes the exercise of such power in the course of trafficking in persons, in particular women and children;
   (d) "Deportation or forcible transfer of population" means forced displacement of the persons concerned by expulsion or other coercive acts from the area in which they are lawfully present, without grounds permitted under international law;
   (e) "Torture" means the intentional infliction of severe pain or suffering, whether physical or mental, upon a person in the custody or under the control of the accused; except that torture shall not include pain or suffering arising only from, inherent in or incidental to, lawful sanctions;
   (f) "Forced pregnancy" means the unlawful confinement of a woman forcibly made pregnant, with the intent of affecting the ethnic composition of any population or carrying out other grave violations of international law. This definition shall not in any way be interpreted as affecting national laws relating to pregnancy;
   (g) "Persecution" means the intentional and severe deprivation of fundamental rights contrary to international law by reason of the identity of the group or collectivity;
   (h) "The crime of apartheid" means inhumane acts of a character similar to those referred to in paragraph 1, committed in the context of an institutionalized regime of systematic oppression and domination by one racial group over any other racial group or groups and committed with the intention of maintaining that regime;
   (i) "Enforced disappearance of persons" means the arrest, detention or abduction of persons by, or with the authorization, support or acquiescence of, a State or a political organization, followed by a refusal to acknowledge that deprivation of freedom or to give infor-

mation on the fate or whereabouts of those persons, with the intention of removing them from the protection of the law for a prolonged period of time.

3. For the purpose of this Statute, it is understood that the term "gender" refers to the two sexes, male and female, within the context of society. The term "gender" does not indicate any meaning different from the above.

Article 8
War crimes

1. The Court shall have jurisdiction in respect of war crimes in particular when committed as part of a plan or policy or as part of a large-scale commission of such crimes.

2. For the purpose of this Statute, "war crimes" means:
   (a) Grave breaches of the Geneva Conventions of 12 August 1949, namely, any of the following acts against persons or property protected under the provisions of the relevant Geneva Convention:
       (i) Willful killing;
       (ii) Torture or inhuman treatment, including biological experiments;
       (iii) Willfully causing great suffering, or serious injury to body or health;
       (iv) Extensive destruction and appropriation of property, not justified by military necessity and carried out unlawfully and wantonly;
       (v) Compelling a prisoner of war or other protected person to serve in the forces of a hostile Power;
       (vi) Wilfully depriving a prisoner of war or other protected person of the rights of fair and regular trial;
       (vii) Unlawful deportation or transfer or unlawful confinement;
       (viii) Taking of hostages.
   (b) Other serious violations of the laws and customs applicable in international armed conflict, within the established framework of international law, namely, any of the following acts:
       (i) Intentionally directing attacks against the civilian population as such or against individual civilians not taking direct part in hostilities;
       (ii) Intentionally directing attacks against civilian objects, that is, objects which are not military objectives;
       (iii) Intentionally directing attacks against personnel, installations, material, units or vehicles involved in a humanitarian assistance or peacekeeping mission in accordance with the Charter

of the United Nations, as long as they are entitled to the protection given to civilians or civilian objects under the international law of armed conflict;

(iv) Intentionally launching an attack in the knowledge that such attack will cause incidental loss of life or injury to civilians or damage to civilian objects or widespread, long-term and severe damage to the natural environment which would be clearly excessive in relation to the concrete and direct overall military advantage anticipated;

(v) Attacking or bombarding, by whatever means, towns, villages, dwellings or buildings which are undefended and which are not military objectives;

(vi) Killing or wounding a combatant who, having laid down his arms or having no longer means of defence, has surrendered at discretion;

(vii) Making improper use of a flag of truce, of the flag or of the military insignia and uniform of the enemy or of the United Nations, as well as of the distinctive emblems of the Geneva Conventions, resulting in death or serious personal injury;

(viii) The transfer, directly or indirectly, by the Occupying Power of parts of its own civilian population into the territory it occupies, or the deportation or transfer of all or parts of the population of the occupied territory within or outside this territory;

(ix) Intentionally directing attacks against buildings dedicated to religion, education, art, science or charitable purposes, historic monuments, hospitals and places where the sick and wounded are collected, provided they are not military objectives;

(x) Subjecting persons who are in the power of an adverse party to physical mutilation or to medical or scientific experiments of any kind which are neither justified by the medical, dental or hospital treatment of the person concerned nor carried out in his or her interest, and which cause death to or seriously endanger the health of such person or persons;

(xi) Killing or wounding treacherously individuals belonging to the hostile nation or army;

(xii) Declaring that no quarter will be given;

(xiii) Destroying or seizing the enemy's property unless such destruction or seizure be imperatively demanded by the necessities of war;

(xiv) Declaring abolished, suspended or inadmissible in a court of law the rights and actions of the nationals of the hostile party;

(xv) Compelling the nationals of the hostile party to take part in the operations of war directed against their own country, even if they were in the belligerent's service before the commencement of the war;

(xvi) Pillaging a town or place, even when taken by assault;

(xvii) Employing poison or poisoned weapons;

(xviii) Employing asphyxiating, poisonous or other gases, and all analogous liquids, materials or devices;

(xix) Employing bullets which expand or flatten easily in the human body, such as bullets with a hard envelope which does not entirely cover the core or is pierced with incisions;

(xx) Employing weapons, projectiles and material and methods of warfare which are of a nature to cause superfluous injury or unnecessary suffering or which are inherently indiscriminate in violation of the international law of armed conflict, provided that such weapons, projectiles and material and methods of warfare are the subject of a comprehensive prohibition and are included in an annex to this Statute, by an amendment in accordance with the relevant provisions set forth in articles 121 and 123;

(xxi) Committing outrages upon personal dignity, in particular humiliating and degrading treatment;

(xxii) Committing rape, sexual slavery, enforced prostitution, forced pregnancy, as defined in article 7, paragraph 2 (f), enforced sterilization, or any other form of sexual violence also constituting a grave breach of the Geneva Conventions;

(xxiii) Utilizing the presence of a civilian or other protected person to render certain points, areas or military forces immune from military operations;

(xxiv) Intentionally directing attacks against buildings, material, medical units and transport, and personnel using the distinctive emblems of the Geneva Conventions in conformity with inter national law;

(xxv) Intentionally using starvation of civilians as a method of warfare by depriving them of objects indispensable to their survival, including wilfully impeding relief supplies as provided for under the Geneva Conventions;

(xxvi) Conscripting or enlisting children under the age of fifteen years into the national armed forces or using them to participate actively in hostilities.

(c) In the case of an armed conflict not of an international character, serious violations of article 3 common to the four Geneva Conventions of 12 August 1949, namely, any of the following acts committed against persons taking no active part in the hostilities, including members of armed forces who have laid down their arms and those placed *hors de combat* by sickness, wounds, detention or any other cause:

   (i) Violence to life and person, in particular murder of all kinds, mutilation, cruel treatment and torture;

   (ii) Committing outrages upon personal dignity, in particular humiliating and degrading treatment;

   (iii) Taking of hostages;

   (iv) The passing of sentences and the carrying out of executions without previous judgement pronounced by a regularly constituted court, affording all judicial guarantees which are generally recognized as indispensable.

(d) Paragraph 2 (c) applies to armed conflicts not of an international character and thus does not apply to situations of internal disturbances and tensions, such as riots, isolated and sporadic acts of violence or other acts of a similar nature.

(e) Other serious violations of the laws and customs applicable in armed conflicts not of an international character, within the established framework of international law, namely, any of the following acts:

   (i) Intentionally directing attacks against the civilian population as such or against individual civilians not taking direct part in hostilities;

   (ii) Intentionally directing attacks against buildings, material, medical units and transport, and personnel using the distinctive emblems of the Geneva Conventions in conformity with international law;

   (iii) Intentionally directing attacks against personnel, installations, material, units or vehicles involved in a humanitarian assistance or peacekeeping mission in accordance with the Charter

of the United Nations, as long as they are entitled to the protection given to civilians or civilian objects under the international law of armed conflict;

(iv) Intentionally directing attacks against buildings dedicated to
religion, education, art, science or charitable purposes, historic monuments, hospitals and places where the sick and
wounded are collected, provided they are not military objectives;

(v) Pillaging a town or place, even when taken by assault;

(vi) Committing rape, sexual slavery, enforced prostitution, forced
pregnancy, as defined in article 7, paragraph 2 (f), enforced
sterilization, and any other form of sexual violence also constituting a serious violation of article 3 common to the four
Geneva Conventions;

(vii) Conscripting or enlisting children under the age of fifteen years
into armed forces or groups or using them to participate
actively in hostilities;

(viii) Ordering the displacement of the civilian population for reasons
related to the conflict, unless the security of the civilians
involved or imperative military reasons so demand;

(ix) Killing or wounding treacherously a combatant adversary;

(x) Declaring that no quarter will be given;

(xi) Subjecting persons who are in the power of another party to
the conflict to physical mutilation or to medical or scientific
experiments of any kind which are neither justified by the
medical, dental or hospital treatment of the person concerned
nor carried out in his or her interest, and which cause death to
or seriously endanger the health of such person or persons;

(xii) Destroying or seizing the property of an adversary unless such
destruction or seizure be imperatively demanded by the necessities of the conflict;

(f) Paragraph 2 (e) applies to armed conflicts not of an international
character and thus does not apply to situations of internal disturbances and tensions, such as riots, isolated and sporadic acts of violence or other acts of a similar nature. It applies to armed conflicts
that take place in the territory of a State when there is protracted
armed conflict between governmental authorities and organized
armed groups or between such groups.

QUESTIONS FOR DISCUSSION

1. Should the definition of genocide in the UN Convention be amended? If so, why and in what ways?

2. Why might governments be reluctant to revise the UN's definition of genocide?

3. If identifying genocide continues to depend on demonstrating the intent of potential or actual perpetrators, how likely is it that genocide can be prevented or checked before it is too late?

4. What kinds of early intervention might prevent genocide?

5. How is genocide different from mass civilian deaths or other wartime atrocities?

6. Do we need a notion of a *genocidal society* as well as of a *genocidal state?*

7. What long-term social, economic, and historical conditions allow genocidal political movements to thrive?

8. Which of the following should one study in order to understand the dynamics of genocide: the perpetrators, the victims, or the bystanders? Why?

9. Why is sexual violence an inevitable part of genocide?

10. What role has religious fundamentalism played in genocides in the twentieth and twenty-first centuries?

11. What are some of the moral, psychological, and political consequences of genocide?

12. If the prosecution and punishment of war crimes and crimes against humanity have so little deterrent effect, why establish international tribunals? Are they a waste of time and money?

13. What is the role of apology and reconciliation in the aftermath of a genocide?

14. Does seeking financial compensation from the perpetrator group demean the memory of the victims and cheapen the tragedy of genocide?

15. What is the cause of popular indifference to genocide? What could help overcome that indifference?

SELECTED GENOCIDE
WEBSITES

Today, the use of the world-wide web (www) by teachers, students, and scholars is indispensable to the study of genocide(s). Literally, there are thousands of sites one can access on the web. The following are only a few of the many available, selected to provide the reader-researcher with a broad and complementary perspective on various issues and questions related to genocide and its recurrence throughout history in many parts of the world.

Aegis Trust
www.aegistrust.org
Information about genocide and genocide prevention; good links to websites.

Amnesty International
www.amnesty.org
Information, reports, documentation about human rights abuses worldwide; many links.

BBC - British Broadcasting Corporation
www.news.bbc.co.uk
BBC news reports, in-depth essays; links to relevant sites.

The Danish Center for Holocaust and Genocide Studies
www.dchf.dk
Independent institution with the Danish Ministry of Foreign Affairs; many links.

End Genocide
www.endgenocide.org
Site contains information about genocides around the world.

Forum on Early Warning and Early Response (FEWER)
www.fewer.org
Information, perspective, analysis, options for response to conflict; many links.

Holocaust and Genocide Studies
www.webster.edu/~woolflm/holocaust.html
Teaching and academic resources; links to genocide web sites.

Human Rights Watch
www.hrw.org
Information, reports, documentation about human rights abuses world-wide; many links.

Institute for the Study of Genocide / International Association of Genocide Scholars
www.isg-ags.org/index.htm/
Information about genocide(s); teaching materials; many links.

International Monitor Institute
www.imisite.org
Identifies and acquires visual and audio evidence of human rights violations.

Montreal Institute for Genocide and Human Rights Studies
www.migs.concordia.ca
Site contains analytical papers and other information; very good web links.

PBS - Public Broadcasting System
www.pbs.org
American non-commercial television site; documents, essays, and links about genocide.

Prevent Genocide
www.preventgenocide.org
Source of information on genocides worldwide.

Teaching and Research on Genocide
www.people.memphis.edu/~genocide
Information, papers, and research on genocides; links to legal issues about genocide.

United Nations
www.un.org
Reports and information from the UN; portal to all UN organizations.

Web Documentation Centre
www.ess.uwe.ac.uk/genocide.htm
Data on individual countries; information on war crimes and legal issues.

Acronyms

APFO	Africa Peace Forum
FCO	Foreign and Commonwealth Office, UK
CGP	Cambodian Genocide Program (Yale University, USA)
CNN	Cable News Network
DPKO	Department of Peace Keeping Operations, UN
EAWARN	Ethnological Monitoring & Early Warning of Conflict Network
EPRP	Ethiopian People's Revolutionary Party
ETO	Ecole Technique Officielle
FEWER	Forum on Early Warning and Early Response
GSP	Genocide Studies Program (Yale University, USA)
HCNM	High Commissioner for National Minorities
ICG	International Crisis Group
ICRC	International Committee of the Red Cross
ICTR	International Criminal Tribunal for Rwanda
ICT	International Criminal Tribunal for Yugoslavia
IGO	Inter-governmental Organization
IMT	International Military Tribunal
MAAG	Military Advisory Assistance Group
NATO	North Atlantic Treaty Organization
NGO	Non-governmental organization
OAU	Organization of Africa Unity
OSCE	Organisation for Security and Co-operation in Europe
PCIA	Peace and Conflict Impact Assessment Methods
PMAC	Provisional Military Administrative Council
RPF	Rwandan Patriotic Front
RTLM	Radio-Télévision Libre des Mille Collines
UN	United Nations
UNAMIR	United Nations Assistance Mission for Rwanda
UNDP	United Nations Development Programme
UNGC	United Nations Convention on the Prevention and Punishment of the Crime of Genocide
US	United States
USA	United States of America

BIBLIOGRAPHY

Adelman, Howard and Astri Suhrke, eds. *The Path of a Genocide: The Rwanda Crisis from Uganda to Zaire.* Princeton, New Jersey: Transaction Publishers, 2000.

African Rights. *Confessing to Genocide: Responses to Rwanda's Genocide Law.* London, UK, 2000.

Alker, Hayward R., T. R. Gurr, and Kumar Rupesinghe, eds. *Journeys Through Conflict: Narratives and Lessons.* Lanham, MD: Rowman & Littlefield, 2001.

Allen, Beverly. *Rape Warfare: The Hidden Genocide in Bosnia-Herzegovina and Croatia.* Minneapolis, MN: University of Minnesota Press, 1996.

Allen, Tim and Jean Seaton, eds. *The Media of Conflict: War Reporting and Representations of Ethnic Violence.* New York, NY: Zed Books, 1999.

Alvarez, Alex. *Governments, Citizens, and Genocide: A Comparative and Interdisciplinary Approach.* Bloomington and Indianapolis: Indiana University Press, 2001.

Andreopoulos, George J. *Genocide: Conceptual and Historical Dimensions.* Philadelphia: University of Pennsylvania Press, 1994.

Auron, Yair. *The Banality of Indifference: Zionism and the Armenian Genocide.* Translated by Maggie Bar-Tura. Princeton, New Jersey: Transaction Publishers, 2001.

Barnett, Michael N. *Eyewitness to a Genocide: The United Nations and Rwanda.* Ithaca, New York: Cornell University Press, 2002.

Barstow, Anne Llewellyn, ed. *War's Dirty Secret: Rape, Prostitution, and Other Crimes Against Women.* Cleveland, Ohio: The Pilgrim Press, 2000.

Bartov, Omer and Phyllis Mack, eds. *In God's Name: Genocide and Religion in the Twentieth Century.* Oxford and New York: Berghahn Books, Incorporated, 2001.

Bauer, Yehuda. *Rethinking the Holocaust.* New Haven, CT: Yale University Press, 2001.

Bell-Fialkoff, Andrew. *Ethnic Cleansing.* New York, NY: St. Martin's Griffin, 1999.

Brooks, Roy L. ed. *When Sorry Isn't Enough: The Controversy Over Apologies and Reparations for Human Injustice.* New York & London: New York University Press, 1999.

Browning, Christopher R. *Ordinary Men.* New York: Harper Collins, 1992.

Brownmiller, Susan. *Against Our Will: Men, Women and Rape.* New York: Ballantine Books, 1975.

Cahill, Kevin M. ed. *Preventative Diplomacy: Stopping Wars Before They Start.* New York: NY: Routledge, 2000.

Campbell, Kenneth J. *Genocide and the Global Village.* Houndmills, Basingstoke, and Hampshire, England: Palgrave Macmillan, 2001.

Cassese, Antonio. ed. *The Rome Statute for an International Criminal Court, A Commentary.* Oxford, UK: Oxford University Press, March 2002.

Chalk, Frank and Kurt Jonassohn. *The History and Sociology of Genocide: Analyses and Case Studies.* New Haven: Yale University Press, 1990.

Charny, Israel W. ed. *Encyclopedia of Genocide.* Santa Barbara, CA: ABC-Clio, 1999.

-------- ed. *Toward the Understanding and Prevention of Genocide.* Boulder: Westview Press, 1984.

Cigar, Norman and Stjepan G. Mestrovic. *Genocide in Bosnia: The Policy of Ethnic Cleansing.* College Station, TX: Texas A & M Press, 1995.

Cushman, Thomas and Stjepan G. Mestrovic. *This Time We Knew: Western Responses to Genocide in Bosnia.* New York: New York University Press, 1996.

Daaider, Ivo H. and Michael E. O'Hanlon. *Winning Ugly: NATO's War to Save Kosovo.* Washington D.C.: Brookings Institution Press, 2000.

Dadrian, Vahakn N. *Warrant for Genocide: Key Elements of Turko-Armenian Conflict.* New Brunswick, NJ: Transaction Publishers, 1999.

Davies, John and Ted Robert Gurr, eds. *Preventive Measures: Building Risk Assessment and Crisis Early Warning Systems.* Lanham, MD: Rowman and Littlefield, 1998.

Davis, G. Scott, ed. *Religion and Justice in the War Over Bosnia.* New York and London: Routledge, 1996.

Des Forges, Alison. *Leave None To Tell The Story.* New York: Human Rights Watch, 1999.

Dobkowski, Michael N. and Isidor Wallimann, eds. *On the Edge of Scarcity: Environment, Resources, Population, Sustainability, and Conflict.* Syracuse, NY: Syracuse University Press, 2002.

Feil, S. R. *Preventing Genocide: How the Early Use of Force Might Have Succeeded in Rwanda,* Report to the Carnegie Commission on Preventing Deadly Conflict. New York: Carnegie Corporation, 1998.

Fein, Helen, ed. *The Prevention of Genocide.* New York Institute for the Study of Genocide, 1998.

-------- *Genocide: A Sociological Perspective. London: Sage Publications, 1993.*

-------- ed. *Genocide Watch.* New Haven: Yale University Press, 1991.

Gourevitch, Philip. *We Wish to Inform You That Tomorrow We Will Be Killed With Our Families: Stories from Rwanda.* London, England: Picador @Pan Macmillan, 1999.

Grenke, Arthur. *Holocaust and Genocide: Motivation and Ideology.* Ontario, Canada: Wilfrid Laurier University Press, 2001.

Gurr, Ted Robert. *Peoples Versus States: Minorities at Risk in the New Century.* Washington, D.C.: United States Institute of Peace Press, 2000.

Gutman, Roy. *A Witness to Genocide.* New York: Macmillan Publishing Company, 1993.

Gutman, Roy and David Rieff, eds. *Crimes of War.* New York: W.W. Norton & Co, 1999.

Hayner, Priscilla B. *Unspeakable Truths: Confronting State Terror and Atrocity: How Truth Commissions Around the World Are Challenging the Past and Shaping the Future.* New York, NY: Routledge, 2001.

Heidenrich, John G. *How to Prevent Genocide: A Guide for Policymakers, Scholars, and the Concerned Citizen.* Westport, CT: Praeger Publishers, 2001.

Helmick, S. J. and R. L. Petersen, eds. *Forgiveness and Reconciliation: Religion, Public Policy and Conflict Transformation.* Radnor, PA: Templeton Foundation Press, 2001.

Hinton, Alexander Laban, ed. *Genocide: An Anthropological Reader.* Oxford, England: Blackwell Publishers, 2002.

Hirsch, Herbert. *Genocide and the Politics of Memory: Studying Death for the Sake of Life.* Chapel Hill: University of North Carolina Press, 1995.

Horowitz, D. L. *The Deadly Ethnic Riot.* Berkeley, CA: University of California Press, 2001.

Horowitz, Irving W. *Taking Lives: Genocide and State Power.* New Brunswick, NJ: Transaction Books, 1980. New Brunswick, NJ: Transaction Publishers, 2001.

Human Rights Watch. *Kosovo: Rape as a Weapon of "Ethnic Cleansing".* New York: Human Rights Watch, 2000.

-------- *Shattered Lives: Sexual Violence during the Rwandan Genocide and its Aftermath*. New York: Human Rights Watch, 1996.

-------- *Slaughter Among Neighbors: The Political Origins of Communal Violence*. New York, 1995.

Jok, Madut Jok. *War and Slavery in Sudan*. Philadelphia, PA: University of Pennsylvania Press, 2001.

Jokic, Aleksander. *War Crimes and Collective Wrongdoing: A Reader*. Malden, MA: Blackwell Publishers, 2001.

Jongman, Albert J., ed. *Contemporary Genocides: Causes, Cases, Consequences*. Leiden: PIOOM, 1996.

Kaye, James and Bo Strath, eds. *Enlightenment and Genocide, Contradictions of Modernity*. Brussels, Belgium: Peter Lang, 2000.

Kennan, George F. *The Other Balkan Wars: A 1913 Carnegie Endowment Inquiry in Retrospect with a New Introduction and Reflection on the Present Conflict*. Washington, D.C.: Carnegie Endowment, 1993.

Kiernan, Ben. *The Pol Pot Regime: Race, Power and Genocide in Cambodia under the Khmer Rouge, 1975-1979*. New Haven: Yale University Press, 1996. Yale Nota Bene edition, 2002.

-------- *How Pol Pot Came to Power: A History of Communism in Kampuchea, 1930-1975*. London: Verso, 1985.

Kimenyi, Alexandre and Otis L. Scott. *Anatomy of Genocide: State-Sponsored Mass-Killings in the Twentieth Century*. Wales, England and New York: Edwin Mellen Press, 2001.

Krasner, Stephen D. *Sovereignty: Organized Hypocrisy*. Princeton, NJ: Princeton University Press, 1999.

Kressel, Neil J. *Mass Hate: The Global Rise of Genocide and Terror*. Colorado, USA: Westview Press, 2002.

Kuper, Leo. *The Prevention of Genocide*. New Haven, CT: Yale University Press, 1985.

-------- *Genocide: Its Political Use in the Twentieth Century*. Penguin Books, 1981. New Haven, CT: Yale University Press, 1982.

Kuperman, Alan J. *The Limits of Humanitarian Intervention: Genocide in Rwanda*. Washington, D.C.: Brookings Institution Press, 2001.

Lemkin, Raphael. *Axis Rule in Occupied Europe: Laws of Occupation, Analysis of Government, Proposals for Redress*. Washington, D.C.: Carnegie Endowment for International Peace, 1944.

Lifton, Robert Jay. *The Nazi Doctors: Medical Killing and the Psychology of Genocide.* New York: Basic Books, 1986.

Lifton, Robert Jay and Eric Markusen. *The Genocidal Mentality: Nazi Holocaust and Nuclear Threat.* New York: Basic Books, 1990.

Lindquist, Sven. *Exterminate the Brutes.* New York: The New Press, 1992.

Lorey, David E. and William H. Beezley, eds. *Genocide, Collective Violence, and Popular Memory: The Politics of Remembrance in the Twentieth Century.* Wilmington, Delaware: Scholarly Resources, Inc., 2001.

Mamdani, Mahmood. *When Victims Become Killers: Colonialism, Nativism, and the Genocide in Rwanda.* Princeton, NJ: Princeton University Press, 2001.

Martin, Ian. *Self-Determination in East Timor: The United Nations, the Ballot, and International Intervention.* International Peace Academy Occasional Paper Series. Boulder, CO: Lynn Rienner Publishers, 2001.

McCuen, Marnie J. *The Genocide Reader: The Politics of Ethnicity and Extermination.* Hudson, WI: Gem Publishers, 2000.

Melson, Robert. *Revolution and Genocide: On the Origins of the Armenian Genocide and the Holocaust.* Chicago: University of Chicago Press, 1992.

Milgram, S. *Obedience to Authority.* New York: Harper & Row, 1974.

Mojzes, Paul, ed. *Religion and the War in Bosnia.* Atlanta, GA: Scholars' Press, 1998.

-------- *Yugoslavian Inferno: Ethnoreligious Warfare in the Balkans.* New York: Continuum, 1994.

Mousavizadeh, Nader, ed, *The Black Book of Bosnia: The Consequences of Appeasement.* New York: Basic Books, 1996.

Neuffer, Elizabeth. *The Key to My Neighbor's House: Seeking Justice in Bosnia and Rwanda.* New York, NY: Picador USA, 2001.

Newman, Leonard S. and Ralph Erber, eds. *Understanding Genocide: The Social Psychology of the Holocaust: Contemporary Analyses of the Perpetrators of Genocide.* Oxford, UK: Oxford University Press, July 2002.

Paust, Jordan J. and M. Cherif Bassiouni et al. *Human Rights Module: On Crimes Against Humanity, Genocide, Other Crimes Against Human Rights, and War Crimes.* Durham, NC: Carolina Academic Press, 2001.

Physicians for Human Rights. *War Crimes in Kosovo: A Population-Based Assessment of Human Rights Violations against Kosovar Albanians.* Boston, August 1999.

Power, Samantha. *"Problem from Hell": America and the Age of Genocide.* Cambridge, Massachusetts: Perseus Books Group, 2002.

Prunier, Gerard. *The Rwanda Crisis: History of a Genocide.* New York: Columbia University Press, 1995.

Rawson, Claude. *God, Gulliver, and Genocide: Barbarism and the European Imagination, 1492-1945.* New York, NY: Oxford University Press, 2001.

Reynolds, Henry. *An Indelible Stain?: The Question of Genocide in Australia's History.* Ringwood, Vic: Viking, 2001.

Riemer, Neal. *Protection Against Genocide: Mission Impossible.* Westport, Connecticut: Greenwood Publishing Group, Incorporated, 2000.

Ronayne, Peter. *Never Again? The United States and the Prevention and Punishment of Genocide since the Holocaust.* Lanham, Maryland: Rowman & Littlefield Publishers, Inc., 2001.

Roth, John K. and Elisabeth Maxwell-Meynard eds. *Remembering for the Future: The Holocaust in an Age of Genocides.* New York: Palgrave, 2001.

Rubenstein, Richard L. *The Age of Triage: Fear and Hope in an Overcrowded World.* Boston: Beacon Press, 1983.

Rubenstein, Richard L. *The Cunning of History: Mass Death and the American Future.* New York: Harper and Row, 1975.

Rummel, R. J. *Death by Government.* New Brunswick, NJ: Transaction Publishers, 1997.

Rupesinghe, Kumar. *Toward the Understanding and Prevention of Genocide.* Boulder, CO: Westview Press, 1984.

Schabas, William A. *Genocide in International Law: The Crime of Crimes.* Cambridge: Cambridge University Press, 2000.

Scherrer, Christian P. *Genocide and Crisis in Central Africa: Conflict Roots, Mass Violence and Regional War.* Westport, CT: Greenwood Publishers, 2001.

Sells, Michael. *The Bridge Betrayed: Religion and Genocide in Bosnia.* Berkeley, CA: University of California Press, 1998.

Sinner, Samuel D. *The Open Wound: The Genocide of German Ethnic Minorities in Russia and the Soviet Union, 1915-1949 and Beyond.* Fargo, ND: North Dakota State University Libraries, 2000.

Spangenburg, Ray and Kit Moser. *Crime of Genocide: Terror Against Humanity.* Berkeley Heights, New Jersey: Enslow Publishers, Incorporated, 2000.

Staub, Ervin. *The Roots of Evil: The Origins of Genocide and Other Group Violence.* Cambridge: Cambridge University Press, 1989.

Stiglmayer, Alexandra, ed. *Mass Rape: The War against Women in Bosnia-Herzegovina.* Lincoln, NE: University of Nebraska Press, 1994.

Strozier, Charles B. and Michael Flynn. *Genocide, War, and Human Survival.* New York: Rowman and Littlefield, 1996.

Szayna, T. S. *Identifying Potential Ethnic Conflict: Application of a Process Model.* San Diego, CA: Rand Corporation, 2000.

Taylor, John G. *East Timor: The Price of Freedom.* London: Zed Books, 1999.

Tschuy, Théo. *Ethnic Conflict and Religion: Challenge to the Churches.* Geneva, Switzerland: WCC Publications, 1997.

Totten, Samuel. *First-Person Accounts of Genocidal Acts Committed in the Twentieth Century: An Annotated Bibliography.* New York, Westport, CT: London: Greenwood Publishing Group, 1991.

Totten, Samuel, ed. *Intervention and Prevention of Genocide: An Annotated Bibliography.* Westport, CT: Greenwood Publishers, forthcoming.

Totten, Samuel, and Steven Leonard Jacobs, eds. *Pioneers of Genocide Studies.* New Brunswick, NJ: Transaction Publishers, 2002.

Totten, Samuel, William S. Parsons and Israel W. Charny, eds. *Century of Genocide: Eyewitness Accounts and Critical View.* New York: Garland Publishers, 1997.

United Nations. *Report of the Independent Inquiry in the Actions of the United Nations during the 1994 genocide in Rwanda.* New York: United Nations, Office of the Secretary General, 15 December 1999. Available at www.un.org/News/ossg/rwanda_report.htm

Wallimann, Isidor and Michael Dobkowski, eds. *Genocide and the Modern Age.* Westport, CT: Greenwood Press, 1987.

Waters, Tony. *Bureaucratizing the Good Samaritan: The Limitations of Humanitarian Relief Operations.* Boulder, CO: Westview Press, 2001.

Weindling, Paul. *Epidemics and Genocide in Eastern Europe, 1890-1945.* Oxford, England: Oxford University Press, 2000.

Weine, Stevan M. *When History is a Nightmare: Lives and Memories of Ethnic Cleansing in Bosnia-Herzegovina.* New Brunswick, NJ: Rutgers University Press, 1999.

Wheeler, Nicholas J. *Saving Strangers: Humanitarian Intervention in International Society.* Oxford, UK: Oxford University Press, 2000.

Woodruff, Paul and Harry A. Wilmer, eds. *Facing Evil: Confronting the Dreadful Power behind Genocide, Terrorism, and Cruelty.* Chicago, Illinois: Open Court Publishing Company, 2001.

CONTRIBUTORS

Editors

Carol Rittner, R.S.M., a Sister of Mercy, is Distinguished Professor of Holocaust and Genocide Studies at The Richard Stockton College of New Jersey (USA). She is the author, editor, or co-editor of numerous publications, including most recently (with John K. Roth), *Pius XII and the Holocaust.*

John K. Roth is Russell K. Pitzer Professor of Philosophy at Claremont McKenna College, California (USA), where he has taught since 1966. He has published hundreds of articles and reviews and more than thirty books, including *Ethics after the Holocaust* and, most recently, *Holocaust Politics.*

James M. Smith is co-founder and Executive Director of the Aegis Trust, a UK-based NGO devoted to genocide prevention, and co-founder of Beth Shalom Holocaust Centre (UK). He also is an emergency medicine doctor, currently working at Queen's Medical Centre, Nottingham.

Contributors

Michael J. Bazyler is Professor of International Law at Whittier Law School, in Costa Mesa, California (USA) and a Research Fellow with the London-based Holocaust Educational Trust. His specialty is human rights law. He has been involved in various lawsuits filed in the United States representing human rights victims.

Helen Fein is the Executive Director of the Institute for the Study of Genocide and an Associate of the Belfer Center for Science and International Affairs of the Kennedy School of Government of Harvard University, Cambridge, MA (USA). She is the author and editor of many articles, books, and monographs on genocide, collective violence, collective altruism, human rights and antisemitism. She was a founder and first President of the International Association of Genocide Scholars (1995-97).

Stephen C. Feinstein is Emeritus Professor of History, University of

Wisconsin-River Falls (USA). In 1999, Feinstein was appointed Director of the Center for Holocaust and Genocide Studies at the University of Minnesota. He was the guest curator for the 5,000 square foot exhibition, "Witness and Legacy: Contemporary Art About the Holocaust."

Nicole Fritz served as law clerk to Justice Richard J. Goldstone between July 1999 and August 2000. She is now Crowley Fellow in International Human Rights at Fordham Law School (USA).

Richard J. Goldstone is a South African jurist. A justice of the Constitutional Court of South Africa since 1994, he has served as chairperson of the Commission of Inquiry Regarding the Prevention of Public Violence and Intimidation in South Africa and chief prosecutor of the United Nations International Criminal Tribunals for the former Yugoslavia and Rwanda. He is the author of *For Humanity: Reflections of a War Crimes Investigator.*

Barbara Harff is Professor of Political Science at the US Naval Academy in Annapolis, Maryland and senior consultant to the White House initiated State Failure Task Force. Dr. Harff's books include *Genocide and Human Rights: International Legal and Political Issues* (1984) and, with T. R. Gurr, *Ethnic Conflict in World Politics* (1994).

John G. Heidenrich is an independent scholar. He has been a consultant to the US Government on genocide, early warning and prevention issues since 1998. Mr. Heidenrich is the author of *How To Prevent Genocide: A Guide for Policymakers, Scholars, and the Concerned Citizen.*

Herbert Hirsch is Professor of Political Science at Virginia Commonwealth University (USA) where he teaches courses on the politics of war, violence and genocide. He is the author or editor of several books including *Genocide and the Politics of Memory: Studying Death to Preserve Life.*

Henry R. Huttenbach is Professor of European History at the City College of New York (USA). He is the founder-editor of the bi-monthly, *The Genocide Forum* (1994 –) as well as of the international quarterly, *Genocide Research* (1994 –). He also is the author of several books and articles on genocide.

Steven L. Jacobs holds the Aaron Aronov Chair of Judaic Studies and is Associate Professor of Religious Studies at The University of Alabama,

Tuscaloosa (USA). He is the author, editor, and/or translator of several books and many articles and reviews dealing primarily with the *Shoah* and genocide.

Kurt Jonassohn, Emeritus Professor of Sociology at Concordia University in Montreal (Canada), is a founding member and co-director of the Montreal Institute for Genocide and Human Rights Studies (MIGS). He is also a contributing editor to the *Encyclopedia of Genocide*.

Ben Kiernan is A.Whitney Griswold Professor of History and Director of the Genocide Studies Program at Yale University (USA). His books include *How Pol Pot Came to Power* and *The Pol Pot Regime: Race, Power and Genocide in Cambodia under the Khmer Rouge, 1975-1999*.

Jennifer Leaning is Professor of International Health at the Harvard School of Public Health (USA). She directs the Program on Humanitarian Crises, based at the FXB Center for Health and Human Rights, and the Human Security Program at the Harvard Center for Population and Development Studies. She is lead editor of *Humanitarian Crises: The Medical and Public Health Response*.

Mark Levene is Reader in Comparative History at the University of Southampton and the Parkes Centre for the Study of Jewish/non-Jewish Relations (UK). He has been working on *Genocide in the Age of the Nation-State*, a three volume history of the phenomenon. The first volume, *The Coming of Genocide*, will be published in 2002. Dr. Levene is also a peace and environmental campaigner.

Hubert G. Locke is Dean Emeritus, and John and Marguerite Corbally Professor of Public Service, University of Washington (USA). A member of the Committee on Conscience of the United States Holocaust Memorial Museum and Chair of the Board of Trustees of the Pacific School of Religion, California. His latest book is *Learning from History: A Black Christian's Perspective on the Holocaust*.

Eric Markusen is Research Director of the Danish Center for Holocaust and Genocide Studies, Copenhagen, and Professor of Sociology and Social Work at Southwest State University, Marshall, Minnesota (USA). He served as associate editor and contributing editor of the two-volume *Encyclopedia of Genocide*.

Clark McCauley is Professor of Psychology at Bryn Mawr College, and Co-director of the Solomon Asch Center for Study of Ethnopolitical Conflict at the University of Pennsylvania (USA). His research interests include stereotypes and the psychology of group identification, group dynamics and intergroup conflict, and the psychological foundations of ethnic conflict and genocide.

Robert Melson is Professor of Political Science and founding member of the Jewish Studies Program at Purdue University (USA). His most recent publication is *False Papers: Deception and Survival in the Holocaust*.

Linda Melvern, a Fellow of the University of Wales, Aberystwyth (UK), Department of International Politics, is an investigative journalist. Her account of the 1994 genocide in Rwanda, *A People Betrayed: The Role of the West in Rwanda's Genocide*, was published in 2000.

Paul Mojzes is Professor of Religious Studies at Rosemont College, Rosemont, Pennsylvania (USA). He is the co-editor of the *Journal of Ecumenical Studies*, and founder and former editor of *Religion in Eastern Europe*. He is the author of five books, including *Yugoslavian Inferno: Ethno-religious Warfare in the Balkans*, and the editor of several other books, including *Religion and the War in Bosnia*.

David Nyheim is the Director of the FEWER Secretariat, London (UK). He is trained in political economy, medical sciences and epidemiology and has published on a range of issues, covering early warning and conflict prevention, as well as humanitarian and public health issues.

Ahmedou Ould-Abdallah, Executive Secretary of the Global Coalition for Africa, Washington, D.C., was UN Secretary-General Special Representative for Burundi (1993-1995) and, from 1984-1991, a high-level official for energy and economic issues at UN Headquarters in New York. Prior to that, he was Minister of Foreign Affairs (1979-80), Mauritania, Ambassador of Mauritania to the United States (1973-76), and Ambassador to the European Union (1976-1979).

Richard L. Rubenstein, theologian and educator, is President Emeritus and Distinguished Professor of Religion at the University of Bridgeport (USA). He is also Distinguished Professor Emeritus of Religion at Florida State University. His many books include *After Auschwitz, The Cunning of History, The Age of Triage,* and *Approaches to Auschwitz,* co-authored with John K. Roth.

Roger W. Smith is Professor Emeritus of Government at the College of William and Mary, Williamsburg, Virginia (USA), and co-founder and past president of the International Association of Genocide Scholars. He has written on the history of genocide, women and genocide, denial of the Armenian Genocide, and responsibility for genocide.

Stephen D. Smith is co-founder of Britain's first Holocaust Memorial Centre, Beth Shalom, and co-founder of the Aegis Trust (UK). He is editor of the Witness Collection series (Quill Press) and writer/director of several film documentaries, including *Wasted Lives*; *Survivors: Memories of the Past: Lessons for the Future*; and *Britain and the Holocaust*. Dr. Smith is a member of the International Task Force on Holocaust Education (Sweden).

Ervin Staub is Professor of Psychology at the University of Massachusetts at Amherst (USA). In addition to his work on genocide, other group violence and their prevention, he has written extensively about the origins of helping, and altruism. Dr. Staub is the author of *The Roots of Evil: The Origins of Genocide and Other Group Violence*.

Samuel Totten, a member of the Council of the Institute on the Holocaust and Genocide, Jerusalem, Israel, is the compiler of *First-Person Accounts of Genocidal Acts Committed in the Twentieth Century*, the is co-editor of *Genocide in the Twentieth Century: Critical Essays and Eyewitness Accounts*, a co-editor of *Century of Genocide*, an associate editor of the *Encyclopedia of Genocide*, and the editor of *Pioneers of Genocide Studies*.

INDEX